MIGRATION
DEBATE

THE MIGRATION DEBATE

Sarah Spencer

First published in Great Britain in 2011 by

The Policy Press
University of Bristol
Fourth Floor, Beacon House
Queen's Road
Bristol BS8 1QU

Tel +44 (0)117 331 4054
Fax +44 (0)117 331 4093
e-mail tpp-info@bristol.ac.uk
www.policypress.co.uk

North American office:
The Policy Press
c/o International Specialized Books Services (ISBS)
920 NE 58th Avenue, Suite 300
Portland, OR 97213-3786, USA
Tel +1 503 287 3093
Fax +1 503 280 8832
e-mail info@isbs.com

British Library Cataloguing in Publication Data
A catalogue record for this book is available from the British Library

Library of Congress Cataloging-in-Publication Data
A catalog record for this book has been requested

ISBN 978 1 84742 285 9 paperback

Cover design by The Policy Press
Front cover: photograph kindly supplied
by www.istock.com
Printed and bound in Great Britain by
TJ International, Padstow

Contents

Acknowledgements

I am grateful to the former Ministers, special advisors and officials who agreed to be interviewed in the course of research for this book, and for an earlier chapter on which it draws, including David Blunkett, Barbara Roche and Fiona McTaggart, Nick Pearce, Maeve Sherlock, Stephen Boys Smith, Chris Hedges and Mark Kleinman; to Alessio Cangiano and Isabel Shutes for their insights in our collaboration on migrant workers, which informed my thinking; to Don Flynn, and Gay Moon and to Allan Findlay, Katharine Charsley, Lisa Doyle and my colleagues Ben Gidley, Hiranthi Jayaweera, Michael Keith, Martin Ruhs, Nando Sigona and Nick van Hear for their hugely valuable comments on draft chapters. My thanks go to Vanessa Hughes for her considerable research skills in tracking down sources of material; to Rachel Humphris for research assistence on asylum and refugee policy and to Amber Stechman likewise on family migration. My thanks to the Economic and Social Research Council (ESRC) for the financial support that enabled me to write the book at the ESRC Centre on Migration, Policy and Society, University of Oxford; and to Alison Shaw and Jo Morton at The Policy Press (and their anonymous peer reviewers) for their patience and skill. Finally, thanks to the British Library for providing a brilliant resource for authors and an inclusive public space in which to work.

Glossary

A2	Bulgaria and Romania, which joined the EU in January 2007
A8	Eight Central and Eastern European countries that joined the EU in May 2004 (Czech Republic, Estonia, Hungary, Latvia, Lithuania, Poland, Slovakia and Slovenia)
BIS	Department for Business, Innovation and Skills
CBI	Confederation of British Industry
CIC	Commission on Integration and Cohesion
CLG	Department for Communities and Local Government
DCSF	Department for Children, Schools and Families
DfID	Department for International Development
DWP	Department for Work and Pensions
e-Borders	A system of collection and analysis of data provided by transport providers in respect of journeys to and from the UK
ECJ	European Court of Justice, now the Court of Justice of the European Union
EEA	European Economic Area, a free trade area made up of the (now) 27 EU member states plus Iceland, Liechtenstein and Norway
EEC	European Economic Community
EU	European Union
FCO	Foreign and Commonwealth Office
GATS	General Agreement on Trade in Services
GDP	Gross Domestic Product
HRA	Human Rights Act 1998
HSMP	Highly Skilled Migrant Programme
ILO	International Labour Organisation
ILR	Indefinite Leave to Remain
IND	Immigration and Nationality Department

IOM	International Organisation for Migration
JCHR	Joint Committee on Human Rights
LFS	Labour Force Survey
MAC	Migration Advisory Committee
NGO	Non-governmental organisation
NHS	National Health Service
NQF	National Qualifications Framework
OECD	Organisation for Economic Cooperation and Development
ONS	Office for National Statistics
PAC	Public Accounts Committee
PBS	Points-Based System
PSA	Public Service Agreement
RLMT	Resident Labour Market Test
SAWS	Seasonal Agricultural Workers Scheme
TCN	Third Country National (not a citizen of a country in the EU)
TUC	Trades Union Congress
UASC	Unaccompanied Asylum Seeking Children
UKBA	United Kingdom Border Agency
UNHCR	United Nations High Commissioner for Refugees
WRS	Workers Registration Scheme

1

Introduction: migration policy in the 21st century

Migration presents us with a paradox. The vast majority of the public say that fewer migrants should be allowed to come to the UK and each new government promises tighter controls, yet a significant number of people continue to come. That divergence alone makes migration an intriguing area of public policy to explore.

Of those born in the UK, 83% want fewer migrants (foreign born) to come, as do a majority of those who were themselves born abroad (Lloyd, 2010:Table 73). More than a third of the public now regularly cite race and immigration as among the most important issues facing the country, significantly higher than in most European countries and a sharp increase from a decade ago (Eurobarometer, 2009: 11; MORI, 2009). During that time, national policies on labour migration, asylum, family migrants and international students have been radically overhauled. Yet the public is evidently far from reassured.

Nor is the UK alone in this experience. No country in Europe set out to expand its post-war population through permanent migration or made a conscious choice to become a multicultural country. Yet, by 2008, more than 30 million foreign citizens were living in the 27 member states of the European Union (EU), 6.4% of its population, of whom two thirds were citizens of countries outside the EU (Eurostat, 2010b). The social, economic and political effects of migration are inextricably interwoven into the fabric of Europe and its future (Hansen, 2002).

In the decade 2000–09, towards 1.9 million more people came to live in the UK than left to live abroad (ONS, 2010a). A British immigration minister insisted in 2009 that 'The British people can be confident that immigration is under control' (Woolas, 2009) but they

—

were not, 71% rating the government's management of immigration as poor (Transatlantic Trends, 2009). Migration was a salient issue in the 2010 general election and the Conservative policy to set tighter limits was popular on the doorstep. Yet its manifesto anticipated the tensions it would face:

> We want to attract the brightest and the best people who can make a real difference to our economic growth. But immigration is too high and needs to be reduced.... We want to encourage students to come to our universities and colleges, but our student visa system has become the biggest weakness in our border controls. (Conservative Party, 2010)

No sooner had the Coalition government taken office than its policy faced opposition at home and abroad that it could not afford to ignore.

Competing policy objectives

Migration has a significant bearing on many of the core responsibilities of government and therein, for politicians, lies the rub. Government choices are constrained by the significance of migration to competing policy objectives: from economic competitiveness and capacity to deliver public services to international relations and compliance with human rights law. There is, however, no consensus on the weight that should be placed on those priorities: should we value the remittances migrants send home as a contribution to international development (Van Hear et al, 2009), for instance, or bemoan them as a loss to the British Exchequer (Migration Watch, 2009)? Options are further constrained by the legacy of migration trends and legal precedents from the past; and immigration controls cannot always deliver what governments aspire. These constraints, however, are rarely transparent. Eager to reassure, governments over-promise and under-inform. A polarised, highly charged public and media discourse inhibits reasoned debate on policy options. The public does not know why governments cannot simply shut the door.

–

2

Ask why migration should be curbed and the answer, with differing emphases, focuses on the impact on jobs, public services, community cohesion and the environment. While critics near-universally acknowledge that migration has brought economic and social benefits, the suggestion that it will be the primary cause of the UK population rising to an estimated 70 million prompts tabloid headlines that it is 'a time-bomb ticking under our environment' (*Daily Mail*, 2009), putting pressure on housing (Green, 2009), stretched public services and natural resources (Balanced Migration, 2010). Some argue that migrants damage the employment prospects for British workers (Migration Watch, 2010) or undermine the trust and mutual belonging on which support for the welfare state depends (Goodhart, 2004). Tight restrictions are also, critics argue, what the public want, and failing to respect their views fuels support for the far right.

These claims have been seriously challenged by scholars, questioning the data, assumptions and value judgements on which they are based and the fearful tone in which they are expressed. It is argued that the UK experience of migration is unremarkable in an international and European context; that claims about the impact of migration on population growth are based on a questionable use of statistics; that evidence on the economic impact of migration is finely balanced (Chapter 3); and that migrants take up less space and use no more resources than other residents. Members of minorities are not choosing to live parallel lives, neighbourhoods are becoming more ethnically mixed not more segregated and diversity has not threatened support for the welfare state (eg Banting and Kymlicka, 2006; Phillips, 2006, 2007; Peach, 2009; Finney and Simpson, 2009). NGOs have similarly been sceptical of claims about the impact of migration on the environment (FOE, 2006).

Nor are public attitudes as clear-cut as they might seem. Dig beneath the headlines and we find that opposition to migration is not uniform or consistent. The government's own Citizenship Survey found young people less likely than their elders to be hostile to migration and no less than 84% of the public in England (2008–09) see their local area as a place where people from different backgrounds get on well together

(Lloyd, 2010). The public are considerably less concerned about legal migration than illegal migrants and fewer than half believe migrants bring down wages. Just 54% think migrants reduce the number of jobs available, despite mistakenly believing that they comprise 27% of the population, almost three times the actual figure (Transatlantic Trends, 2009).

Migration is, moreover, a freedom many British people want for themselves: the freedom to study in Japan, work in Canada, retire to Spain or have a gap year in Africa and to bring home the soulmate they meet on the way. Every year, thousands of British citizens leave the UK to live abroad (some 364,000 in the year to March 2010), around 5.5 million living permanently overseas and a further 500,000 for part of the year (Sriskandarajah and Drew, 2006; ONS, 2010c). As an employer, moreover, we want the freedom to employ a brilliant scientist from China or migrant carer to look after our kids; freedoms that require reciprocity: British citizens free to live and work in the other 26 EU member states, for instance, in return for the freedom of their citizens to live and work here. Some UK residents, however, have not themselves benefited from migration and question the impact on Britain and their neighbourhoods of those who do come to work, study or seek refuge here.

This book

No student of public policy would suggest that strengthening the evidence base will in itself be sufficient to reconcile these conflicting views. This book, nevertheless, in providing an overview of policies, their development and some alternative options, aims to put the debate on a more informed footing and to throw light on the politics of migration policymaking: the conflicting objectives, constraints and trade-offs from which policies and practices emerge (Spencer, 2003). As in earlier volumes in this series, the intention is thus not simply to set out what policy is and how it has developed but to explain *why*, to explore whose interests it serves and the ways in which the concepts and language used in policy discourse can privilege certain ideas over others (Ball, 2008), a process that can accord the status of 'common sense' to views which are not necessarily highly evidence-based.

While the central focus of the book is on the UK, its experience can only be understood in a global and European context. The UK itself, moreover, is not one nation, but four. While the central tenets of migration policy are not devolved, the text notes some policy divergence in Scotland in particular, as well as the central importance of local policymaking in relation to migrants living across the UK. The book makes reference to policies towards source countries and to emigration, but focuses primarily on entry to the UK and on policies towards migrants remaining on a temporary or permanent basis. It notes evidence on policy outcomes and considers alternative options that academic, parliamentary and civil society critics have proposed.

In this chapter I begin by identifying the global migration trends that provide part of the context for migration policy. I move on to show how our understanding is enhanced by migration theory, enabling us to critique some common perceptions about migrants, their motivations and future intentions. Mistaken assumptions and a poor evidence base are by no means the only hazards for policymakers in this field. The section that follows, drawing on the emerging literature on migration policymaking, sets the context for understanding the politics and process of policymaking itself. We cannot understand policy today without knowing something of its history and the chapter continues with a brief review of how we came to this juncture. It concludes with an explanation of the significance of recent data on migration and migrants before outlining the structure of the rest of the book.

Terminology

Before we continue, it is necessary to clarify what is meant by the terms used in the text and their significance. Why 'migration', for instance, rather than 'immigration'?

Immigration is defined by the International Organisation for Migration (IOM) as 'a process by which non-nationals move into a country for the process of settlement' (IOM, 2004: 31). Thus, *immigrant* has connotations of long-term stay. In more common usage in recent times is *international migrant*, defined by the UN (and in UK statistics) as someone who changes their country of residence for at least a year so that their destination effectively becomes their country of usual residence. Unlike *immigrant*, it encompasses those whose movement is relatively temporary or circular (moving on or back home). It can also refer to those leaving to live abroad; unless they are citizens or long-term residents, referred to as *emigrants*. Technically, those who come to the UK from other parts of the EU are not migrants but *EU citizens* exercising their right to free movement within its borders.

Whether the term *migrant* refers to foreign nationals (non-citizens) or the foreign born depends on the data available. UK data (where it exists) is generally on the foreign born (thus including UK citizens born abroad). While *migrant* can refer to all those born abroad, it is used in common parlance to refer to those who have relatively recently arrived. *Refugees* are often identified separately because of their distinct legal status (see Chapter 2). An *asylum seeker* is someone who has applied, or intends to apply, for that status.

Migration is 'a process of moving, either across an international border or within a state' – reminding us that the impact of the latter can also be significant, if beyond the remit of this book – the term 'encompassing any kind of movement of people, whatever its length, composition and causes' (IOM, 2004: 41). It is in that inclusive sense that I use the term and equally *migration policy*. *Irregular migration*, the term I use in preference to its many alternatives (see Chapter 5), is movement that takes place outside of the regulatory norms of the sending, transit and receiving countries. There are other terms, like '*integration*', the meaning of which I shall explore in Chapter 6.

A global phenomenon

The UK is far from alone in experiencing migration on a significant scale. Across the world, only 3.1% of the world's population are living abroad and that percentage has barely risen in the past two decades. In that sense, migration remains the exception, not the norm. Absolute numbers, however, grew from 155 million in 1990 to 214 million in 2010, and in Europe (including Russia) from 49 million to 70 million (UNDESA, 2009). Of the world's migrant population, 16 million people (8%) are refugees, most remaining near the country from which they fled (with a further 26 million internally displaced). Just over one third of international migrants have moved from a developing to a developed country. An estimated 50 million people are living abroad with irregular migration status (UNDP, 2009).

International mobility has become easier since the 1980s because of political reform, cheaper transport and a communications revolution that has opened up access to information, ideas and networks hitherto the prerogative of the few. As before, people migrate to work, study, and rejoin their families or to find a safe place to start a new life; but now we also see new reasons for moving: for retirement in sunnier climes, commuting across borders to work, the temporary migration of young working holidaymakers and migration within what was once but is no longer the same country. In the new global and European map of migration, the old dichotomies of migration analysis – forced versus voluntary, temporary versus permanent, legal versus illegal – blur as the motivations for migration and the forms it takes have become much more diverse (King, 2002: 89). People in the poorest countries remain the least mobile. Rather than development reducing the likelihood of migration, however, development and migration can go hand in hand (UNDP, 2009).

Castles and Miller (2009), in their classic text in migration studies, *The Age of Migration*, identify six broad trends in current patterns of migration: *globalisation*, the tendency for ever more countries to be affected and to receive migrants from a large range of source countries; *acceleration* in the number of people involved; growing *differentiation* in the range of categories of migrant; *feminisation*, the significance of women in current migration flows; *politicisation*, in its impact on domestic politics and prominence in bilateral and international agreements; and *transition*, where countries of emigration become countries of immigration. The outcome is societies that look very different from those in which the older generation grew up. Migrants

–

can be distinct in terms of ethnicity, culture, faith, physical appearance, language, legal status and residential concentration, but the social relevance of this depends on a changing economic, social and political context over time and on the significance attached to it by existing residents (Castles and Miller, 2009: 10). It is likely, moreover, that migration will continue, shaped by a complex interplay of economic, geopolitical, social, technological and environmental factors, though it is difficult to forecast either its scale or direction (OECD, 2009).

Understanding the dynamics of migration

Migration policies can be posited on unspoken assumptions about the reasons why people move, choose to come to Britain or their behaviour after arrival. Migration theory provides a lens through which we can interpret more accurately what is happening and help to explain why, as so often the case, policies do not achieve their stated objectives (Massey et al, 1993; Brettel and Hollifield, 2000; Castles and Miller, 2009).

Decision to migrate

From the 'new economics of migration' theorists (eg Stark and Bloom, 1985), for instance, we see that the decision to migrate may not be that of an individual but part of a collective strategy of a family or household to enhance its economic security; a strategy in which risk may be spread by other members remaining to work in the local labour market. Equally, the viability of a refugee's return to a post-conflict society may be predicated on other family members retaining their capacity to send remittances from abroad (Van Hear et al, 2009). It is thus the household that needs to be the unit of analysis in explaining motivations, and for policy interventions intended to attract migrants (when competing for skilled workers for instance) or to deliver durable solutions for refugees.

Those considering migration, however, are not necessarily in a position to make rational choices. Neoclassical economics originally envisaged individuals weighing up the costs and benefits, moving from areas with high population density, low living standards or political repression to areas in which they could maximise their economic opportunities and political freedoms. Yet few can in practice assess potential relative earnings in different countries, still less know the rules governing access to their welfare systems (as has at times been assumed in the UK in relation to asylum seekers).

Nor can migrants necessarily exercise choice at all. While it is possible to identify migrations that are unequivocally forced (as from ethnic cleansing) or voluntary, the distinction between choice and compulsion is often less clear. Entry channels label them as labour migrants, asylum seekers, students or dependants, masking the overlapping reasons why people have left their homes and their experiences on arrival. Some of those who anticipate temporary residence will change their intentions as job opportunities or relationships lead them to stay (whether or not with permission). In the chapters of this book I separate out the main categories of entry to enable readers to access quickly the material they need, but those labels can make more sense to policymakers than to migrants themselves.

Structural causes

Neither 'voluntary' nor 'forced' migration can in fact adequately be explained at the level of individual or household decision-making, but instead require an understanding of the structural conditions in sending and destination countries that set the context in which those decisions are made. In sending countries, conflict may be a trigger to move but poverty, insecurity, lack of the rule of law, environmental degradation, youthful populations and the income differential between the developing and developed world can be underlying structural factors (Malmberg et al, 2006; OECD, 2009). Migration can in turn be part of the development process. It can hinder development through loss of highly skilled people ('brain drain') but can also make a vital contribution through acquisition of skills, trading and investment connections. Remittances from within the EU to non-EU countries totalled €21.5 billion in 2009, with a further €8.1 billion to countries within its borders (Eurostat, 2010a). It is regularly argued that migration policies could more effectively take into account development outcomes and, in the UK, that the Department for International Development should therefore be more centrally involved in their formulation (Select Committee on International Development, 2004; Chappell and Glennie, 2009; UNDP, 2009).

In destination countries, a key insight, initially from dual-labour market theory (Piore, 1979), is that demand for migrant labour is a structural feature of advanced industrial economies in which there is a permanent demand for workers willing to accept poor conditions, low wages and lack of security. The decline in women fulfilling that role is one factor increasing demand for migrant labour. Another 'pull factor' is ageing populations, creating a demand to replace the declining numbers of young workers as well as for caregivers to look after the elderly (OECD, 2009: 10). The emphasis in this analysis on demand rather than an exclusive focus on 'push factors' in source countries is highly relevant to analysis of the UK's reliance on labour migration today (see Chapter 3).

A structural analysis of supply and demand in individual source and destination countries does not, however, give us the full picture. World systems or globalisation theory (eg Sassen, 1988; Castells, 1989) has shown that migration is grounded in the operation of the global market economy – shaped in part by foreign investment in developing countries and the disruption that ensues – and that the extent and direction of global migration flows can reflect the consequent cultural, communications and transport links between the industrialised and developing world. As many European countries have found, mobility is particularly evident between former colonial powers and colonies because of the trade, transport, communication, cultural and linguistic ties that remain. The implication of these structural analyses is that if the intention is to change migration patterns, then the fundamental solution lies not in regulating the symptom, migration, but in addressing the underlying conditions that drive it.

Finally, there is a further factor with which policymakers have to contend. From within and beyond migrant communities, a 'migration industry' of recruitment agencies, lawyers, advisers, travel agents and smugglers has emerged to provide services for profit (see Chapter 5). As organisations that depend on migration proliferate, it becomes more institutionalised and independent of the underlying structural factors that originally caused it (Massey et al, 1993; Salt and Stein, 2002).

Self-perpetuating dynamic of social networks

If we want to understand the direction and continuity of migration to particular destination countries, we need to take on board a further significant dimension. Network theory drew on the earlier concept of 'chain migration' to explore the ways in which networks of kin and shared community of origin can incentivise both migration and choice of destination. Networks, a form of social capital (Portes, 1998), reduce both the cost and risk of migration by helping migrants secure access to jobs and accommodation, providing information, contacts and support. Access to networks can contribute to a migrant's decision to remain, start a family or be joined by dependants; while the presence of children with evolving networks of their own further reduces the likelihood of return. As the network is reinforced, migration becomes self-perpetuating because new migrants in turn reduce the costs for later arrivals. Thus migration can become progressively more independent of its original drivers; new arrivals less reflective of economic demand in the destination country and more representative of the sending community from which they come. This analysis has particular resonance in family migration (Gurak and Caces, 1992; Haug, 2008):

> It is this powerful internal dynamic of the migratory process that often confounds expectations of the participants and undermines the objectives of policy-makers in both sending and receiving countries. (Castles and Miller, 2009: 33)

The trend for some migrants to retain political, economic and social links with their country of origin led to a new body of thinking on transnational communities, which built on earlier work on diasporas (Vertovec, 1999). Transnational links facilitate circular migration and transnationalism has helped to raise awareness that migrants cannot be categorised as temporary or permanent settlers. Patterns of migration are now more fluid over time and migrants' intentions on arrival are a poor predictor of long-term behaviour. Significantly, while governments may fear that retaining transnational connections will reduce migrants' motivation to participate in the economic and social life of the country, studies have shown that this is not necessarily the case (eg Jayaweera and Choudhury, 2008). It is thus important not to overestimate the significance of continuing transnational links for migrants whose primary focus may nevertheless be their lives and aspirations in their country of residence. I look at what the literature tells us about 'integration' processes in Chapter 6.

Impact of policy intervention

Early theories of migration tended to overlook a further factor: the impact of the state on migration flows. Political scientists have sought to address this omission, arguing that:

> the speeding train of international migration is fuelled by economic and social forces, but it is the state that acts as a switching mechanism, which can change the course of the train, or derail it altogether. (Hollifield, 2008: 196)

Migration analysts disagree, however, on the extent to which states can regulate migration. Some argue there is in fact a pattern of states failing to prevent unwanted flows: 'The more that states and supranational bodies do to restrict and manage migration, the less successful they seem to be' (Castles, 2004: 205). The extent of irregular migration in particular can suggest that migration is driven by forces governments cannot control. This is attributed to a range of causes including a failure to take account of the long-term dynamic of migration processes (including the actual motivations of migrants and demand for their labour); a tendency to overestimate the efficacy of regulation; and constraints within the policymaking system itself, leading to 'poorly conceived, narrow and contradictory policies, which may have unintended consequences' (Castles, 2004: 222).

Policy failure in liberal democracies has been attributed in part to 'political hyper activism', when politicians gain 'points' with the media and party colleagues from new initiatives but see less political mileage in efficient implementation or in evaluating past initiatives (Dunleavy, 1995: 61). Political hyper activism is indeed evident in the recent history of migration in the UK: no less than seven major pieces of legislation in the decade 1999–2009[1] and 47 changes to the Immigration Rules in the five years 2004–09 alone (UKBA, 2010). The consistency with which government policy on most aspects of migration is criticised from all sides suggests that the policy failure thesis has some traction in the UK.

In contrast, however, there are scholars who argue that far from exhibiting weakness, states have recently been intent on maximising their intelligence, technical efficiency and inter-agency collaboration to strengthen border and internal surveillance, blurring the boundary between immigration controls and other law enforcement (Bigo, 2002; Bigo et al, 2009). There is evidence to support this 'securitisation' thesis in the UK (see Chapter 5), notwithstanding that it may attribute greater coherence to policymaking than is always the case.

State capacity subject to constraints

What is clear is that states' capacity to manage migration is not unfettered. They operate within political, legal, economic, technical and evidential constraints and are trying – through a process of trade-offs that are rarely explicit – to achieve differing and sometimes competing policy objectives. Motivations and capacity to intervene effectively can differ significantly in relation to different categories of migrants, combining openness to skilled migrants, for instance, with highly restrictive regimes in other respects. Some of the constraints derive from the dynamics of migration processes: the demand generated within

---

13

domestic labour markets, for instance and, as we saw, the impact of social networks. A further constraint derives from the history of migration to the country and past legislative and institutional responses, because the cost of reversal can be high or future options have been closed off by past choices, thus encouraging continuity along the original path (Hansen, 2002).

Academics seeking to explain a gap between restrictive public demands and the measures implemented by their governments (or between restrictive policies and their outcomes) have focused on the competing interests served by migration and the interest groups and state institutions that articulate them (Facchini and Mayda, 2009). While the impact of economic interests has had most attention, suggesting for instance that those who benefit from immigration are more influential than those who are 'cost-bearers', economic models have been found only partially to account for policies adopted (Freeman and Kessler, 2008).

We might expect labour market interests to be more evident in relation to some dimensions of migration than others, such as asylum policy. We might also expect that the capacity of some sections of society to articulate their interests will be less than that of the business sector, and not only because of the differing resources at their disposal. Research has found that collective action by interest groups is not a direct outcome of the costs and benefits of immigration 'but of the extent and way immigration is politicised and publicly mediated, and how certain positions are made to appear more feasible, reasonable, and legitimate, compared to alternative definitions of political reality' (Statham and Geddes, 2006: 251). States play a key role in setting that context. Far from merely reflecting the views of pressure groups, the interests of the state itself (and conflicts of interest within it) need to be explained if we are to understand why particular policies emerge in the form they do (Boswell, 2007; Hollifield, 2008).

Impact of international, European and domestic law

Obligations under international human rights law can be one significant constraint: foreigners now enjoy rights of entry and within the country that were once exclusive to citizens. States' autonomy has, in this respect, been curtailed (Soysal, 1994). That impact can be overstated but when rights are anchored in *national* legal systems they can impose limits on states' capacity to restrict entry, family reunion and the social rights of migrants after arrival (Joppke, 1998; Hollifield, 2008: 211). Governments can be further restrained by public adherence to the ethics on which these international standards are based, requiring respect (as we shall see, for instance, in relation to family life or deportation) beyond rights enforceable in any court of law.

In the UK, the UN Convention on Refugees has required successive governments to consider the protection needs of those who claim asylum; and the recent Council of Europe Convention on trafficking influenced the support provided for its victims (see Chapter 5). With these notable exceptions there has been limited endorsement of international standards protecting the rights of migrants per se. The UK is not among the minority of states that have ratified the UN Convention on the Rights of Migrant Workers and their Families (1990). States can also enter reservations on their compliance with international standards as the UK did for many years, in this context, in relation to the UN Convention on the Rights of the Child.

Both before and since it was brought into UK law by the Human Rights Act 1998 (HRA), the European Convention on Human Rights (ECHR) has imposed a range of constraints, in relation to family reunion for instance and to the return of foreign nationals to countries where they could face torture. The courts do from time to time ensure that these constraints are keenly felt. Nevertheless, most rights in the ECHR are not absolute and states have considerable leeway in their implementation (Jackson et al, 2008).

UK domestic law beyond the HRA has also constrained the government's options, notably in relation to asylum seekers within the UK (see Chapter 2). Race discrimination law, on the other hand, has not prevented a disproportionate indirect impact of immigration controls on Black and Asian migrants, the law specifically providing a broadly worded exemption in relation to immigration control, carried forward by the Equality Act 2010. It was argued in 2002 that the absence of a Bill of Rights, a weak legislature and 'a timid judiciary' had 'allowed British policy makers to translate public preferences into public policy more directly than in any other liberal democracy', resulting in one of the tightest immigration control regimes in the Western world (Hansen, 2002: 265). Recent Home Secretaries, consistently challenged in the courts, might not share that view.

International governance framework

Recognition that neither migration flows nor their socio-economic and political impacts can be managed by the UK in isolation has led to negotiation of bilateral and multilateral agreements, the former including a 'Common Travel Area' allowing free movement to and from Ireland[2] and readmission agreements to return irregular migrants.

Multilateral migration governance, however, is limited. Responsibility at UN level is spread across institutions, including the UN High Commissioner for Refugees (UNHCR). The International Labour Organization (ILO) includes only limited categories of migrants within its focus; and the IOM was established in 1951 to promote practical solutions and provide services to member states, not binding agreements. Despite the very nature of migration necessitating cooperation across borders, states have been unwilling to commit fully to international cooperation because controlling who enters the territory is seen as integral to state sovereignty. Yet it is argued that neither sovereignty nor competition between states for skilled migrants need be undermined by more systematic sharing of information and expertise or greater policy coordination. The absence of a UN framework of governance has led to a proliferation of regional and international mechanisms for interstate dialogue, including the Global Forum on Migration and Development since 2007 (GFMD, 2010), demonstrating that migration cannot be addressed effectively on a unilateral basis (GCIM, 2005: 66; Betts, 2008).

European Union

Highly significant in this context is the role of the European Union, the impact of which we shall see throughout this book. A core purpose of the EU is free movement of European citizens within its borders, a right extended in 1994 to the other three European Economic Area (EEA) countries, Iceland, Liechtenstein and Norway. At enlargement of the EU from 15 to 25 states in 2004, the UK could have chosen to restrict access to the UK labour market for a transitional period, but in this instance did not do so (see Chapter 3). With the right of free movement for EU nationals come associated rights that differ from those of other 'migrants', for instance, in relation to family reunion (see Chapter 4).

Cooperation in relation to migration of 'third-country nationals' from beyond the EU is unavoidable as many of those arriving in the UK have travelled through other member states. The 1997 Amsterdam Treaty established EU competency to legislate on international migration, replacing earlier intergovernmental arrangements such as the 1985 Schengen Agreement (to remove checks at internal borders), to which the UK was not a party. With Ireland it negotiated a selective opt-out from EU law which has enabled it to maintain a strongly national approach when it chooses to, while opting to collaborate where that helps to achieve its objectives, as on asylum and irregular migration (Geddes, 2005; Peers, 2009).

The EU's policy framework was set out in 1999 (Tampere), and revised in the Hague Programme of 2004 (CEU, 2004) and later the Stockholm Programme of 2009 (CEU, 2009). The aim is to work towards a comprehensive asylum, migration and border policy, from the root causes of forced migration through to integration or return, based on common standards and on cooperation with third countries. An early priority was establishing a mechanism for allocating responsibility among member states for handling asylum applications (the 'Dublin system', under which the UK returns asylum seekers to other states on a monthly basis) with separate Directives providing common procedures in the refugee determination process (to deter 'asylum shopping') and minimum standards for the reception and treatment of asylum seekers (see Chapter 2).

EU law now sets out conditions for the admission and residence of third-country nationals including, for instance, Directives governing admission for study and for highly skilled workers. The UK opted out of these measures, as it did from the 2003 Directive on family reunification. It has shown more enthusiasm for cooperating with FRONTEX, an agency set up in 2007 to strengthen the EU's external borders (see Chapter 5); and opted in to Directives in 2002 providing a level of harmonisation on offences and penalties for illegal entry and trafficking, but not to a further Directive in 2009 covering sanctions on employers who employ those not entitled to work. Meanwhile, the EU has sought the cooperation of source countries in reducing irregular migration and provides some practical assistance, to which the UK contributes.

The UK's self-interested opt-out arrangement causes some resentment and hence resistance when it chooses to engage (Peers, 2009). The 2007 Lisbon Treaty increased EU competence to develop common standards on immigration and asylum, extended the jurisdiction of the European Court of Justice (ECJ)[3] and made all decisions subject to qualified majority voting. When the UK now decides to opt in, it can thus be outvoted.

The policymaking process

To understand migration policies, we also need to look at the complex processes through which they emerge. This is far removed from an idealised process of logical 'stages': from recognition of a problem, through consideration of the options, agreement on the way forward, to implementation. While it is possible in broad terms to identify these stages they do not necessarily occur sequentially. Moreover, a key stage occurs before that process begins: the way in which an issue is perceived ('socially constructed') and the language in which it is discussed is hugely important in setting the terms on which policy options are considered. Thus, for European countries that see migration through the prism of nation-states with distinct territories and citizens, it is an anomaly. Hence, migration policies have largely been reactive and defensive in contrast to North America where immigrants have long been seen as central to the process of nation-building (Penninx and Martiniello, 2004). A further example is the aquatic language of 'flows' and 'floods', regularly used in relation to migration, which clearly carries connotations of threat rather than of the social, economic and cultural benefits that migration can bring.

Policy silos

UK policymaking has since the 1980s become increasingly fragmented between the international, European, national, regional and local levels, and involves a more diverse set of actors from the public, private and voluntary sectors. This is true in relation to migration, if less so than in some other fields, central government retaining a high level of control within the UK and negotiating an opt-out, as we have seen, from EU decisions not to its liking. Devolution of power to Scotland, Northern Ireland and Wales has led to policy divergence less than in other fields because immigration control is not devolved (Kyambi, 2009).

Early studies of national policymaking in the UK emphasised the vertical fragmentation of policymaking into discrete Whitehall departments (Jordan and Richardson, 1982). Serious attempts have been made in recent years to overcome departmental boundaries including cabinet subcommittees, interdepartmental taskforces and, under Labour, cross-cutting Public Service Agreement (PSA) targets (HM Government, 2009). Nevertheless, Whitehall's 'federal' structure continues to impede the handling of cross-cutting issues (Parker et al, 2010). On migration, the dominance of the Home Office has limited the influence of other departments and agencies keenly affected by it.

When Labour took office in 1997, the Home Office was the lead department on immigration, asylum and citizenship policy, the responsibility of its then Immigration and Nationality Department (IND). Policy on work permits, international students and seasonal agricultural workers (SAWs) had, however, long been in the hands of the departments leading on employment, education and rural affairs, respectively. In 2001, Home Secretary David Blunkett took responsibility for those entry channels with him to the Home Office, making it possible, in theory, to develop a holistic migration policy for the first time: an ambition reflected in his 2002 White Paper (Home Office, 2002). The downside, reflected in the chapters that follow, is that each element of migration policy is isolated from the mainstream economic and social policies that it affects, and is affected by. No effective governance arrangement has been established to address that gap, nor the equally problematic isolation from the devolved administrations and local services.

The extent to which public policy in Britain is formulated within the executive has tended to marginalise the direct influence of Parliament, though its voice has been strengthened by the growing influence of Select Committees. On migration and integration, we shall see that Select Committees have indeed called government to account and have on occasion been highly critical, influencing aspects of policy if not the central thrust of its direction.

Party politics and personal influence

Studies have found a tendency for the Opposition to retain their rivals' legislation when elected to govern, ensuring continuity and incremental change where party politics might suggest there would be a sharp disjuncture (Dorey, 2005: 267–70). This will be evident when we look at the early years of the Blair government in its handling of the asylum crisis; yet significant shifts in policy were seen elsewhere, as with the subsequent Coalition government, and require explanation.

Analysis of recent policymaking in the UK has revealed the close working relationship between 'policy networks' and government in some policy fields and much greater distance in others. The literature highlights the influence of ministers' special advisers after Labour's election in 1997 (evident in the shift towards 'managed migration' during Labour's second term) and the continuing role of 'think tanks' as a source of policy ideas. Significantly, it also suggests that the exercise of power by the executive 'is heavily dependent on circumstances, personalities, styles of leadership and the type of issues or policies involved' (Dorey, 2005: 2). The priorities of successive Home Secretaries and indeed of the Prime Minister have at times been highly significant in migration, within the broader context of the economic, political and international pressures to which they had to respond (Spencer, 2007).

Evidence base

The Labour government elected in 1997 was committed to greater use of evidence in the policymaking process, but was slow to apply this to migration. A Home Office conference in 2001, 'Closing the Information Gap', first signalled to researchers that policymakers were now interested in developing an evidence base on migration and government has contributed through research and funding of external studies. There has also been greater willingness to learn from policy experiences abroad and to pilot initiatives to assess impacts before deciding whether to roll out policies nationwide.

While evidence now plays a greater part in migration policy and political debates, the nature of its utilisation in the UK and at EU level has been found to be highly selective. Knowledge is rarely deployed in a politically neutral way and the validity of data and research findings (for instance, on the economic impact of labour migration) are frequently contested (Boswell, 2008, 2009). One former advisor on migration to the Conservative administration in the 1980s observed with some irony that 'the only decisions that are made primarily on the basis of research findings are politically unimportant ones' (Coleman, 1991: 420). This, he argued, is in part because some social and economic questions are not capable of effective testing, produce contested results or are overlooked in the truncated timescale in which policies are developed. There is, moreover, the primacy of politics: all governments are devoted to staying in office and options indicated by research may look unappealing to the electorate. The Coalition government's newly appointed Immigration Minister, in a tongue-in-cheek reference to his predecessors, nevertheless promised he would be 'relying more on evidence than is customary in this role' (Green, 2010).

Implementation

The policies that emerge in legislative and broader forms evolve in the course of their implementation (Hill, 2009). Writing on education, but of a process that is equally true in migration and integration, Stephen Ball says:

> Policies are contested, interpreted and enacted in a variety
> of arenas of practice and the rhetorics, texts and meanings of
> policy makers do not always translate directly and obviously
> into institutional practices. They are inflected, mediated,
> resisted and misunderstood, or in some cases simply prove
> unworkable. (Ball, 2008: 7)

Implementation is often the stage at which policies unravel, are abandoned or have unforeseen consequences that become apparent when faced with the reality of the issues they are intended to address (Dorey, 2005: 3). This will be evident in the implementation of asylum policy, for instance, at the local and national level. It has been argued by immigration lawyers that the effectiveness and fairness of immigration control can depend as much on the quality and efficiency of those who are engaged in operating the system as the structure of the system itself (Jackson et al, 2008: 5).

Historical overview

To understand policy today it is necessary to step back and remind ourselves how we came to be here. In the chapters that follow, I shall take account in particular of policy development since 1997, but those developments were constrained by the legislation, institutions and paradigms shaped in earlier years. It is striking how themes that emerge from this early history resonate with the policy debates and practices of today.

Parts of the UK have experienced migration for centuries. 'Immigrants, refugees and sojourners', as one social historian writes, 'have been continually present' (Holmes, 1988: 276). The origins of our plurality lie in conquest, flight from persecution, slavery, trade and even in the Middle Ages in the search for employment. While cities such as London and Cardiff had a long, pre-war, historical experience of migration, however, for other parts of the UK it has been a more recent development. Nevertheless, no one who has read a social history of immigration will doubt the pervasive if immeasurable influence that people from abroad have had for centuries on all aspects of British life, including employment, literature, entertainment and the culture, attitudes and identities of their fellow residents.

Commonwealth immigration

It was the arrival of Jewish people fleeing pogroms in Eastern Europe that led to the first modern legislative controls on immigration in the form of the Aliens Act 1905, providing the Home Secretary with considerable powers to control entry, residence and deportation. British subjects from the colonies and later the Commonwealth continued, on paper, to enjoy a right of entry but there was a de facto policy between the wars to 'keep out Asian and black settlers'. Historian Ian Spencer, drawing on cabinet papers released under the 30-year rule, found administrative barriers to prevent would-be migrants obtaining travel documents, the instructions for which were secreted in circulars and letters to officials. Documents revealed this to be prompted in part by fears of a repeat of inter-racial violence that had occurred in 1919, but also by 'underlying assumptions about the general undesirability of physically and culturally distinct groups', whether British subjects or not (Spencer, 1997: 8–24).

This account challenges the perception that Commonwealth citizens had free access to the UK until 1962 and that, facing labour shortages post-1945, the government welcomed their arrival. Labour

—

23

shortages were intense and it was this that drew in immigrants from the Commonwealth (Rose et al, 1969). Notwithstanding limited recruitment initiatives to meet shortages in the health and transport sectors, the government discouraged immigration from the New Commonwealth while actively recruiting white people from the 'Old Dominions' and Europe. Relations with the Commonwealth required that the 'illusion' of openness be maintained but officials in the 1950s:

> raised the invention of techniques to keep Britain white without using legislation almost to the level of an art form. The contrast between the public face of a mother country open to all and the private calculation to exclude was sharp. (Spencer, 1997: 153)

For the Labour and Conservative administrations of the early post-war years, the benefits of legislation to limit entry did not outweigh the costs for Britain's standing in the Commonwealth if legislation were to appear racially discriminatory. Only when a formula was found that avoided that appearance, a system of employment vouchers restricting the entry of those without a job offer or skills in short supply, was the Commonwealth Immigrants Act 1962 brought onto the statute book.

Contemporary relevance of the 1962 Act

The politics of the 1962 Act, despite the passage of time, is instructive. First, approaches taken within Whitehall were strongly affected by departmental interests. While the views of the then Commonwealth and Colonial Offices were tempered by their need to maintain good relations with governments highly sensitive to restrictions applied only to their citizens, the Home Office was 'singularly and unrestrainedly opposed' to further immigration, believing it likely to lead to unrest. The Treasury, in contrast, argued that there was no economic justification for restrictions as immigration had been beneficial for the economy and there would be costs if it were curtailed (Spencer, 1997: 45, 115).

Second, this period demonstrates how shifts in foreign policy can alter the balance of policy options. In the 1950s, the political cost to Commonwealth relations of legislation to exclude New Commonwealth citizens was too high; by the 1960s, that cost was outweighed by domestic considerations and the shift in focus towards Britain's place in Europe, consolidated by entry into the then Common Market in 1971. While in 1945 Commonwealth citizens had (at least in theory) free access to live and work in the UK, by the 1970s their position was largely reduced to that of aliens; while the fortunes of Europe's citizens was the mirror opposite: aliens in 1945 but enjoying free movement within the European Economic Community (EEC) three decades later (Spencer, 1997: 150).

The unintended outcome of the Act is also instructive: contrary to intention, it marked the *beginning* of the process of significant Black and Asian immigration, not the end. By the 1981 Census, well over three quarters of Asian immigrants had arrived after the 1962 Act, not before. There were three reasons for this: a 'beat the ban rush' in the many months between announcement of the Bill and the Act coming into force; that the law encouraged those in the UK to stay as it would prevent re-entry; and, as migrants could bring their families, each voucher issued led on average to 3.7 people arriving to settle (Rose et al, 1969: 77; Spencer, 1997: 129–55).

Immigration becomes an electoral issue

The strength of anti-immigrant feeling and overt racism in the 1964 general election led the incoming Labour government to impose further restrictions on entry, with all-party support. Setting a pattern to become familiar in subsequent years, rights of entry were often curtailed not through primary legislation but Immigration Rules. Low-skilled permits were no longer issued, the definition of family members was more tightly drawn, the standard of proof required to establish family relationships was made more rigorous and administrative delays were used to regulate entry numbers.

The year 1968 saw the passing in just three days of legislation to curb the entry of UK passport-holders after 10,000 Kenyan Asians arrived in one month (prompted by hostility in Kenya and fears that their bolt-hole to Britain would soon close). Using a formula that was later to form the basis of comprehensive reform in 1971, the Act made British citizens subject to immigration control (with access controlled by an annual quota) unless they, a parent or grandparent were born, adopted or naturalised in the UK. When Enoch Powell made his 'Rivers of Blood' speech one month after the Act came into force calling for an end to all non-white immigration, his was not an isolated voice. In 1969, 327 out of 412 Conservative constituency associations surveyed wanted all 'coloured' immigration stopped indefinitely (Dummett and Nicol, 1990; Spencer, 1997: 143; Hansen, 2002).

At the 1970 general election, immigration was the fourth most salient issue. The seminal Immigration Act 1971 consolidated the now tight restrictions on all primary immigration, allowing access for work only through a work permit system linked to specific jobs. The grandparent rule, allowing not only access but also a 'right of abode', was a qualification far more likely to be met by would-be migrants from Old Commonwealth countries such as Canada than by their New Commonwealth counterparts. The Act gave the Home Secretary huge discretion to make further changes under Immigration Rules: those governing the entry of husbands, for instance, changed five times between 1974 and 1985 (Dummett and Nicol, 1990).

Symbolically, the 1971 Act came into force on the day the UK entered the EEC, 1 January 1973, giving freedom to live and work to people from countries with which, in some cases, the UK had been at war less than 30 years before. Yet this huge shift in the parameters of immigration control attracted little political or public attention. It led initially to modest and largely unnoticed numbers of people, not withstanding enlargement of the EU to include countries less prosperous than the UK: Greece in 1981 and Spain and Portugal five years later (Rechi, 2008).

Meanwhile, Commonwealth citizens within the UK retained rights that they had previously enjoyed, including access to employment in most parts of the civil service and to be a candidate and to vote in parliamentary and local elections. For those seeking to be joined by their dependants from abroad, however, entry was rationed by long delays and intrusive procedures to establish identity (see Chapter 4). Nevertheless, grants of settlement to Commonwealth citizens continued at an average of over 30,000 per year throughout the 1970s, and political controversy focused heavily on these numbers and on the queues of families waiting to enter, rather than on any larger policy objective (Dummett and Nicol, 1990: 234).

Family migration was not, however, the only issue. Within a year of the 1971 Act, a military coup in Uganda and subsequent expulsion of British nationals, mostly of Indian origin, led 30,000 people to seek sanctuary in the UK. Despite their British citizenship, Ugandan Asians were met by high levels of public and media hostility, reception camps in former military barracks and attempts to prevent them settling in cities such as Leicester which had significant Asian populations and where they subsequently made a substantial economic contribution.

Community relations rationale

The rationale for tighter controls was that it was necessary to improve community relations. That was consistently challenged on the grounds that they would increase the insecurity of immigrants already living in the UK (Dummett and Nicol, 1990: 220) and undermine the positive perception of minorities on which good relations depends. Writing in 1996, with the benefit of hindsight, former Labour Minister Roy Hattersley spelt out that contradiction:

> Good community relations are not encouraged by the promotion of the idea that the entry of one black immigrant to this country will be so damaging to the national interest that husbands must be separated from their wives, children denied the chance to look after their aged parents and sisters prevented from attending their brothers' weddings ... if we

cannot afford to let them in, those of them who are here already must be doing harm. (Hattersley, 1996)

Nevertheless, from the end of the 1970s there was a bipartisan consensus that increasingly tight controls were necessary. Nostalgia among some Conservatives for the Commonwealth, still evident in the 1971 debate, was no longer voiced and Labour's enthusiasm for controls was curbed only occasionally by pressure from ethnic minority constituents; to relax restrictions on foreign husbands, for instance, in 1974.

Conservative era

The choice of Margaret Thatcher as leader of the Conservative Party in 1975 marked the shift to a more populist, less inclusive, form of conservatism. Immigration policy was no exception. The British people, Mrs Thatcher famously said before the election, fear 'being swamped' by people with 'alien cultures'.[4] Elected in 1979, the government moved quickly to impose further restrictions on fiancés, spouses and elderly relatives and to limit visitors and students switching to another status in Immigration Rules the following year. In its 1981 Nationality Act, it brought nationality and immigration law into line by redefining British citizenship more narrowly to match those who now had the right to live in the UK and creating subcategories of citizenship for many who did not.

Further legislation followed in 1987 to penalise airlines and shippers that transported passengers without required visas, and in 1988 to impose additional restrictions on family reunion. When asylum seekers began to arrive from Commonwealth countries such as Sri Lanka, visa requirements were introduced to limit their capacity to reach the UK. A rise in the number of people seeking asylum after 1990, including from the former Yugoslavia, Somalia and former Soviet countries, prompted increasingly restrictive legislation in 1993 and 1996 to prevent and deter people reaching the UK (see Chapter 2).

Immigration and asylum were salient if not definitive electoral issues in the 1990s and were used overtly in the 1992 general election and

1994 European election campaigns, a Conservative party official later reported to have observed that the issue had 'played particularly well in the tabloids and has more potential to hurt'.[5] It was during this period that new vocabulary entered the discourse on asylum, of Britain as a 'soft touch' for 'bogus refugees' perceived to be 'abusing' the system and taking advantage of the goodwill of the British people (Spencer, 1998). While rising asylum numbers caused consternation, some 32,500 applying in 1997, little attention was paid to the far greater number of work permit-holders and their dependants, 63,000 approved that year (Home Office, 2001).

Neither asylum nor immigration were, nevertheless, major issues in the 1997 election. Only 3% of the public then cited race and immigration as among key issues facing the country (MORI, 2009) and Labour's manifesto gave migration little coverage beyond assurances that it would remove certain 'arbitrary and unfair' impacts of immigration control. Just six lines were devoted to asylum, the issue that would dominate its first term in office, and none to labour migration where it would fundamentally change the parameters of policy and debate.

The story from here is taken up in the chapters that follow, first setting out Labour's inheritance and the policies it adopted on asylum, labour migrants, students, family migrants, irregular migration and integration, before in turn handing over to the Coalition government in May 2010. We see that the Coalition has retained the thrust of much of Labour's approach but with some elements of reversal to Labour's early thinking in relation to labour migration, students and citizenship, a new 'cap' on labour migration, and steps to sever the link between temporary migration and settlement: to retain access to the 'brightest and the best' while curbing the impact of migration on population growth (May, 2010).

Migration and migrants in the UK

Before I turn to a few facts on recent migration trends there are points to note about the data and its political significance. A key difference

—

is between 'flow' data, showing the number who enter and leave, and 'stock' figures, showing the number present within the country at a given time. On flows, we know most about those from outside the European Economic Area (EEA) who are subject to immigration control and least about EEA nationals who are not. The UK also has limited 'stock' data on foreign nationals (non-citizens) within the UK, with a little more on those who are foreign-born, which includes those who were always or have become British citizens. Many data sources, however, only record those who identify themselves as from an ethnic minority, a majority of whom are not migrants but born in the UK. The paucity of data on those who have migrated to the UK, particularly on recent migrants, is a significant limitation on our knowledge of what happens to those who enter through various migration channels.

The political fallout of inadequate migration data, including the implications for a local authority funding system reliant on accurate local population figures, led the Office for National Statistics (ONS) to establish a taskforce to improve national and local statistics (2008–12). An e-Borders system recording entry and exit (see Chapter 5) may provide more comprehensive data by 2014.

Turning to the data we do have we should note, first, the sheer number of *arrivals* at the UK's borders each year: 101.6 million in 2009,[6] of whom 12.3 million were not EEA nationals (Home Office, 2010). It is this volume of arrivals, many of them short-stay visitors, which is relevant to any discussion on the operation of border controls – how feasible it is to carry out checks on each person who enters, for instance and to monitor whether those given temporary residence do leave when that time has expired.

Controversy often focuses on a quite separate figure, that of *net migration*: the total number of those arriving with the intention of staying for more than a year, less the number who leave with that intention. It is this figure that is relevant if the focus is on the overall number of people living in the UK, and in the Coalition government's commitment to bring net migration down to 'tens of thousands'. In most years until 1993, fewer people came to live in the UK than left, but net migration subsequently rose over the next decade to a peak of 245,000 in 2004. In 2008, as Figure 1.1 shows, it fell during the recession but rose again to 242,000 in the year to September 2010. Significantly, this was largely because of a decline in emigration from the UK (Horsfield, 2005; ONS, 2011). Emigration levels are thus crucial to the 'net' migration figure, yet not subject to policy control – and woe betide the government that suggested more British people should leave to help bring net migration down!

If the focus is on the impact or needs of new arrivals, it is not net migration that is relevant but *immigration*: not only those arriving with the intention of staying more than a year but arguably those here for shorter periods as seasonal agricultural workers for instance or on short courses. In the year to September 2010, an estimated 586,000 people came to live in the UK for more than a year: contrary to public

Figure 1.1: Net migration to the UK 2000–10

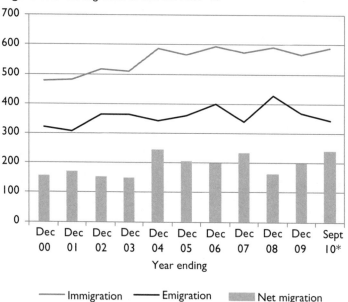

Year ending

——— Immigration ——— Emigration ▓▓ Net migration

Note: *Year includes provisional estimate for 2010.

Source: ONS estimates of long-term international migration to September 2010 (ONS, 2011)

perception, a level similar to the annual intake since 2004 (ONS, 2011). A striking feature in recent years has been the number of people coming from the eight accession countries of the EU ('A8'), the vast majority from Poland (Matheson, 2009), although entry declined significantly during the recession.

After varying periods of time, some migrants can apply to remain in the long term. In the year to September 2010, 239,000 people successfully applied for settlement, a significant increase on the previous year and, as Figure 1.2 shows, continuing an upward trend. The largest category is those who had originally come to the UK through a work channel (including dependants), followed by those who had come for family reasons, few having come as asylum seekers (ONS, 2010c). Those whose predominant concern is to limit population growth have increasingly focused on this settlement figure, arguing that the UK could continue to benefit from labour migration if there were tighter limits on those subsequently allowed to stay (Balanced Migration, 2010).

Figure 1.2: Grants of settlement 2005–10 (excluding EEA and Swiss nationals)

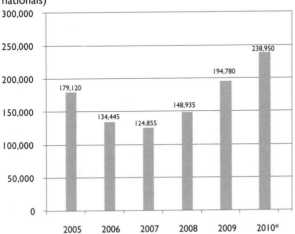

Note: *Year to September 2010
Source: Home Office Control of Immigration Statistics UK (2009, Table 4.4), Control of Immigration Quarterly Statistical Summary Q3 (2010, Table 4.3)

32

For those British citizens emigrating to live abroad (in 2004–08), the most popular destinations were Australia, Spain, Germany, France and the USA. Work was the main reason for leaving, followed by family or education (ONS, 2009). We know surprisingly little about those who emigrate, although there was a net loss of 2.7 million British citizens between 1966 and 2006, nor about those migrants who in turn re-emigrate, although both have potential policy implications (Sriskandarajah and Drew, 2006; Finch et al, 2009).

The UK's diverse, ageing population

Net migration was the primary driver of the growth in the UK's population for much of the past decade, natural change (the difference between births and deaths) once again becoming the main driver in 2007 (ONS, 2010b). The UK population was 61.8 million in 2009, up from 56.3 million in 1983. During that time, the proportion of the population under 16 years fell and those over 85 grew, an ageing process that will continue, leaving a smaller proportion of people of working age. Migration has helped to offset demographic ageing but cannot be the sole solution to that problem (Münz, 2007; Matheson, 2009).

At the time of the 2001 Census, around 8% of the UK population had been born abroad. By March 2010, this had risen to 11.4%, of whom a little under half were British citizens. India was the most common country of birth for those born abroad and Polish now the most common non-British nationality (ONS, 2010c). By 2008, migrants from the A8 European countries accounted for 10% of the foreign-born population. Half of them are in the 16–29 age group, but there has been an increase in family migration, raising the number of A8 child migrants under 16 in the UK to 75,000 (Matheson, 2009): small numbers in the overall migration picture but more significant for schools and other service providers.

The diversity of countries from which migrants now come is a very different picture from the post-war period. Britain's foreign-born population has also become more diverse in terms of religion, language, socio-economic status, immigration status, transnational connections and location in the UK. By 2001, there were already people from 179 nations in London, 45% of whom had arrived since 1990, and 300 languages were spoken in the capital's schools. Dubbed 'super-diversity', a 'level and kind of complexity surpassing anything the country has previously experienced', this is significant because it has brought new patterns of inequality and prejudice, differing needs and barriers to service delivery (including the implications of language diversity for translation and interpretation services), and requires new modes of consultation with migrant communities (Vertovec, 2007: 1024).

Chapters of this book

I began this chapter with a paradox – the gap between public demands for tighter controls on migration and successive governments' reluctance or failure to deliver – and suggested that, in this experience, the UK is no exception. I set out the range of conflicting policy objectives and constraints which in practice limit both the policy options and the efficacy of controls, including limitations within the policymaking system itself, and argued that the options and constraints are rarely transparent to the public, nor the rationale for decisions clearly explained. I drew on migration theory to show that policymakers need to take account of the powerful structural drivers of migration and the actual motivations of migrants if they are to design appropriate policy levers, but also need to acknowledge the limits on their capacity to manage this complex, global process. Finally, I gave a brief overview of the history that precedes the chapters in this book, drawing out themes from decades past with surprising resonance for migration debates and policy interventions today.

In the next chapter I turn to the issue that dominated the decade to 2004, asylum, showing how the unprecedented number of arrivals and the media and public reaction to it shifted first a Conservative and then a Labour government to deploy extreme measures to deter and remove people perceived to be abusing British hospitality rather than in need of protection. In Chapter 3, I shift focus to look at policy on labour migration, tracing the way in which policy has both shaped and responded to demand for skilled and low-skilled labour through the shift to 'managed migration' to maximise the UK's economic interests a decade ago and the enlargement of the EU in 2004, to the Points-Based System and its subsequent reversal in some respects by the Coalition government. I am also concerned here with policy on international students, the largest intake of migrants to the UK and, like labour migration, overtly geared towards maximising economic benefits for the UK and its education providers until competing policy objectives brought the primacy of those objectives into question.

In Chapter 4 I turn to family migration which highlights themes that have already emerged in earlier chapters: the gap between the rights enjoyed by EU nationals and other migrants; the close relationship between entry and post-entry restrictions on access to jobs and services; the impact of the courts in curbing government policy options; and the stark contrast between the perspectives of policymakers seeking to regulate entry and those of individuals whose lives can be deeply affected by the rules that they make.

In Chapter 5 I focus on irregular migrants, finding that most of this eclectic category of people came legally and overstayed or are in breach of their conditions of stay. We see that the enforcement measures used to deter, detect, detain and remove them can be disproportionate and of limited effect set against the limited priority attached to tackling the structural causes of irregularity. As in other chapters, we find that there are conflicting interests at play, constraining in some crucial respects the extent to which governments have been willing or able to intervene; and suggest that a note of realism needs to be injected into the promises that are made to the public and in the approach to more than half a million irregular migrants currently living in the UK.

The intensity of political debate on the numbers who enter reflects concern about impacts after arrival, not least on the labour market, public services and relationships with existing residents. Chapter 6 is devoted to policies relating to the participation and inclusion of newcomers and those who settle in the UK, or rather in significant respects to explaining a policy vacuum in that field. The Conclusion draws together key themes that emerge and suggests reforms that could help to shift both the politics of migration and the outcomes of the migration process.

Notes

[1] The Immigration and Asylum Act 1999; Nationality, Immigration and Asylum Act 2002; Immigration and Asylum (Treatment of Claimants etc) Act 2004; Immigration, Asylum and Nationality Act 2006; UK Borders Act 2007; Criminal Justice and Immigration Act 2008; and Borders, Citizenship and Immigration Act 2009.

[2] Including the Channel Islands and the Isle of Man.

[3] Now the 'Court of Justice of the European Union'.

[4] *World in Action*, January 1978.

[5] Head of the Conservative Party Research Department, quoted in the *Observer*, 3 September 1995.

[6] Not including Ireland. Note that throughout the book migration statistics are rounded to the nearest thousand.

References

Balanced Migration (2010) 'Our Case'. Available at: http://www.balancedmigration.com/ourcase.php

Ball, S. J. (2008) *The Education Debate*. Bristol: The Policy Press.

Banting, K. and Kymlicka, W. (2006) *Multiculturalism and the Welfare State: Recognition and Redistribution in Contemporary Democracies*. Oxford: OUP.

Betts, A. (2008) 'Global Migration Governance', GEG Working Paper 2008/43, University of Oxford.

Bigo, D. (2002) 'Security and Immigration: Toward a Critique of the Governmentality of Unease', *Alternatives* 27: 63.

Bigo, D., Carrera, S., Guild, E. and Walker, R.B.J. (2009) 'The Changing Landscape of European Liberty and Security: The Mid-Term Report of the CHALLENGE Project', *International Social Science Journal* 59(192): 283–308.

Boswell, C. (2007) 'Theorising Migration Policy: Is There a Third Way?' *International Migration Review* 41(1): 75–100.

Boswell, C. (2008) 'The Political Functions of Expert Knowledge: Knowledge and Legitimation in European Union Immigration Policy', *Journal of European Public Policy* 15(4): 471–88.

Boswell, C. (2009) 'Knowledge, Legitimation and the Politics of Risk: The Functions of Research in Public Debates on Migration', *Political Studies* 57(3): 165–86.

Brettel, C.B. and Hollifield, J. (2000) *Migration Theory: Talking across Disciplines*. New York: Routledge.

Castells, M. (1989) *The Informational City: Information Technology, Economic Restructuring and the Urban-Regional Process*. Oxford: Oxford University Press.

Castles, S. (2004) 'Why Migration Policies Fail', *Journal of Ethnic and Racial Studies* 27(2): 205–27.

Castles, S. and Miller, M. J. (2009) *The Age of Migration: International Population Movements in the Modern World*, 4th edition. Basingstoke: Palgrave Macmillan.

CEU (Council of the European Union) (2004) *The Hague Programme: Strengthening Freedom, Security and Justice in the European Union*, JAI 559. Brussels: Council of the European Union.

CEU (2009) *The Stockholm Programme: An Open and Secure Europe Protecting the Citizens*, JAI 896. Brussels: Council of the European Union.

Chappell, L. and Glennie, A. (2009) *Maximising the Development Outcomes of Migration: A Policy Perspective*. London: Institute for Public Policy Research.

Coleman, D. (1991) 'Policy Research – Who Needs It?', *Governance: An International Journal of Policy and Administration* 4(4): 420–55.

Conservative Party (2010) *Invitation to Join the Government of Britain: The Conservative Manifesto 2010*, London: Conservative Party.

Daily Mail (2009) 'Playing into the Hands of Racists', 22 October.

Dorey, P. (2005) *Policy Making in Britain: An Introduction*. London: Sage.

Dummett, A. and Nicol, A. (1990) *Subjects, Citizens, Aliens and Others: Nationality and Immigration Law*. London: Weidenfeld and Nicolson.

Dunleavy, P. (1995) 'Policy Disasters: Explaining the UK's Record', *Public Policy and Administration* 10: 52–70.

Eurobarometer (2009) 'Eurobarometer 72 First Results Public Opinion in the European Union'. Available at: http://ec.europa. eu/public_opinion/archives/eb/eb72/eb72_first_en.pdf (accessed 4 January 2010).

Eurostat (2010a) 'Remittances from the EU Down for the First Time in 2009, Flows to Non-EU Countries More Resilient', *Statistics in Focus* 40/2010. Brussels: Eurostat.

Eurostat (2010b) 'Population of Foreign Citizens in the EU27 in 2008', 129/2010. Brussels: European Commission.

Facchini, G. and Mayda, A. M. (2009) *The Political Economy of Immigration Policy*, Human Development Research Paper 2009/03, United Nations Development Programme.

Finch, T., Latorre, M., Pollard, N. and Rutter, J. (2009) *Shall We Stay or Shall We Go? Re-Emigration Trends among Britain's Immigrants.* London: Institute for Public Policy Research.

Finney, N. and Simpson, L. (2009) *Sleepwalking to Segration? Challenging Myths about Race and Migration.* Bristol: The Policy Press.

FOE (Friends of the Earth) (2006) 'Immigration, Population and the Environment', Briefing Note, Friends of the Earth.

Freeman, G.P. and Kessler, A.E. (2008) 'Political Economy and Migration Policy', *Journal of Ethnic and Migration Studies* 34(4): 655–78.

GCIM (Global Commission on International Migration) (2005) *Migration in an Interconnected World: New Directions for Action.* Geneva: Global Commission on International Migration.

Geddes, A. (2005) 'Getting the Best of Both Worlds? Britain, the EU and Migration Policy', *Journal of International Affairs* 81(4): 723–40.

GFMD (Global Forum on Migration and Development) (2010) 'Global Forum on Migration and Development'. Available at: http://www. gfmd.org/en/home.html (accessed 9 September 2010).

Goodhart, D. (2004) 'Too Diverse?', *Prospect* 95 (February).

Green, A. (2009) 'Presentation to the National Housing Federation on 23 September 2009', Briefing Paper 165. London: Migration Watch UK.

Green, D. (2010) 'The Real Immigration Question', Speech to the Royal Commonwealth Society, London, 7 September.

—

Gurak, D.T. and Caces, F. (1992) 'Migration Networks and the Shaping of Migration Systems', in M. Kritz, L.L. Lim and H. Zlotnik (eds) *International Migration Systems: A Global Approach*. Oxford: Clarendon Press, pp. 150–76.

Hansen, R. (2002) 'Globalisation, Embedded Realism and Path Dependence: The Other Immigrants to Europe', *Comparative Political Studies* 35(3): 259–83.

Hattersley, R. (1996) 'Endpiece', *The Guardian*, 26 February.

Haug, S. (2008) 'Migration Networks and Migration Decision-Making', *Journal of Ethnic and Migration Studies* 34(4): 585–6.

Hill, M. (2009) *The Public Policy Process*, 5th edn. Harlow: Pearson Education.

HM Government (2009) 'PSA Delivery Agreement 3: Ensure Controlled, Fair Migration That Protects the Public and Contributes to Economic Growth'. London: Home Office.

Hollifield, J. (2008) 'Politics of Migration: How Can We "Bring the State Back in"?' in C.B. Brettel and J.F. Hollifield (eds) *Migration Theory*, 2nd edn. New York and London: Routledge, pp. 183–239.

Holmes, C. (1988) *John Bull's Island: Immigration and British Society 1871–1971*. Basingstoke: Macmillan.

Home Office (2001) *Control of Immigration: Statistics United Kingdom 2000*. London: Home Office.

Home Office (2002) *Secure Borders, Safe Haven: Integration with Diversity in Modern Britain*. London: HMSO.

Home Office (2010) *Control of Immigration: Quarterly Statistical Summary United Kingdom July–September 2010*. London: Home Office.

Horsfield, G. (2005) 'International Migration', in *Focus on People and Migration*. London: Office for National Statistics, Chapter 7.

IOM (International Organisation for Migration) (2004) *International Migration Law Glossary on Migration*. Geneva: IOM.

Jackson, D., Warr, G., Onslow, J. and Middleton, J. (2008) *Immigration Law and Practice*, 4th edn. Haywards Heath: Tottel Publishing.

Jayaweera, H. and Choudhury, T. (2008) *Immigration, Faith and Cohesion: Evidence from Local Areas with Significant Muslim Populations*. York: Joseph Rowntree Foundation.

—

Joppke, C. (1998) 'Why Liberal States Accept Unwanted Immigration', *World Politics* 50: 266–93.

Jordan, A.G. and Richardson, J. (1982) 'The British Policy Style or the Logic of Negotiation?' in J. Richardson (ed) *Policy Styles in Western Europe*. London: George, Allen and Unwin.

King, R. (2002) 'Towards a New Map of European Migration', *International Journal of Population Geography* 8(2): 89–106.

Kyambi, S. (2009) *Room for Manoeuvre? The Options for Addressing Immigration Policy-Divergence between Holyrood and Westminster*. Glasgow: Equality and Human Rights Commission Scotland.

Lloyd, C. (2010) *2008–09 Citizenship Survey Community Cohesion Topic Report*, Department for Communities and Local Government.

Malmberg, B., Tamas, K., Bloom, D., Münz, R. and Canning, D. (2006) *Global Population Ageing, Migration and European External Policies*. Stockholm: Institute for Future Studies.

Massey, D. S., Arango, J., Hugo, G., Kouaouci, A., Pellegrino, A. and Taylor, J.E. (1993) 'Theories of International Migration: A Review and Appraisal', *Population and Development Review* 19(3): 421–66.

Matheson, J. (2009) 'National Statistician's Annual Article on the Population: A Demographic Review', *Population Trends* 138 (Winter): 7–21.

May, T. (2010) The Home Secretary's Immigration Speech', 5 November. London: Home Office.

Migration Watch UK (2009) *The Invisible Cost of Immigration*, Briefing Paper Economics 1.23. Available at: http://www.migrationwatchuk. org/briefingpaper/document/157 (accessed 29 August 2010).

Migration Watch UK (2010) 'Immigration has Damaged Employment Prospects for British Workers', Press release, 12 August.

MORI, I. (2009) 'Trends since 1997: The Most Important Issues Facing Britain Today'. Available at: http://www. ipsos-mori.com/researchpublications/researcharchive/poll. aspx?oItemId=56&view=wide (accessed 4 January 2010).

Münz, R. (2007) 'Ageing and Demographic Change in European Societies: Main Trends and Alternative Policy Options', Social Protection Discussion Paper. Washington, DC: World Bank.

—

OECD (Organisation for Economic Cooperation and Development) (2009) *The Future of International Migration to OECD Countries*. Paris: Organisation for Economic Cooperation and Development.

ONS (Office for National Statistics) (2009) *Migration Statistics 2008*. London: ONS.

ONS (2010a) 'Provisional Estimates of Long-Term International Migration, Year Ending March 2010'. Available at: http://www.statistics.gov.uk/downloads/theme_population/provisional-estimates-longterm-international-migration.xls (accessed 10 January 2011).

ONS (2010b) 'Population Change', National Statistics Online. Available at: http://www.statistics.gov.uk/cci/nugget.asp?id=950 (accessed 9 September 2010).

ONS (2010c) *Migration Statistics Quarterly Report*, No 7: November. London: ONS.

ONS (2011) *Migration Statistics Quarterly Report*, No 9: May. London: ONS.

Parker, S., Paun, A., McClory, J. and Blanchford, K. (2010) *Shaping Up: A Whitehall for the Future*. London: Institute for Government.

Peach, C. (2009) 'Slippery Segregation: Discovering or Manufacturing Ghettos?', *Journal of Ethnic and Migration Studies*, 35(9): 1381-95.

Peers, S. (2009) *EU Treaty Analysis No 4: British and Irish Opt-outs from EU Justice and Home Affairs (JHA) Law*. London: Statewatch.

Penninx, R. and Martiniello, M. (2004) 'Integration Processes and Policies: State of the Art and Lessons', in R. Penninx, K. Kraal, M. Martiniello and S. Vertovec (eds) *Citizenship in European Cities: Immigrants, Local Politics and Integration Policies*. Aldershot: Ashgate.

Phillips, D. (2006) 'Parallel Lives? Challenging Discourses of British Muslim Self-Segregation', *Environment and Planning D: Society and Space* 24(1): 25–40.

Phillips, D. (2007) 'Ethnic and Racial Segregation: A Critical Perspective', *Geography Compass* 1(5): 1138–59.

Piore, M. J. (1979) *Birds of Passage: Migrant Labour in Industrial Societies*. Cambridge: Cambridge University Press.

Portes, A. (1998) 'Social Capital: Its Origins and Applications in Modern Sociology', *Annual Review of Sociology* 24: 1–14.

Rechi, E. (2008) 'Cross-State Mobility in the EU', *European Societies* 10(2): 197–224.

Rose, E.J.B. and associates (1969) *Colour and Citizenship: A Report on British Race Relations*. London: Oxford University Press.

Salt, J. and Stein, J. (2002) 'Migration as a Business: The Case of Trafficking', *International Migration* 35(4): 467–94.

Sassen, S. (1988) *The Mobility of Labour and Capital: A Study in International Investment and Labor Flow*. Cambridge: Cambridge University Press.

Select Committee on International Development (2004) *Migration and Development: How to Make Migration Work for Poverty Reduction, Volume 1*, 6th Report Session 2003–04, HC 79-1. London: House of Commons.

Soysal, Y.N. (1994) *Limits of Citizenship: Migrants and Postnational Membership in Europe*. Chicago: University of Chicago Press.

Spencer, I. R. G. (1997) *British Immigration Policy Since 1939: The Making of Multi-Racial Britain*. London: Routledge.

Spencer, S. (1998) 'The Impact of Immigration Policy on Race Relations', in T. Blackstone, B. Parekh and P. Sanders (eds) *Race Relations in Britain: A Developing Agenda*. London and New York: Routledge.

Spencer, S. (2003) 'Introduction', in S. Spencer (ed) *The Politics of Migration: Managing Opportunity, Conflict and Change*. Oxford: The Political Quarterly, Blackwell.

Spencer, S. (2007) 'Immigration', in A. Seldon (ed) *Blair's Britain 1997–2007*. Cambridge: Cambridge University Press.

Sriskandarajah, D. and Drew, C. (2006) *Brits Abroad: Mapping the Scale and Nature of British Emigration*. London: Institute for Public Policy Research.

Stark, O. and Bloom, D. (1985) 'The New Economics of Labor Migration', *American Economic Review* 75: 173–8.

—

Statham, P. and Geddes, A. (2006) 'Elites and the "Organised Public": Who Drives British Immigration Politics and in Which Direction?' *West European Politics* 29(2): 248–69.

Transatlantic Trends (2009) *Immigration: Key Findings 2009*. Washington, DC: German Marshall Fund.

UKBA (UK Border Agency) (2010) 'Statements of Changes in Immigration Rules'. Available at: http://www.ukba.homeoffice. gov.uk/sitecontent/documents/policyandlaw/statementsofchanges/

UNDESA (UN Department of Economic and Social Affairs) (2009) 'Trends in International Migration Stock: The 2008 Revision'. Available at: http://www.un.org/esa/population/migration/UN_ MigStock_2008.pdf (accessed 19 May 2011).

UNDP (UN Development Programme) (2009) 'Overcoming Barriers: Human Mobility and Development', *Human Development Report 2009*. New York: UNDP.

Van Hear, N., Brubaker, R. and Bessa, T. (2009) *Managing Mobility for Human Development: The Growing Salience of Mixed Migration*, UN Development Programme Human Development Reports Research Paper 2009/20. New York: UNDP.

Vertovec, S. (1999) 'Conceiving and Researching Transnationalism', *Journal of Ethnic and Racial Studies* 22(2): 447–62.

Vertovec, S. (2007) 'Super-Diversity and Its Implications', *Journal of Ethnic and Racial Studies* 30(6): 1024–54.

Woolas, P. (2009) 'Immigration and Asylum Statistics Released', Home Office press release, 27 August.

2

Protection: asylum and refugee policy

In this chapter I explore policy towards people who apply for refugee status, 'asylum seekers', and those who are refused. Tracing the rapid rise in asylum applications from the late 1980s, we see the responses of Conservative and Labour administrations: from measures to prevent asylum seekers reaching the UK, through procedural reforms of the refugee determination system to curtailment of access to work and benefits, noting parallel developments across the EU. We see how policy was shaped by factors external and internal to the UK that differ in degree from those we shall see in other chapters: the constraints imposed by international and European human rights law, high levels of cooperation at EU level, vitriolic coverage in the tabloid press, and major capacity failings within the bureaucracy. It is also here that we see exclusion from the welfare state used as a primary lever of immigration control:

> The utilisation of the welfare state as a device to deter asylum seekers added a new weapon to the armoury of post-war immigration controls and redefined the relationship between migrants and the welfare state. (Geddes, 2000: 142)

To understand how that could emerge and be reinforced by a Labour government we need to explore the tension between the UK's legal and ethical responsibility to those in need of protection and the political, economic and practical challenges to which that obligation gives rise (Law, 2009).

Legal and ethical constraints

It is in relation to people seeking protection that government is most constrained by commitments under international and European human rights law, and it is on human rights and ethical grounds that, from one side of a highly polarised debate, criticism has been based. The basis of international refugee law is the 1951 Geneva Convention on the Status of Refugees (and subsequent 1967 Protocol) to which the vast majority of member states of the United Nations (UN) are signatories. Agreed at the height of the Cold War, it defines a refugee as someone who:

> owing to a well-founded fear of persecution for reasons of race, religion, nationality, membership of a particular social group or political opinions, is outside of the country of his nationality and is unable or, owing to such fear, is unwilling to avail himself of the protection of that country ... [1]

It will be immediately apparent that the definition is a narrow one, excluding those who, fleeing civil war or famine for instance, would in common parlance be called refugees. Under the Convention, however, states must provide an impartial process to determine whether an individual qualifies for protection and must not return a refugee to a place where they could face persecution (*refoulement*). Interpretation of the Convention falls to the agency set up to safeguard the well-being of refugees, the Office of the UN High Commissioner for Refugees (UNHCR), to the governments of member states and to the courts: the UK Supreme Court ruling in July 2010, for instance, that persecution on grounds of homosexuality falls within the terms of the Convention, a decision accepted by the Coalition government.[2]

The causes of conflict are often related to poverty and to the collapse of effective government and the rule of law, conditions that can contribute to the motivation to move (Van Hear et al, 2009). Applicants for refugee status can thus include some whose flight is entirely because of persecution; some who are fleeing violence that falls outside of the Convention definition of refugee; and others who have less need of a safe haven than of economic opportunities for which they have found no other channel to migrate. An application for refugee status can be made after the person has been in the host country for some time. The situation in their country of origin may have deteriorated or their application may be 'opportunistic' if their permission to stay is about to expire (Home Office, 2005: 36). Their claim must nevertheless be considered, leading some governments to question not the narrowness of the Convention but the constraint it imposes on their capacity to control their borders. The judicial nature of the process ensures that it is expensive and time-consuming. Legal and practical barriers can then make it difficult to remove those whose applications are refused (Gibney, 2008: 150).

The UNHCR finds critics of the Convention arguing that it is 'outdated, unworkable, irrelevant and inflexible' and that the protection regime globally is threatened by the economic cost of offering asylum, by security fears in the context of the 'war on terror' and concerns regarding mixed motives for migration: 'States that once had generous refugee policies now see the costs of asylum as outweighing its benefits ... [and] refugees as a burden rather than an asset' (UNHCR, 2006: 1). UK leaders have been among those critics, Prime Minister Blair arguing: 'The Convention was drawn up for a vastly different world.... The UK is taking a lead in arguing for reform, not of the Convention's values but of how it operates' (Blair, 2001). The Conservative manifesto in 2005 promised to pull out of the Convention and allow only an annual quota of refugees to enter, but Labour's Home Secretary rejected that as 'unworkable, unjust and counterproductive', arguing that it would destroy the international cooperation the UK needs to return those whose applications are refused (Home Office, 2005). A House of Lords inquiry found that 'The 1951 Convention regime has stood the test of time. There is no viable alternative to it as the principal international instrument of protection for those at risk of persecution' (HLSC on European Union, 2004: para 125).

The government has found itself less constrained by the UN Convention on the Rights of the Child because, when ratifying it

47

in 1991, it entered a reservation in relation to immigration control. In face of criticism from the UK's Children's Commissioners and parliament's Joint Committee on Human Rights that this 'sends out a powerful signal that the rights of asylum seeking children are less important than those of other children' (JCHR, 2007: 176), the government withdrew that reservation in 2009, a notable example of the influence of such bodies. Significantly, the government has found itself forcefully constrained by the European Convention on Human Rights (ECHR, enforceable in the UK courts through the Human Rights Act 1998), which requires government to secure the rights in the Convention 'to everyone within their jurisdiction', thus including refused asylum seekers. The courts have consistently challenged aspects of asylum legislation and practice as in breach of the Convention so that anticipation of what a court decision *might* be has in itself been a constraint on the options government has felt able to pursue.[3]

Rise in asylum applications in Europe

The rising number of people seeking protection in the 1990s was a global phenomenon. Large population displacements were less a consequence of persecution per se than of armed conflict and communal violence, as in Somalia and Afghanistan. In some cases, as in the former Yugoslavia, ethnic displacement was not a by-product of conflict but an intended weapon of war. In the decade to 2001, 70% of the world's refugee population was accommodated in developing countries but others sought asylum in industrialised states (Crisp, 2003). The UNHCR found that this led to a marked shift in approach across receiving states: more restrictive policies; curtailment of due process; greater use of detention and expulsion; greater collaboration between asylum authorities, intelligence and enforcement agencies; and a proliferation of alternative, discretionary protection mechanisms in sending and receiving states according fewer entitlements than guaranteed by the Convention (UNHCR, 2006: 1–2).

As numbers rose in Europe (Figure 2.1), governments did indeed respond with measures to deter asylum seekers reaching their borders, to reform asylum procedures, increase capacity to detain and remove and to limit access to welfare support. Exclusion from work and the welfare system has been used not only to deter future arrivals but arguably to exclude asylum seekers from social integration so that the migration process could be reversed, while reassuring 'legitimate welfare receivers' that this is the intention (Geddes, 2000: 143).

Figure 2.1: Asylum applications in the EU27, 1998–2009

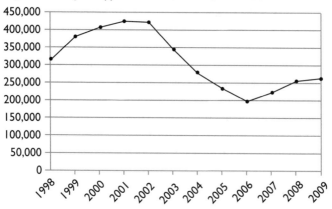

Note: Applications relate to main applicant only.

Source: Eurostat Statistics Explained: Asylum Statistics November 2010; Asylum applications in the European Union 110/ 2007

EU member states, recognising that an effective response required cooperation, began to work towards a Common Asylum System, the EU being given legal competence to develop binding provisions by the Amsterdam Treaty in 1997. The priority was to stop 'asylum shopping' by setting minimum standards for refugee determination procedures and preventing asylum seekers making successive claims in more than one state. Successive UK governments, normally keen to present policy as entirely home-grown, wanted to ensure that the UK was no more attractive to asylum seekers than its neighbours and to be able to return them to an EU country through which they had travelled. Moreover, it helped if rising asylum numbers was seen as a European problem, not a failing of UK immigration control. Hence it signed up to key EU provisions, between 1999 and 2004 opting into all seven asylum measures in contrast to only one in four on regular migration and six out of 21 provisions on border controls (Geddes, 2005).

While the UK was in tune with the restrictive aims at the heart of the EU agenda, it also opted into the 2003 Reception Directive that set down minimum standards on education, health care and legal advice (2003/9/EC). Contrary to UK policy at the time, it also allowed asylum seekers to work if their application had been under consideration for more than 12 months (European Commission, 2003). The Supreme Court has ruled that this includes refused asylum seekers who have made a further claim that remains unresolved – an instance of EU law requiring a change in UK policy (UKBA, 2010a). Recent plans to revise the Directive saw the UK depart from its earlier cooperation, concerned that the definition of family members was too wide and that the grounds on which it could fast-track cases would be curtailed (HLSC on European Union, 2009).

UK destination

The UK was consistently among the top three EU countries in the number of asylum applications over the decade 1999–2008, and in 2000–03 received more than any other EU country. The political impact of that headline was not mitigated by the fact that, per capita, the UK did not make the top five, or that the lead countries from which they came, Iraq, Zimbabwe, Afghanistan and Somalia, were all well-known conflict zones (Home Office, 2009: Tables 2.1a, 2.3).

Conservative and Labour administrations were convinced that asylum seekers 'chose' the UK as their destination because jobs and welfare support were too readily available – that Britain was 'a soft touch'. Research did not support that view, finding that linguistic and cultural affinities with the UK and existing social networks were the key factors. Many 'sending' states, like Sri Lanka and Zimbabwe, had long ties with the UK. For many, the circumstances of departure, lack of travel documents and reliance on others for transport were found in practice to limit any 'choice' of destination (Robinson and Segrott, 2002; Zetter et al, 2003; Crawley, 2010). The ending of Britain's geographic isolation with the opening of the Channel Tunnel in the 1990s, its strong economy and ease of access to the labour market, as well as increasing restrictions on access to other EU states, were nevertheless thought to be contributory factors (Gibney, 2004). A major plank of policy since the 1990s has rested on the premise that the opportunity to work or access welfare support made the UK a destination of choice, and that any such incentive must therefore be removed.

Development of asylum policy

Britain had been a destination for those seeking a safe haven long before the arrival of Jewish people fleeing pogroms in Eastern Europe prompted the passage of the Aliens Act 1905. The anti-Semitism vocalised then and in relation to the arrival of Jewish refugees in the 1930s somewhat belies a national perception that Britain's record in 'providing hospitality to men, women and children fleeing persecution … is rightly a source of national pride' (Hague, 2000). After the Second World War, uprisings against Soviet domination did lead to the acceptance of many thousands of refugees from Eastern Europe, decisions relying on executive discretion. Procedure for determination of refugee status was not standardised until the 1980s, a decade in which applications averaged less than 4,000 a year.

Occasions arose when the government succumbed to pressure from the international community to accept refugees from camps in regions of conflict, including a quota of Vietnamese 'Boat People' in the early 1980s. Recently released cabinet papers record the then Prime Minister's reluctance to agree and her insistence that it was 'wrong that immigrants should be given council housing whereas white citizens were not', a foretaste of debates to come (Travis, 2009). The policy towards refugees that developed in the UK was not, however, focused on settlement programmes of that kind but a reaction to the spontaneous arrival of people claiming asylum on or after arrival in the UK.

When the annual numbers of applications rose to more than 26,000 in 1990 and towards 45,000 the following year, the Conservative government responded with measures to 'fast-track' cases, returning some to a 'safe' country they came through en route without a full examination of the case or guarantee that that country would do so (Asylum and Immigration Appeals Act 1993). In that reaction it preceded public concern (Gibney, 2004: 121). Meanwhile, welfare benefits for asylum seekers were set at 70% of standard levels. The 1993 Act introduced compulsory fingerprinting of applicants, removed any requirement to house those waiting for a decision and provided a power to detain when an application was refused. It nevertheless brought the UN Convention on Refugees into UK law and provided an 'in-country' right of appeal against refusal. The time subsequently taken to resolve the growing volume of cases was then unacceptable for all concerned and the integrity of the process became a focus of political and media debate (Billings, 2006).

Within three years, the government legislated again to address the delays, expediting and truncating the determination process by deeming categories of applications 'unfounded', triggering an accelerated procedure with limited rights of appeal (Asylum and Immigration Act 1996). In so doing, it was not out of line with the practice of its European neighbours. It also took steps to deny welfare support to applicants who did not apply on entry and to those appealing against refusal, convinced that Britain was attracting 'bogus' asylum seekers, for which the evidence was the rejection of 81% of applications that year. Asylum seekers were portrayed as undeserving, a drain on a welfare state to which they had not contributed (Macdonald and Billings, 2007). NGO critics challenged the assumption that a 'genuine' applicant would necessarily declare their intention to apply on arrival (rather than wait, for instance, to get advice); that welfare entitlements drove migration; and that low success rates indicated that the majority were abusing the system, recalling the narrow criteria for entitlement to refugee status (Refugee Council, 1996).

The Conservative period also saw measures to prevent asylum seekers reaching the UK: the extension of visa requirements, as for those from Yugoslavia during its civil war in 1992, and penalties on airlines and shipping companies that brought travellers without necessary documentation (Carriers' Liability Act 1987). Labour, in opposition, argued that this would impede access to the UK of those in genuine need of protection who might have no choice but to use false documents to travel. Nevertheless it endorsed the perception that 'bogus' claimants were abusing the system, repeatedly using that 'rhetoric of disbelief' in debates on the Bill and contributing to a highly exclusionary discourse on asylum emerging across the EU (Spencer, 1998; Bloch, 2000; Squire, 2009).

Figure 2.2: Asylum applications in the UK 1992–2009 (excluding dependants)

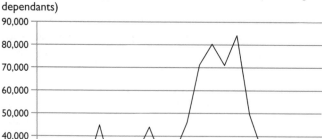

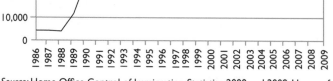

Source: Home Office Control of Immigration Statistics 2000 and 2009; House of Commons Library Standard Note SN/SG/1403 (2010) *Asylum Statistics*

Labour, moreover, shared the Conservative view that public hostility to asylum seekers could harm race relations. Blair was later to say: 'unless we act to tackle abuses it could be increasingly exploited by extremists to promote their perverted view of race' (Home Office, 2005). Asylum policy in the 1990s was, in this way, 'bolted on' to the existing framework of immigration policy, its rationale and its policymaking system. Although firmly underpinned, as in no other area of migration, by international human rights law, asylum was subsumed within the existing immigration *problematique* as a challenge to border controls and good race relations. Parliament, moreover, continued to provide 'blank cheques' for the Home Office to fill in with secondary legislation – Labour's subsequent Immigration and Asylum Act 1999 alone containing 50 such provisions (Geddes, 2000: 135). The courts were less forgiving, the European Court of Human Rights ruling in 1997 that the ECHR prohibited returning refugees to any country where the individual could face torture or inhuman or degrading treatment.[4]

For the Conservatives in the 1990s, cutting asylum seekers' access to welfare support resonated with their rolling back of the welfare state. The effect of their asylum reforms, opposed but later taken forward by Labour, was a short-term reduction in applications (Zetter et al, 2003) and a marked, ongoing inequality between asylum seekers and others living in the UK (Bloch, 2000). This also did not go unchallenged by the courts,[5] however, which required local authorities to support those who would otherwise be destitute (under domestic law this time – the National Assistance Act 1948), shifting some of the cost of support to local authorities in the South East where most asylum seekers were living. In Scotland, local authorities were already shouldering some responsibility under similar provisions (the Social Work (Scotland) Act 1968).

Policy under Labour

This was the legacy Labour inherited in 1997, along with a highly polarised debate: 'All asylum seekers are "bogus" to one group', the new administration was to rue, 'or almost all genuine to another'. It also inherited a backlog of 50,000 applications, some dating back to 1990, caused in part by a major computerisation failure. A further 20,000 were in the queue for an appeal, then taking up to 15 months to list in London (Home Office, 1998: paras 8.5, 8.7). An election promise to maintain tight controls on public expenditure meant no new resources to front-load the refugee determination system and the government was unwilling at that stage to fast-track the backlog through to refugee status. The lack of capacity to deal with the volume of applications meant that the backlog grew to 125,000 in 1999, drawing criticism for the cost to the taxpayer of supporting those waiting for a decision, then some £400 million a year (Home Office, 1998), and for the insecurity and hardship it meant for the individuals concerned.

As new applications rose to a peak of 84,000 in 2002, including many from Iraq, Zimbabwe and Afghanistan, the tabloid press and the Opposition put the government under intense pressure to bring the numbers under control, with little effective counter-pressure (other than the courts and NGOs' vocal concerns) to protect the integrity of the asylum system. The perception that the system was out of control was compounded by the low number of refused asylum seekers subsequently removed from the UK. When in opposition, Labour had not highlighted the Conservatives' 'deportation gap' as the thrust of its critique was that the government was too harsh on asylum seekers. With the shoe on the other foot, the Conservative Opposition felt no such compunction (Gibney, 2008: 155).

Media factor

It is difficult to overestimate the pressure ministers felt from hostile national and local press coverage during this period. Their concern was threefold: its potential electoral impact; the loss of public confidence in government to control 'immigration'; and the threat hostile attitudes posed to public order at community level. Ministers and their special advisors speak of this period as 'extraordinarily tense'; the 'media onslaught unrelenting. By the end of 2002 the situation was unsustainable', one special advisor said. 'We were just getting slaughtered on asylum. It wasn't unusual for there to be an asylum story on the front page of a tabloid everyday of the week' (Spencer, 2007: 343-5). Asked why asylum was such a priority, a senior official told the author:

> "It was the *Daily Mail* factor. Despite Labour having a big majority, asylum exposed its political flank. Here was something that a lot of people thought was wrong and demonstrated a government unable to do anything about it. A demonstration of the powerlessness of government is never comfortable for a Minister."[6]

A former *Sun* journalist, Roy Greenslade, argues that the tabloids were engaged in a 'distasteful contest' to boost their readership: the *Daily Express* for example, in one 31-day period in 2003 running 22 front-page lead stories on asylum seekers and one popular columnist making 88 disparaging references to them in the three years from January 2001. Alarmist stories, some exaggerated and others entirely fabricated (as in the *Sun*'s 'Callous Asylum Seekers are Barbecuing the Queen's Swans' in 2003: Greenslade, 2005: 25), associated 'asylum seeker' with crime and welfare fraud so that a humanitarian label became a term of abuse. Public hostility is nevertheless not simply the result of what people read. Rather, 'the press both reflects and enhances public attitudes and thereby sets up a chain reaction ... until reality is buried under layers of myth and prejudice' (Greenslade, 2005: 6). The four tabloids most prolific in running anti-asylum stories then had combined sales of 7.5 million and a readership of 22 million, more than a third of the British population.

David Blunkett, Home Secretary from 2001 to 2004, said he feared the impact of asylum on a public already unsettled by the pace of change, fearful of crime and resentful of newcomers accessing resources they themselves needed. With an eye to growing support for right-wing parties in other parts of Europe, he saw a reduction in asylum numbers as essential to prevent such a drift in the UK. In failing to support him in that approach, Blunkett felt 'grossly misinterpreted by the liberal left' (Spencer, 2007: 343). The Prime Minister drove the agenda, giving asylum an extraordinary amount of his personal attention: more than 50 meetings between 2001 and 2004, with some lasting three to four hours (Spencer, 2007: 359).

The terms in which the Conservative Opposition criticised the government for a 'chaotic system ... both ineffective and unfair' exacerbated the polarity of the debate: both through the sharpness of their criticism and in proposing unworkable but superficially attractive alternatives including detention of all asylum seekers in 'reception centres' (Hague, 2000; Ward, 2000). Nevertheless, there is a strong argument that government policy and the rhetoric with which it was delivered exacerbated its own predicament: a vicious circle in which government announcements reinforced public concern and thus increased the pressure it was under. Both Labour and its predecessor fuelled 'the potent myth of the welfare-scrounging bogus asylum seeker' that has polluted immigration-related political discourse, playing a key role in shifting public perceptions of refugees from people deserving of protection to abusers of Britain's generosity (Geddes, 2000: 139–40). With the benefit of hindsight, a government special advisor later observed to the author that:

> "the effect of the tough rhetoric was to wind up their concerns, not reassure them. We should have taken down the temperature and worked with local authorities and the local press to change attitudes. But the pressures at the time were immense." (Cited in Spencer, 2007: 349)

A parliamentary inquiry in 2007 urged ministers to: 'recognise their responsibility to use measured language so as not to give ammunition to those who seek to build up resentment against asylum seekers, nor to give the media the excuse to write inflammatory or misleading articles' (JCHR, 2007: 367).

Threefold strategy

Labour never failed to insist that it would honour the UK's obligation to protect those in genuine need of sanctuary. Its stated rationale was the need to weed out those who could have sought protection at an earlier stage in their journey or who did not need protection at all

(Home Office, 2002). As numbers rose its focus broadened nevertheless from fraudulent claims to reducing the number of applications per se. To that end, its strategy was threefold:

- To raise the barriers to asylum seekers reaching the UK: through extension of 'carrier sanctions' and visa requirements, posting UK immigration staff at border posts abroad and providing protection in regions of origin.
- To disperse asylum applicants to designated local authority areas and extend restrictions on access to work and benefits as a deterrent to new applicants, to encourage refused asylum seekers to leave, and to assure the public that Britain's largesse was not being abused.
- To speed up the throughput of applications and removal of refused asylum seekers through reform of the determination system and increasing detention capacity.

In this strategy, Labour did not change the direction of policy set in place by its predecessor but its approach was distinct in the extraordinary lengths to which it was prepared to go.

As we look now at the measures adopted we find that it is not only policy instruments found wanting but major failures in implementation that have thwarted government intentions and exacerbated their impact on the individuals concerned. This suggests, as we saw in Chapter 1, that it is only through studying the operation and politics of implementation that we can truly gauge the capacity of the state in this field (Ellerman, 2006: 294).

Barriers to arrival

The first arm of Labour's strategy was thus to prevent would-be asylum seekers reaching the UK. As a special advisor told the author:

> "The Government realised that if you want to get numbers down you have to prevent people arriving in the first place. You can do what you like to try to make life more unpleasant for people once they got here but that was never going to

---

reduce the overall numbers." (Special advisor, cited in Spencer, 2007: 343)

Labour's first years thus saw the further extension of visa requirements, a significant 'upstream' means of preventing asylum seekers from reaching the UK. Their application to citizens of Zimbabwe in 2003 contributed to halving the number of Zimbabwean applicants of the previous year. Requiring protection is not accepted as grounds for a visa, assuming the individual is even able to reach a UK visa post. As there is thus no legal means of travel, those determined to do so use the same means as irregular migrants and face the same hazards.

Carrier sanctions were meanwhile extended to rail and road transport, with airlines already reported to be paying significant fines, although some passengers without proper documentation are subsequently found to be entitled to refugee status (Guiraudon, 2006). Carrier sanctions externalise the cost and responsibility for entry control to private carriers untrained to make informed decisions, preventing those with a legitimate claim from having it heard so that asylum seekers are forced to use forged documents or the services of a 'people smuggler'. This increases the criminalisation of migration and the industry of false documents, the existence of which is then used to justify further controls. A senior official at the time carrier sanctions were extended argues that it is the requirement in the Refugee Convention that government considers every claim that forced them 'to do things that were against the interests of genuine refugees because it meant they could never reach the UK'.[7]

There is a concern in relation to all external controls that there is no monitoring of who is stopped, whether they need protection or what happens to them; and that NGOs and the UNHCR are regularly denied access to the border areas where individuals are intercepted. Taken together these measures have the effect of transferring responsibility for refugees to regions of origin less equipped to provide the support they need (Reynolds and Muggeridge, 2008). Government has responded that it works through the Department for International Development (DfID) to improve protection for refugees in regions of origin and in alleviating the poverty and conflict that create pressures to migrate (Home Office, 2005: 18).

The year 2004 saw visitors from some Asian and African countries required to provide fingerprints, justified as a response to asylum applicants destroying their travel documents after arrival or claiming false identities and heralded as 'the next step in the Government's phased roll out of biometric technology to tackle immigration abuse' (Home Office, 2004). Meanwhile, to end nightly television pictures of would-be asylum seekers scaling fences to board trains bound for Dover, closure of the Sangatte refugee camp near Calais had been negotiated with France in 2002. Securing an agreement to post UK immigration staff in France and Belgium, and the use of technology to detect those travelling illegally in freight vehicles, were among measures credited in 2005 with reducing asylum applications by 67% from their peak in 2002 (Home Office, 2005: 12).

Protection in regions of origin

Blair unsuccessfully sought EU agreement in 2003 to take external controls one step further: a system of protection centres in regions of origin (and 'transit' centres nearer the external borders of the EU) where claims could be assessed without claimants ever reaching the UK. Most controversially, asylum seekers arriving in the UK would be transported to such centres for 'extra-territorial processing'. It was unclear which state would have responsibility for the application and, to deter spontaneous arrivals, applicants would have to be transferred to camps on a huge scale (UNHCR, 2006: 38). Consideration was also given to the possibility of 'EU Reception Centres', rejected by a House of Lords Select Committee that saw more merit in using resources to accelerate the handling of asylum applications, firmly believing that the quality of initial decision-making is the single most important component of an effective asylum system (HLSC on European Union, 2004: 108).

The EU did initiate a limited Regional Protection Programme from 2005, assisting transit countries such as the Ukraine and Moldova to set up systems for handling asylum claims. It is also suggested that protection in regions of origin could genuinely offer the prospect of honouring humanitarian obligations while reducing the pressure of numbers arriving in Europe: 'protection is exported in order to maintain security inside', with the two agendas moving forward hand in hand but occupying different spaces (Haddad, 2008).

Curtailing access to work and welfare support

The second arm of the strategy was to ensure that access to work and welfare support provide no incentive to choose the UK as a destination, or subsequently to remain following refusal of any right to stay. It was also intended to send a signal to the public 'that people who have not established their right to be in the UK should not have access to welfare provision on the same basis as those whose citizenship or status here gives them an entitlement to benefits when in need' (Home Office, 1998: 18). As in many EU countries by that time, welfare support would be separate from mainstream provision and at a lower level. The corollary was that decisions should be made more quickly and those refused entry removed from the UK. In practice it was easier to set that goal than to achieve it.

A concession that asylum seekers were allowed to work after six months was withdrawn (until, as we saw, the EU's 2003 Reception Directive meant that principal applicants could again apply to work after 12 months). Labour was convinced this was essential to avoid making the UK more attractive than its European neighbours, despite public hostility to asylum seekers' inactivity and its impact on the job prospects of those subsequently granted refugee status (Bloch, 2002). A Conservative-led think tank, no doubt mindful that the UK was at this time seeking to attract skilled labour migrants (Chapter 3), argued that it is 'not only immensely damaging to an individual's mental health but is also de-skilling very motivated and qualified workers who could be making a contribution to the UK economy and paying their own way' (CSJ, 2008: 16).

Dispersal

The Immigration and Asylum Act 1999 paved the way for dispersal of asylum seekers in order to relieve 'the burden' on local authorities near ports and airports and in London, where the Opposition claimed that there were boroughs 'spending more on supporting asylum seekers than on residential and nursing placements for elderly people' (Hague, 2000). Labour set up the National Asylum Support System (NASS, within what is now the UK Border Agency (UKBA)) to arrange accommodation and provide support directly rather than through the benefit system; support that is withdrawn if the asylum seeker leaves the accommodation provided. Home Secretary David Blunkett proposed an alternative system of accommodation centres housing around 3,000 asylum seekers in total, and removing them from local health and education provision (Home Office, 2002). In this he was thwarted by the Treasury on cost grounds, by community opposition in the areas chosen and opposition from refugee NGOs on many grounds.

While some refugee organisations accepted the rationale for dispersal there has been widespread criticism of its implementation. Highly centralised with little consultation or buy-in from local authorities, the system was from the start beset with difficulties for local agencies, asylum seekers and community relations. Areas were chosen in part because of the availability of (often substandard) housing in areas otherwise lacking capacity to provide jobs or specialist services. Some local publics were unfamiliar with ethnic diversity and asylum seekers were not always well received by their neighbours. Whereas the skills and previous work experience of asylum seekers and refugees suggests that they could have contributed to the regeneration of these areas, their exclusion from employment has exacerbated existing levels of deprivation and, arguably, negative attitudes towards them (Phillimore and Goodson, 2006; Robinson and Reeve, 2006; PAC, 2009). At the end of 2009, 23,845 asylum seekers were being supported in dispersed accommodation across the UK and a further 4,670 were receiving subsistence support (Home Office, 2010: Table 2.6).

—

Limited welfare support

Support was initially provided by NASS through vouchers, a system roundly condemned and largely replaced in 2002 with cash benefits. That support was subsequently removed from those who did not apply 'as soon as reasonably practicable after arrival' (Nationality, Immigration and Asylum Act 2002, s 55), once again proving a step too far for the courts which required support to be restored to those who would otherwise be destitute in breach of the 'inhuman and degrading treatment' provision of the ECHR.[8] Prior to that decision, s 55 cases led to a quarter of all judicial review cases lodged in the High Court (JCHR, 2007: paras 89–92).

Refused asylum seekers facing destitution may receive 'Section 4' accommodation and subsistence support (£35.39 per week in 2010). Intended as a short-term measure for people who agree to leave and are taking steps to do so, it is also used where UKBA accepts that return is not a viable option. Payment was switched from vouchers to a pre-payment card usable in a wider range of shops after the Joint Committee on Human Rights (JCHR) had judged vouchers to be 'inhumane and inefficient', for failing to provide for basic living needs, and discriminatory on grounds of nationality (JCHR, 2007: para 110). NGOs are critical of delays in assessing claims and of a high rate of errors. Where support is refused it can fall to local authorities to provide it in order to avoid breaching the ECHR, leading to disagreement in individual cases over who should pay.

Steps have also been taken to exclude refused asylum seekers from free hospital treatment, endorsed by the Court of Appeal in March 2009, although health providers retain discretion to provide care if urgent and must do so if immediately necessary (DH, 2009). There is evidence of asylum seekers being denied access to care in hospitals because staff are uncertain as to their entitlement and the cost implications. Rather than saving public funds, however, this may prove more costly if the condition deteriorates to the extent that emergency treatment is needed (Macdonald and Billings, 2007). This issue is explored further in Chapter 5.

—

The Centre for Social Justice (CSJ) criticised the speed with which support is withdrawn following the refusal of a claim. It found evidence that many asylum seekers 'go underground into a world of illegal work, prostitution and destitution' rather than apply for the limited support available with its condition of voluntary return attached. It deemed this 'utterly inhumane' but also counterproductive in that it provides no time to work with individuals to overcome their concerns about returning home. This contrasts to Sweden's 82% success rate in securing voluntary returns (UK 21%) in 2008, and the UK's overall low return rate compared to its European neighbours. CSJ's then chair, later Conservative Secretary of State for Work and Pensions, Iain Duncan Smith, argued that:

> UK policy is still driven by the thesis, clearly falsified, that we can encourage people to leave by being nasty. The result is that we rely heavily on forcible return, which is both very costly and time-consuming, and engages only a small proportion of those whose claims are refused. (CSJ, 2008: 4)

The CSJ advocated intense work with refused asylum seekers to identify and overcome their concerns about voluntary return, estimating that sufficient savings would be made by increasing the rate of return to enable financial support to continue for 16 weeks after refusal at no extra cost.

Use of destitution to deter?

Government is caught between public and media perceptions that the system is too generous and criticism that destitution is used deliberately to deter future applications and encourage refused asylum seekers to leave the UK. A JCHR inquiry concluded that by refusing permission for most asylum seekers to work and operating a system of support that results in widespread destitution, the treatment of asylum seekers in a number of cases reached the ECHR Article 3 threshold of inhuman and degrading treatment:

> We have been persuaded by the evidence that the Government has indeed been practising a deliberate policy of destitution of this highly vulnerable group. We believe that the deliberate use of inhumane treatment is unacceptable. (JCHR, 2007: para 120)

Evidence of destitution is substantial. A survey in 2008 by UKBA-funded service providers, for instance, found widespread and long-term destitution among refused asylum seekers. Although destitute people came from more than 40 countries, most were from countries where there is well-documented human rights abuse, persecution and/or conflict. Long-term destitution (more than two years) suggested that individuals are prepared to endure it for long periods rather than leave the UK (Smart, 2009). Further studies found destitute asylum seekers, some with professional backgrounds, sleeping rough and surviving on less than £5 per week (Lewis, 2009; Taylor, 2009). Labour disputed the evidence and rejected the suggestion that it used destitution as a means to deter (Woolas, 2010).

Fast throughput to refugee status or removal

In the third leg of Labour's approach, the goal was to speed up the decision-making process: 'the key to restoring effectiveness to our asylum system and to tackling abuse is swifter determination of applications and appeals' (Home Office, 1998: para 8.7). From an average of 22 months to resolve a case in 1997, it intended to complete most cases in six months by 2001; recommitting itself in 2007 to resolve 60% in six months by the end of 2008 and 90% by 2011 (HM Government, 2007: 9; Home Office, 2009: 41). The intention was to achieve this by fast-tracking 'unfounded' applications, introducing rule changes to limit times allowed for preparation of claims, making case management more effective and cutting back rights to appeal. Meanwhile capacity to detain applicants pending a final decision was expanded and steps were taken to increase the rate of removal, including bilateral agreements with source countries to facilitate return.

—

Curtailing the refugee determination system

By 2006, asylum was deemed '*the* most fertile and controversial area of public law' (Billings, 2006: 197, emphasis in original). Legislation in 1999 (the Immigration and Asylum Act) and 2002 (the Nationality, Immigration and Asylum Act) had extended the practice of categorising certain claims from 'safe countries' as 'unfounded', fast-tracking their processing through to removal with a right of appeal only after leaving the UK. The list of countries considered safe included some with a poor human rights record. Applicants who had passed through a 'safe third country' were returned there for their application to be processed; EU cooperation (the Dublin Regulation and Eurodac fingerprint database) enabling around 200 people to be returned each month by 2005 (Home Office, 2005). This 'burden-sharing' places additional responsibility on states which, because of their geographic location, experience greater migratory pressures. Those subject to 'Dublin transfers', for instance to Greece, cannot always access a fair determination system (Thielemann, 2009).

Access to judicial review was also curtailed, opening the way to a throughput of cases within days for those in detention. The government subsequently proposed ousting judicial review of tribunal decisions on removal entirely on grounds of speed and cost savings for the taxpayer, but refrained in face of substantial opposition from the judiciary (Billings, 2006). Meanwhile time given for submission of evidence in support of claims was reduced, resulting in a rapid increase in the number deemed non-compliant.

A single tier of appeal, the Asylum and Immigration Tribunal, was created in 2004, coupled with shorter time periods to lodge the appeal and restrictions on legal aid. The rationale was to limit the appeals process to eight weeks and reduce perceived exploitation of the system by applicants using an appeal to extend their stay. The repeated curtailing of appeal rights and in particular its reduction to a single tier has led to criticism that the system falls below government's own insistence that mechanisms of dispute resolution should be proportionate to the seriousness of the claim (Thomas, 2005). Labour sought to go further in its Borders, Citizenship and Immigration Bill 2009, intending once again to limit access to the higher courts for judicial review, but backed down in face of Conservative opposition. It blamed the poor quality of initial decisions for the volume of appeals and argued: 'Home Office failings must not be compensated for by a lessening of appeal rights in those complex cases'.[9]

Some critics have argued that there is a conflict of interest in UKBA having responsibility for the determination system given its role in enforcement, and that case-handlers' judgement may be affected by the political pressure ministers are under to reduce the number given refugee status. Responsibility could be transferred to an independent body: with Canada the oft-quoted example of an independent system reported to work well (JUSTICE et al, 1997; CSJ, 2008).

Until 2005, those granted refugee status were given an indefinite right to settle. Since 2005, however, they have received leave to remain for five years with a view to requiring return to their country of origin if then deemed safe. This followed the practice already in place in Australia but has been criticised as extending the period of insecurity for those concerned and for adding to the cost of the refugee determination system (Macdonald and Billings, 2007).

Case handling

That decisions on cases must be taken more quickly was something on which all could agree. As rates of granting refugee status fell to 13% in 2000 and to 4% in 2004, however (with a further group receiving a discretionary right to stay), criticism mounted that greater speed was being achieved at the expense of the quality of decision-making. The number of those lodging an appeal grew from less than 7,000 in 1999 to more than 74,000 in 2001, indicating that greater throughput at the front end was simply resulting in greater pressure down the line. In the decade to 2008, success rates in appeals averaged more than 20%: applicants thus had a greater chance of success at appeal than in the initial decision. The Home Office increased its acceptance rate, with 20% being granted refugee status in 2008, but the success rate at appeal that year was still 23% (Home Office, 2009: Tables 2.1a, 5.1).

The case handling system had been replaced in 2005 with a 'New Asylum Model', a better resourced 'end-to-end' management system in which a single 'case-owner' handles each application from start to finish. It cost £176 million in 2007–08 (including £80 million on accommodation and welfare support), but staff were still having to cope with separate computer systems that did not communicate and continuing use of manual records (NAO, 2009). The Public Accounts Committee (PAC) found the management of applications improved but that the target of concluding 80% of cases within six months was not yet within reach. Noting that 70% of applicants appeal against a refusal and more than one in five appeals continued to be upheld, it was surprised to find little learning from successful appeals fed back to case-owners handling the initial decisions (PAC, 2009: 6).

Sensitive to criticism of the quality of decision-making, the Home Office allows the UNHCR to monitor and advise. In relation to unaccompanied asylum-seeking children (UASC), where the rate of granting refugee status is exceptionally low (just 11% in 2009), it found that not all staff had the skills required to determine a child's claim. It recommended that each child have an independent Guardian to represent their interests, advice endorsed by the Children, Schools and Families Select Committee which thought that this would also address the particular vulnerability of these children to ongoing exploitation by traffickers (SCCSF, 2009; UNHCR, 2009; Home Office, 2010).

A key concern has been the limited legal support for applicants, a House of Lords inquiry concluding that 'undue restrictions on legal aid and access to qualified legal representation are likely to lead to unfairness and more poor decisions' (HLSC on European Union, 2004: 147). A 'Solihull Pilot' project run by UKBA and the Legal Services Commission demonstrated that when applicants had legal advice before, during and after interview the results were impressive in terms of the quality of decisions, speed of resolution, lower number of appeals and a higher removal rate, deemed to benefit all parties (Aspden, 2008). There is no provision for legal representation for the

2,000 people a year who appeal to the Asylum Support Tribunal against refusal of welfare support. Legal representation of applicants, who are disproportionately poor and lack proficiency in English, significantly increases chances of success, the cost of which, Citizens Advice argues, could be met by improvements in the initial decision-making process (Dunstan, 2009).

Further issues arise in relation to unaccompanied children, more than 3,000 of whom applied for asylum in 2009. These children are entitled to greater welfare support than adults, leading UKBA and Social Services Departments to question the age of many applicants: no less than 1,130 cases were 'age disputed' in that year (Home Office, 2010). Immigration Rules were changed in 2007 to allow the use of X-rays of teeth and wrist and collar-bones, criticised as unsafe by the British Medical Association (Hamm et al, 2008). The procedures used across the UK have been judged to be inconsistent, over-reliant on appearance and failing to recognise that there is no scientific process that can provide a sufficiently accurate assessment. There is also a potential conflict of interest between the requirement of Social Services Departments to undertake age assessments and their obligation to provide services to children in need (Crawley, 2007).

Backlog of cases

The backlog of applications awaiting an initial decision fell from the peak of 125,000 in 1999 to 5,500 in 2005, in part by fast-tracking through to refugee status those who had already been in the UK for many years (Home Office, 2009: Tables 2.1a, 2.2). There was no question of an 'amnesty', government insisted, which would be 'seen as a reward for those who would abuse the system'; but long delays were no fault of the applicant, hence those that applied before a certain date would be allowed to stay (Home Office, 1998: para 8.29). The backlog of applications does not include a legacy of 450,000 'unresolved case records' which UKBA promised to clear by 2011 (HM Government, 2007: 9). These cases cost nearly £600 million in 2007–08, including accommodation and welfare support (NAO,

2009). UKBA's Independent Inspector reported the 2011 target to be unachievable as only 4,500 cases were being resolved each month. The Parliamentary and Health Service Ombudsman, who handles complaints against UKBA, found the continuing delays to be 'serious and far-reaching, both for the individuals caught up in the system and for society as a whole' (ICIUKBA, 2010; PHSO, 2010).

Detention capacity and removal

Dogged by criticism that it was failing to remove from the UK those whose claims were rejected, government expanded the capacity to detain people outside the prison system, opening the first purpose-built detention centre, Oakington, in 2000. By 2009, there were 11 such centres, including Yarlswood, Campsfield House and Harmondsworth, but UKBA will not have the 4,000 places it says are needed until 2013, in part because of the number of foreign prisoners awaiting deportation (PAC, 2009) (Chapter 5).

Detention facilitates a severely truncated determination process of less than a month for 'unfounded cases' from which the rate of awarding refugee status is extremely low. Government justifies detention as essential to remove the risk that those refused will abscond. In the absence of data on the number who do abscond, that rationale is difficult to evaluate. Detention, and the rapid throughput of cases it facilitates, has undoubtedly been a major factor in higher rates of removal (Gibney, 2008). The legality and ethics of detaining people for administrative convenience when it is not necessary to prevent absconding is questioned, particularly for long periods (O'Nions, 2008). NGOs are concerned that some detainees, including unaccompanied minors, lack adequate legal advice as lawyers can be reluctant to take on cases where access to clients is difficult and clients' potential for collecting evidence to support their case is limited.

Labour felt particularly vulnerable to criticism that it failed to remove those whose claims had been rejected. Removal targets offer a tangible way of signalling government success in getting asylum under control but when missed are a clear sign of failure: between 2001 and

—

2004 they were a 'lightening rod for criticism as target after target was missed' (Gibney, 2008). Blair famously committed his government in 2004 to reach the 'tipping point' – more removals each month than 'unfounded applications' – by the end of the following year. Numbers of removals rose but then declined, missing the tipping point target by over 20% in 2007. The majority, moreover, were from legacy cases and those held in detention, not from those handled by the New Asylum Model (NAO, 2009; PAC, 2009). I look further at detention and removal in Chapter 5.

Gateway programme

An alternative to the spontaneous arrival of asylum seekers and the enforcement issues to which they give rise is resettlement programmes in which states, in cooperation with the UNHCR, take a quota of refugees from the region in which they initially seek protection. The UK, like many of its European neighbours, Australia and Canada, agreed a modest 'Gateway programme' in 2004. Relying on local authority willingness to take part, the programme has only seen small numbers relative to asylum applications, rising from 150 arrivals in 2004 to 750 in 2010, some 2,700 in total having been given refuge in that period (UKBA, 2010b). Those on the scheme receive permanent residence on arrival and an 'integration package' of housing, health care, education and casework support. Evaluation found the refugees glad to be settled in the UK but that many experienced the same barriers to integration, including verbal and physical harassment, as other migrants (Evans and Murray, 2009).

Conclusion

The dramatic rise in asylum applications across Europe from the early 1990s led to unprecedented measures to prevent and deter arrivals, to reform refugee determination procedures and remove asylum seekers from mainstream welfare support. In this, the UK was no exception. Labour did not change the direction of policy inherited from its

Conservative predecessor in 1997 but differed in the lengths to which it was prepared to go, not least in using exclusion from the welfare system as a tool of immigration control. In its anxious assurances that it would, with each new measure, finally bring asylum under control, Labour exacerbated its own predicament, reinforcing the public and media hostility that it sought to assuage.

The strategy, as yet continued by the Coalition government, has been threefold: to raise the barriers to asylum seekers reaching the UK; to disperse applicants to designated areas while extending restrictions on their access to work and benefits; and to hasten the throughput of applications in the refugee determination system and removal of those refused. In each case, the reforms and their implementation have given rise to substantial criticism while failing to satisfy those critics whose primary concern was that numbers should fall.

Illustrating the pressures and constraints that shape policy intervention, discussed in Chapter 1, we saw the impact of the UK's obligations under the UN Refugee Convention and the ECHR on the extent to which government could restrict access to the asylum determination system and to welfare support. Successive court judgments and their anticipation curtailed, if only to a degree, the steps government could take. There is an irony that asylum, an institution established to serve humanitarian goals, nevertheless became the catalyst for enhancing the coercive powers of the state (Gibney, 2008: 167). Yet the impact of the courts and the inability of the administration to administer the system with the speed and efficiency it sought, or to remove most of those whose applications are refused, must qualify any analysis of 'executive omnipotence' in this field (Geddes, 2000: 135).

The polarisation of the debate provided an extraordinary context for policymaking: intense media pressure influential in the direction of policy and critical of failure to go further. NGOs provided an alternative critique, replete with evidence and proposals for reform but with little influence, according to a senior official, 'because they didn't help solve the problem as the government perceived it, which was one of numbers'.[10] That these critics were joined by Conservative voices arguing for a more humane system with greater respect for due

72

process, may say more about the lengths to which Labour went to 'bring asylum under control' than any indication that the Coalition government now in power will be willing to dismantle it.

Condemned for failing to control asylum, Labour understandably claimed success for its policies as applications fell after 2002. In broad terms, however, numbers rose because of the rise in refugee-producing conflicts and fell because those conflicts were, at least for the time being, contained. Policy has an impact on numbers but the relationship and the time-lag is not easy to establish (Zetter et al, 2003).

UK asylum policy stands out for an unusual degree of cooperation at EU level. Also notable is the extent to which implementation has been subcontracted to the private sector: transport providers enlisted, through threat of carrier sanctions, to filter out those without valid travel documentation and private firms contracted to run detention centres. The treatment of Unaccompanied Asylum-seeking Children and of children in detention has highlighted the gap between standards required by mainstream law and policy and those in the asylum system. Meanwhile, the 450,000 unresolved 'legacy' cases demonstrate both the immense administrative challenge that UKBA is still struggling to overcome and the excessive periods of insecurity applicants have to endure. Resisting any 'amnesty' while in practice allowing many to stay regardless of the strength of their claim helpfully illustrates that, in the regularisation debate (Chapter 5), there are shades of grey to be explored.

Some 24,500 people applied for asylum in 2009, low relative to labour migration, families and students and a dramatic fall from the numbers that dominated political debate on migration only a few years ago. Across the EU, the UK was second only to France in the number of applications but 13th if measured per capita. Of the decisions taken in that year, less than one in five were granted refugee status, a further 10% were granted a discretionary right to stay and 72% were refused. Just under 11,000 left voluntarily or were removed in 2009 (Home Office, 2010: 3). Despite the fall in applications, the challenge of running a fair and effective asylum system thus remains.

—

There is no shortage of suggestions for reform. Short of an independent determination system, higher levels of training for case-owners, access to independent legal advice and representation from an early stage, abolition of the fast-track process in detention, non-criminalisation of asylum seekers using false documentation, use of alternatives to detention and the ending of forced returns to countries still experiencing widespread violence are among the reforms sought by those working with asylum seekers (see eg Asylum Aid, 2007; RMJ, 2009). For women it is argued that government should ensure that standards of care in relation to domestic violence and maternity care are raised to those for other women in the UK (Singer, 2009); and similarly for children that they should have a Guardian to protect their interests and be able to stay in foster care until 18, not be expected to cope alone after 16 (SCCSF, 2009). There is a further case for ensuring that policy on asylum seekers is more closely aligned with international development objectives (Castles and Van Hear, 2005; Barrow Cadbury Trust, 2009).

As we shall see in the next chapter, the political focus shifted from asylum to labour migration in 2004. The remaining backlog of legacy cases and barriers to removal, plus the ever-present possibility that an escalating conflict will lead to a rise in arrivals, means the Coalition government may nevertheless feel little incentive to look favourably on such reforms. Its predecessor's concern that a rise in numbers would increase public hostility has to be taken seriously but be weighed against the costs, including the hazards for those fleeing without proper documentation and the probability that some who cannot reach safety suffer as a result (Gibney, 2004: 130). No substantive shift in policy can in practice be expected without steps towards a parallel shift across the EU and without a sea-change in the terms of public and political debate. NGOs must have a key role to play in building public awareness and support but government also needs to address the culture of disbelief, acknowledge that the definition of 'refugee' excludes many in genuine need of protection and welcome refugees' economic and social contribution to the UK. There is some recognition that political leaders bear significant responsibility for the terms in

—

which the wider debate on migration is conducted ('how we conduct this debate is as important as the debate itself'; Brown, 2010), but there is no cross-party consensus that political leaders could or should seek to change the terms of debate on asylum that so significantly constrain the policy options they can pursue.

Notes

[1] UN Convention relating to the Status of Refugees, 1951, Article 1(2) .

[2] Judgment available at: http://www.supremecourt.gov.uk/docs/UKSC_2009_0054_Judgment.pdf

[3] Interview with former senior official, Immigration and Nationality Department, 12 October 2009.

[4] *Chahal v the UK* (1997) 23 EHRR 413.

[5] *R v Secretary of State for the Home Department ex p JCWI* [1996] 4 All ER 385; *R v Westminster CC, ex p A; Hammersmith and LBC, ex p M* [1997] EWCA Civ 1032.

[6] Former senior official, Immigration and Nationality Department, interviewed by the author, 12 October 2009.

[7] Interviewed by the author, 12 October 2009.

[8] *R (Limbuela and others) v Secretary of State for the Home Department* [2005] UKHL 66; [2006] 1 AC 396.

[9] Damian Green MP, *Hansard*, HC Committee, Borders, Citizenship and Immigration Bill, sixth sitting, 16 June 2009, cols 184–5.

[10] Interviewed by the author, 12 October 2009.

References

Aspden, J. (2008) *Evaluation of the Solihull Pilot for the United Kingdom Border Agency and the Legal Services Commission*. London: UKBA and LSC.

Asylum Aid (2007) *Asylum Aid's Submission of Evidence to the Independent Asylum Commission*. London: Asylum Aid.

Barrow Cadbury Trust (2009) *Towards a Progressive Framework for Migration*. London: Barrow Cadbury Trust.

Billings, P. (2006) 'Balancing Acts: Six Acts in Search of Equilibrium', *Journal of Immigration Asylum and Nationality Law* 20(3): 197–209.

Blair, T. (2001) 'Immigrants Are Seeking Asylum in Outdated Law', *The Times,* 4 May.

Bloch, A. (2000) 'A New Era or More of the Same? Asylum Policy in the UK', *Journal of Refugee Studies* 13(1): 29–42.

Bloch, A. (2002) *Refugees: Opportunities and Barriers in Employment and Training,* Research Report 179. London: Department for Work and Pensions.

Brown, G. (2010) 'Speech: Controlling Immigration for a Fairer Britain', No 10 Downing Street, London, 31 March.

Castles, S. and Van Hear, N. (2005) *Developing DFID's Policy Approach to Refugees and Internally Displaced Persons, Volume 1: Consultancy Report and Policy Recommendations,* University of Oxford.

Crawley, H. (2007) *When Is a Child Not a Child? Asylum, Age Disputes and the Process of Age Assessment.* London: ILPA.

Crawley, H. (2010) *Chance or Choice? Understanding Why Asylum Seekers Come to the UK.* London: Refugee Council.

Crisp, J. (2003) 'Refugees and the Global Politics of Asylum', in S. Spencer (ed) *The Politics of Migration, Managing Opportunity, Conflict and Change.* Oxford: Blackwell.

CSJ (Centre for Social Justice) (2008) *Asylum Matters: Restoring Trust in the UK Asylum System,* London: Centre for Social Justice, Asylum and Destitution Working Group.

DH (Department of Health) (2009) *Interim Guidance Notes for Failed Asylum Seekers,* 2 April. London: Department of Health.

Dunstan, R. (2009) *Supporting Justice: The Case for Publicly-Funded Legal Representation before the Asylum Support Tribunal. CAB Evidence Briefing.* London: Citizens Advice Bureau.

Ellerman, A. (2006) 'Street-Level Democracy: How Immigration Bureaucrats Manage Public Opposition', *West European Politics* 29(2): 293–309.

European Commission (2003) *EC Directive on the Reception of Asylum Seekers,* 2003/9/EC. Brussels: European Commission.

Evans, O. and Murray, R. (2009) *The Gateway Protection Programme: An Evaluation,* Research Report 12, London: Home Office.

Geddes, A. (2000) 'Denying Access: Asylum Seekers and Welfare Benefits in the UK', in M. Bommes and A. Geddes (eds) *Immigration and Welfare: Challenging the Borders of the Welfare State*. London and New York: Routledge.

Geddes, A. (2005) 'Getting the Best of Both Worlds? Britain, the EU and Migration Policy', *International Affairs* 81(4): 723–40.

Gibney, M. (2004) *The Politics and Ethics of Asylum: Liberal Democracy and Response to Refugees*. Cambridge: Cambridge University Press.

Gibney, M. J. (2008) 'Asylum and the Expansion of Deportation in the United Kingdom', *Government and Opposition* 43(2): 146–67.

Greenslade, R. (2005) *Seeking Scapegoats: The Coverage of Asylum in the UK Press. Asylum and Migration Working Paper 5*. London: Institute for Public Policy Research.

Guiraudon, V. (2006) 'Enlisting Third Parties in Border Control: A Comparative Study of Its Causes and Consequences', in M. Caparini and O. Marenin (eds) *Borders and Security Governance: Managing Borders in a Globalised World*. Geneva: Geneva Centre for the Democratic Control of Armed Forces (DCAF).

Haddad, E. (2008) 'The External Dimension of EU Refugee Policy: A New Approach to Asylum?' *Government and Opposition* 43(2): 190–205.

Hague, W. (2000) 'Common Sense on Asylum Seekers', Speech to the Social Market Foundation, London.

Hamm, C., Harrison, C., Mussell, R., Sheather, J., Sommerville, A. and Tizzard, J. (2008) 'Ethics Briefings', *Journal of Medical Ethics* 34: 125–26.

HLSC (House of Lords Select Committee) on European Union (2004) *Handling EU Asylum Claims: New Approaches Examined*, Eleventh Report Session 2003–04, HL 74. London: House of Lords.

HLSC on European Union (2009) *Asylum Directives: Scrutiny of the Opt in Decisions*, First Report Session 2009–10, HL 6. London: House of Lords.

HM Government (2007) *PSA Delivery Agreement 3*. London: Home Office.

Home Office (1998) *Fairer, Faster, and Firmer: A Modern Approach to Immigration and Asylum*, Cm 4018. London: Home Office.

—

Home Office (2002) *Secure Borders, Safe Haven: Integration with Diversity in Modern Britain*. Cm 5387. London: Home Office.

Home Office (2004) 'Increased Use of Biometrics to Tackle Asylum Abuse', Press release 21 January, London: Home Office.

Home Office (2005) *Controlling Our Borders: Making Migration Work for Britain – Five Year Strategy for Asylum and Immigration*. Cm 472. London: Home Office.

Home Office (2009) *Control of Immigration Statistics 2008*, Home Office Statistical Bulletin 14/09. London: Home Office.

Home Office (2010) *Control of Immigration: Statistics United Kingdom 2009*, Home Office Statistical Bulletin 15/10. London: Home Office.

ICIUKBA (Independent Chief Inspector of the UK Border Agency) (2010) *Asylum: Getting the Balance Right? A Thematic Inspection, July–November 2009*, Home Office, ICUKBA.

JCHR (Joint Committee on Human Rights) (2007) *The Treatment of Asylum Seekers*, 10th Report of 2006–07, HL81/HC 60-1, London.

JUSTICE et al (1997) *Providing Protection: Towards Fair and Effective Asylum Procedures*. London: JUSTICE, ILPA and ARC.

Law, I. (2009) 'Racism, Ethnicity, Migration and Social Security', in J. Millar (ed) *Understanding Social Security*. Bristol: The Policy Press.

Lewis, H. (2009) *Still Destitute: A Worsening Problem for Refused Asylum Seekers*. York: Joseph Rowntree Charitable Trust.

Macdonald, I. and Billings, P. (2007) 'The Treatment of Asylum Seekers in the UK', *Journal of Social Welfare and Family Law* 29(1): 49–65.

NAO (National Audit Office) (2009) *Management of Asylum Applications by the UK Border Agency*, Session 2008–09, HC 124. London: National Audit Office.

O'Nions, H. (2008) 'No Right to Liberty: The Detention of Asylum Seekers for Administrative Convenience', *European Journal of Migration and Law* 10: 149–85.

PAC (Public Accounts Committee) (2009) *Management of Asylum Applications*, 28th Report Session 2008–09, Public Accounts Committee.

Phillimore, J. and Goodson, L. (2006) 'Problem or Opportunity? Asylum Seekers, Refugees, Employment and Social Exclusion in Deprived Urban Areas', *Urban Studies* 43(10): 1–22.

PHSO (Parliamentary and Health Service Ombudsman) (2010) *Fast and Fair? A Report on the UK Border Agency*, HC 329. Parliamentary and Health Service Ombudsman.

Refugee Council (1996) *The State of Asylum: A Critique of Asylum Policy in the UK*. London: Refugee Council.

Reynolds, S. and Muggeridge, H. (2008) *Remote Controls: How UK Border Controls Are Endangering the Lives of Refugees*. London: Refugee Council.

RMJ (Refugee and Migrant Justice) (2009) 'Campaigning for Change'. Has been, but no longer is, available at: http://refugee-migrant-justice.org.uk/downloads/RMJ_CampaigningforChange1.pdf (accessed 6 April 2010).

Robinson, D. and Reeve, K. (2006) *Neighbourhood Experiences of New Immigration*. York: Joseph Rowntree Foundation.

Robinson, V. and Segrott, J. (2002) *Understanding the Decision-Making of Asylum Seekers*. Home Office Research Study 243. London: Home Office.

SCCSF (Select Committee on Children, Schools and Families) (2009) *Looked-after Children*, Third Report Session 2008–09. Select Committee on Children, Schools and Families.

Singer, D. (2009) *Every Single Woman: A Comparison of Standards for Women in the Asylum System with Standards for Women in the Criminal Justice, Prisons and Maternity Systems in the UK*. London: Asylum Aid.

Smart, K. (2009) *The Second Destitution Tally: An indication of the extent of destitution among asylum seekers, refused asylum seekers and refugees*, Asylum Seeker Support Partnership Policy Report, Asylum Seeker Support Partnership.

Spencer, S. (1998) 'The Impact of Immigration Policy on Race Relations', in T. Blackstone, B. Parekh and P. Sanders (eds) *Race Relations in Britain: A Developing Agenda*. London and New York: Routledge.

Spencer, S. (2007) 'Immigration', in A. Seldon (ed) *Blair's Britain 1997–2007*. Cambridge: Cambridge University Press.

Squire, V. (2009) *The Exclusionary Politics of Asylum*. Basingstoke: Palgrave Macmillan.

Taylor, D. (2009) *Underground Lives: An Investigation into the Living Conditions and Survival Strategies of Destitute Asylum Seekers in the UK*. Leeds: PAFRAS.

Thielemann, E. R. (2009) 'The Common European Asylum System: in Need of a More Comprehensive Burden-Sharing Approach', in A. Luedtke (ed) *The Politics of Migration and Migrant Integration*. Cambridge: Scholar Press.

Thomas, R. (2005) 'Evaluating Tribunal Adjudication: Administrative Justice and Asylum Appeals', *Journal of Legal Studies* 25(3): 462–98.

Travis, A. (2009) 'Margaret Thatcher Reluctant to Give Boat People Refuge in Britain: PM Warned of Riots on Streets if Vietnamese Were Given Council Housing, Downing Street Papers Reveal', *The Guardian*, 30 September 2009.

UKBA (United Kingdom Border Agency) (2010a) 'Implementation of the Supreme Court Judgement in ZO (Somalia)', Press notice, 19 August, London, Home Office.

UKBA (2010b) *Second Group of Gateway Refugees Arrive from Nepal*. News update, 2 August. London: Home Office.

UNHCR (United Nations High Commissioner on Refugees) (2006) *The State of the World's Refugees: Human Displacement in the New Millennium*. Oxford: Oxford University Press.

UNHCR (2009) *Quality Initiative Project: Key Observations and Recommendations, 6th Report*. London: UNHCR Representative to the United Kingdom.

Van Hear, N., Brubaker, R. and Bessa, T. (2009) *Managing Mobility for Human Development: The Growing Salience of Mixed Migration*, UN Development Programme Human Development Reports Research Paper 2009/20. New York: UNDP.

Ward, L. (2000) 'Tories Toughen Asylum Line', *The Guardian*, 28 January.

Woolas, P. (2010) 'Election 2010: Where Next for Immigration Policy?', Lecture delivered to the Smith Institute, London, 16 March.

Zetter, R., Griffiths, D., Ferretti, S. and Pearl, M. (2003) *An Assessment of the Impact of Asylum Policies in Europe: 1990–2000.* Home Office Research Study 259. London: Home Office.

3

Migration for work and study

In this chapter I focus on those who enter the UK for work or study, closely related categories because many students also work part time or subsequently stay on to take up employment. While the rationale for attracting international students has not only been economic ('they promote Britain around the world, helping our trade and diplomacy'; Blair, 1999), in both cases the last decade saw a rapid expansion to capitalise on their economic contribution only to be followed by cutbacks in face of recession, public resistance and the susceptibility of these entry channels to abuse. Yet demand from employers in some sectors, and from education providers for students, remains strong. In its commitment to cut net migration, the Coalition government faces a trade-off between the political gains from delivering a sharp drop in numbers and the economic price that employers, education providers and some of its own ministers are saying the country will have to pay.

It is of course not only those migrants who come through work and study entry channels who take up employment. It can be equally important for refugees and for those who come to join family (leaving aside those in other categories who are not allowed to work, but do). Together, the foreign-born comprise just over 13% of people working in the UK (in the third quarter of 2010; see ONS, 2010b). In this chapter we primarily focus on policy relating directly to work or study; but when we consider the labour market conditions that create demand for migrant workers, and in some cases their exploitation, the analysis can be equally relevant to those who were permitted to enter the UK for other reasons.

I look first at the evolution of the UK's labour migration system, showing how selective skill and labour shortages in the late 1990s led to a marked shift in approach to a policy of 'managed migration' to maximise its economic benefits, and to allow immediate access to the labour market for European citizens from the enlarged EU in 2004. I note the factors that subsequently led to the introduction of a 'Points-Based System' (PBS) for non-European workers from 2008, designed in a period of boom but implemented in recession, and look at the policy options for refining that system, for addressing 'demand' for migrant labour and for protecting migrants from exploitation.

In the second part of the chapter I go back to 1999 when Labour set out to capture a greater share of the English-speaking student market, and note the success of that campaign in raising student numbers and the associated economic benefits. I then follow the extension of policy objectives to include the retention of graduates to help fill skill shortages. We see that students were brought within the PBS in 2009, but rules for colleges and students were tightened before the ink was dry in order to reduce the number of students coming to the UK.

Labour migration: ad hoc expansion pre-1997

A modern history of policy towards labour migration would start with Commonwealth immigration in the 1950s–60s (see Chapter 1) and the restrictive policies that accompanied the economic crises that characterised much of the 1970s–80s, where periods of economic growth did not translate into labour shortages of the kind that had encouraged immigration in those earlier decades. By the early 1990s, however, it was apparent that employers' demand for skilled workers to enter on work permits, issued only where no suitable labour in the UK (or EEA) was available, had risen. Only 20,000 permits were issued in 1987 but this had risen to 30,000 five years later[1] (Salt, 2001) and debate had begun on whether the restructuring of the labour market towards higher skills, coupled with an ageing population, meant the UK needed to be more open to labour migrants if it was to remain internationally competitive:

> In the long run new skills can and should be produced as a result of adaptations to the education and training systems of the country, but in the short run and in the medium term

> it is possible, and indeed probable, that skill shortages may occur in certain professional and managerial positions which could be filled to the benefit of the economy by qualified immigrants. (Findlay, 1994: 177)

In the world of politics that was at the time a heretical view, notwithstanding a de facto policy of allowing skilled labour migration to grow, but termed 'mobility' not immigration. The Conservative government quietly streamlined the work permit system to provide quicker access to overseas workers in face of demands from employers to cut red tape, including from multinationals seeking intra-company transfers of staff already employed abroad (Spencer, 1994a: 312). At that time, only employers could initiate entry for a labour migrant, while 86% of work permit-holders also subsequently left the UK: a very different system to the migrant-targeting, points-based systems then in operation in countries like Canada and Australia, seeking to attract skills to their economy for the long term. Moreover, unlike countries such as Germany equipped with an evidence base on the economic impacts of migration, there was a dearth of evidence on which a UK labour migration strategy, as opposed to a reactive, employer-led policy, could then have been based (Findlay, 1994; Spencer, 1994b).

Despite the upward trend in work permits, labour mobility was not contentious. Hence the migration issue on which Labour was fundamentally to change the parameters of policy and debate earned no mention in its 1997 manifesto. Business complaints that the system remained cumbersome and expensive led initially only to steps by the then Department for Education and Employment (DfEE) to make more rapid decisions on applications and to reduce the skill threshold for posts eligible for a permit. It saw the number of permits, swelled by recruitment of IT and health professionals, rise to more than 85,000 in 2000.

Demand for migrant workers

Responding to an employer's application for a work permit, officials had limited means to check whether there was indeed a shortage of the skills needed in that occupation. Nor was there an appetite to second-guess employers deemed the best judge of their business or service needs. There was little focus then on the dilemma that exercises policymakers now: that migrant labour may be optimal for an employer but incur economic and social costs elsewhere.

Anderson and Ruhs argue that there are two underlying factors that must be understood if we are to unravel the nature of 'demand'. First, the demand and supply of migrant workers do not operate independently but are mutually conditioning: 'Employer demand for labour is malleable, aligning itself with supply: "what employers want" can be critically influenced by "what employers think they can get"'. At the same time, supply can in turn adapt to demand. Second, demand is shaped by 'system effects' beyond the control of individual employers but heavily influenced by the state: including levels of investment in skills training, enforcement of employment standards like the statutory minimum wage and welfare policies. These are key to understanding demand for migrant labour in times of economic growth and crisis, and yet are rarely part of the migration policy debate (Anderson and Ruhs, 2010: 16).

Demand for migrants shifts with changes in the structure of the labour market, including the expansion of low-wage service occupations. It is also shaped by employer preferences: for (or against) certain nationalities, for cultural capital or 'soft skills' valued in service delivery, for instance, and for workers willing to accept low pay. In low-skill sectors such as agriculture, construction and hospitality, unfilled vacancies do not necessarily reflect a shortage of people looking for work in the localities where vacancies are located but an unwillingness to consider work at the pay and conditions on which it is offered. Migrant workers, in contrast, may be more open to accepting poor employment conditions. In their eagerness for work they may exhibit a strong 'work ethic' and offer greater 'willingness' to work anti-social hours, particularly if (as often the case) they are agency workers with fewer rights than those directly employed, subject to immigration controls that restrict their job mobility, or have irregular migration status (see Chapter 5) (Anderson et al, 2006; TUC Commission on Vulnerable Employment, 2008; Anderson, 2010).

Employers can make jobs more attractive or accessible to those within the domestic labour force: they can invest in skills training, raise wages, improve conditions, provide access to childcare and flexible working hours; or they can change the production process to make it less labour-intensive in order to avoid reliance on migrant workers. Conversely, the nature of the work, the precarious profitability of a business or the funding source of a service (not least in the face of public expenditure cuts) may provide less scope for employers to make those choices, for instance in the social care sector (Cangiano et al, 2009; Moriarty, 2010). The government can also rebalance the equation by investing in training (as in the significant shift towards self-sufficiency of doctors in the past decade), by facilitating mobility of labour within the UK and helping job seekers reliant on benefits to make the transition into employment.

Whether steps will be taken to address demand for migrant workers and future vacancies will be filled from within the resident population lies at the heart of the current debate on the efficacy of a tight cap on entry of non-EEA workers. In the early years of the Labour government, however, the focus was less on the causes of demand for migrant workers and how it might be ameliorated than on the means to ensure that the demand was met.

Shift to 'managed migration' to maximise economic gains

What had begun in the 1990s as cutting red tape in response to business pressure for flexibility on work permits was cast in a new light, in 2000, by an Immigration Minister keen to strike a markedly different tone on labour migrants from that currently dominating the headlines on asylum:

—

87

> We are in competition for the brightest and the best talents, the entrepreneurs, the scientists, the high technology specialists who make the global economy tick ... the evidence shows that economically driven migration can bring substantial overall benefits both for growth and the economy. (Roche, 2000)

The notion that Britain might want to encourage migrants required some adjustment in the Home Office. It also needed an evidence base: a Cabinet Office study scoured the limited available data and concluded that migration could bring significant economic and social benefits, but more evidence was needed (Glover et al, 2001). The Home Office initiated its own research programme and, as we saw in Chapter 1, for the first time encouraged academics to engage (Home Office, 2001b).

The arrival of David Blunkett as Home Secretary in 2001, bringing responsibility for work permits with him from the DfEE, made it possible, in theory, to develop a more coherent, joined-up approach on entry and settlement policy. It also, however, brought labour migration to a department that itself had no capacity to address the conditions that shaped demand for those workers. Convinced, with the Treasury, that without substantial legal entry routes to work in the UK 'our economy would be closed down' and that the lack of legal channels for migrants to access job vacancies was an incentive to work illegally, Blunkett opened up new routes for skilled workers and a capped, low-skilled, 'Sector Based Scheme' for temporary work in hospitality and food processing to 'undercut the people smugglers' (Home Office, 2002; Spencer, 2007).

Significantly, reform of labour migration did not require primary legislation, enabling rules to be relaxed under the radar of media interest and with tacit Opposition support. A Highly Skilled Migrant Programme (HSMP) now enabled skilled migrants to enter without a job offer (annual entry rising to 28,000 in 2007; see Salt, 2009), but the employer-led work permit system remained the core of the system. Figure 3.1 shows the rapid rise in applications approved in the heart of the period Labour was in power.

—

Figure 3.1: Work permit applications approved 1998–2008*

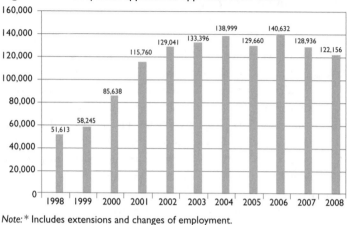

Note: * Includes extensions and changes of employment.

Source: Salt (2009), table 5.1

Employers had to demonstrate that the job was on a skill shortage list or that the post had been advertised but they had been unable to appoint, and that they would pay the going rate for the job. Efficiency of delivery of permits was prioritised in an agency, Work Permits UK (part of what is now the UK Border Agency (UKBA)), reputedly completing 90% of applications in 24 hours by 2003. Meanwhile, restrictions limiting the employment of working holidaymakers were lifted as were those on international students (see later). In a rare divergence in this non-devolved area of policy, the Scottish Executive secured agreement from the Home Office to establish a 'Fresh Talent' scheme allowing international students graduating in Scotland to remain to work for two years. This was successful in attracting additional students to study and work in Scotland, the population of which was in decline (Cavanagh et al, 2008; Kyambi, 2009). Research indicated that migrant workers were a net benefit to the UK economy, bringing significant gains for firms and public services otherwise unable to get staff. 'Our public services', the Prime Minister stated, 'would be close to collapse without their contribution' (Blair, 2004; see also Kempton, 2002).

Impact on source countries

The rationale for labour migration was, in part, to fill a skills gap until the domestic workforce could be trained to do the jobs. The NHS Five Year Plan was explicit, for instance, in anticipating that many of the 9,500 additional doctors and towards 20,000 nurses would have to come from abroad until an expansion in training places would make that unnecessary (DH, 2000: para 5.22). This heightened concern, however, that recruitment of health professionals was denuding developing countries of staff for whose training they had paid and whose skills they needed in order to provide care for their own population.

As recruitment of migrant health professionals rose in the 1990s, the UK had faced criticism for 'poaching' staff from countries experiencing their own skill shortages (Bach, 2003: 21). The response was a modest shift in NHS recruitment policy. Guidelines in 1999 on recruitment from South Africa and the Caribbean were developed into a Code of Practice for the Active Recruitment of Healthcare Professionals in 2001, globally the first code of its kind. Limited to active recruitment by the NHS and lacking effective monitoring, it was strengthened in 2004 but remained voluntary for recruiters in the private sector (DH, 2004).

The relationship between labour migration and development is, however, more nuanced than one of brain drain: source countries can benefit from remittances that generate jobs and from the return of trained staff who bring skills and fresh ideas (UNDP, 2009). Whether labour migration enhances or impedes development reflects differing circumstances, and development policies that operate in tandem can help to shift that equation (SC International Development, 2004; Malmberg et al, 2006: ch 15; Chappell and Glennie, 2009).

New workers from the European Union

It was in the heady days of economic growth during Labour's second term that the decision was taken to allow workers from the newly expanded EU to work in the UK from 1 May 2004 (forgoing the right to curtail that freedom until 2011). As we saw in Chapter 1, free movement of European citizens had long been a condition of membership of the EU but had earlier led only to limited numbers coming to work in the UK. Estimating that arrivals from new member states would again not be high, the government foresaw them helping to address shortages in low-skilled sectors and limiting any future need for the Sector Based Schemes.

Notwithstanding the decision of most other EU countries to delay access to their labour markets, the plan initially aroused little political interest. Only as 1 May approached did media anticipation that these new EU citizens might live on benefits rather than work lead to a hastily constructed Workers Registration Scheme (WRS) to monitor the employment of those from the largest eight of the 10 accession states (hence 'A8'), coupled with a bar on access to benefits or social housing in their first year.[2] While that exclusion led to significant hardship for a minority unable to find work (eg see Homeless Link, 2009) it did not stem arrivals, some 205,000 registering in 2005 and 228,000 the following year, considerably more than the number of non-Europeans who came on work permits but largely heading for low-skilled occupations. The majority came from Poland (UKBA, 2009b).

A8 workers found work in sectors experiencing labour shortages such as construction, agriculture and food processing, with an employment rate of 81.8% (in the first quarter of 2009) compared to 74.1% for the UK-born (MAC, 2009a: table 3.5). Government research suggested that their impact on the economy was positive (Gilpin et al, 2006). The numbers arriving and their impact at the community level, for which no preparation had been made (see Chapter 6), contributed, however, to a heightened political focus on labour migration, for which in 2004 there had been a further cause: the exposure of fraudulent applications for entry to work from Bulgaria and Romania (then outside the EU). Leading to the resignation of an immigration minister, the issue served to expose the complexity of a labour migration system that, coupled with weak enforcement mechanisms, left it vulnerable to abuse.

Points-Based System

A 'top-to-bottom' review led to a new five-year plan three months before the 2005 general election which promised to streamline more than 80 separate channels for entry to work into a five-tier Points-Based System (PBS). With more than 600,000 vacancies in the labour market and unemployment at 'historically low levels', ministers were in no doubt that more labour migrants from beyond the EU would be needed to sustain economic growth:

> Skilled migrants bring new skills, ideas and attitudes to the UK, and help meet skill and labour shortages, easing inflationary pressures and increasing productivity. They make an important contribution to our broader government objectives to increase innovation, to respond to the challenges of global economic change, to shift towards a high-skill economy and to deliver high-quality public services. (Home Office, 2005: 13)

Over the next two years, while the PBS was in the planning phase, the reaction to A8 migration nevertheless ensured that no similar freedom to work was accorded to the Bulgarians and Romanians who joined the EU in 2007, granted only limited access to work in food processing or agriculture (Home Office, 2006b). Meanwhile the automatic right of those on the HSMP to apply to extend their stay after four years was withdrawn in 2006 when it was found that many were not working in high-skilled jobs. The courts, in a rare intervention in this dimension of migration policy, deemed the retrospective application of the rule-change unlawful and ruled that the terms of the original scheme must be honoured (Travis, 2008).

The core rationale for the PBS was to attract and manage the entry of highly skilled workers from beyond Europe: to be more efficient, transparent, objective and easier to enforce and thus increase public confidence that the system was not being abused (Home Office, 2006a). In establishing the scheme, the UK was not constrained by international or EU law in the way that we have seen in relation to asylum and family categories, although it did need to comply with the General Agreement on Trade in Services (GATS), which restricted its capacity to limit intra-company transfers (see MAC, 2009a: para 2.54).

Replacing previous labour migration and student entry routes from outside the EEA[3] with five entry channels, the PBS arguably 'simply "scoops" the existing schemes into five new boxes' (Somerville, 2007: 187). What this system does offer, however, is the capacity to fine-tune entry criteria to reflect changing circumstances or evidence on outcomes: simply by changing the number of points awarded for different migrant characteristics and the conditions that employers must fulfil.

Five tiers of the PBS

The labour migration part of the PBS has been dominated by two entry channels:

- Tier 1 is for the highly skilled, replacing the HSMP and Scotland's 'Fresh Talent' scheme. This is a *supply-side* entry channel in which non-EEA migrants (with dependants) can enter to look for work if they receive sufficient points: awarded for qualifications, prior earnings, prior experience in the UK, age, English language skills and funds to meet maintenance requirements. A post-study route allowed graduates to remain to take up employment and a channel was retained for investors.
- Tier 2, in contrast, is for skilled workers with a job offer from an employer licensed by UKBA to 'sponsor' applicants: where advertising has identified no suitable EEA worker, the occupation is on a shortage occupation list or the worker is on an intra-company transfer. This *demand-led* route replaced the work permit system. 'Skilled' has been flexibly interpreted to include not only professionals but also butchers, sheep-shearers and care assistants where the government has been convinced the jobs will not be filled from within the EEA.

In the first six months of operation, 60% of Tier 2 permits ('certificates of sponsorship') were for intra-company transfers, 32% for jobs unfilled after advertising (dominated by health, social work and education) and 8% for those on the shortage list (MAC, 2009a). Migrants get points for a job offer but must also demonstrate sufficient competency in English to qualify. When the scheme was set up, an accompanying spouse or civil partner was allowed to come, and to work.

Tier 3, for low-skilled workers to enter on a temporary basis, was suspended from the outset in the hope that it would never be needed. Other temporary categories such as people in sports and the creative arts were grouped into Tier 5. A Youth Mobility Scheme, replacing the Working Holiday Scheme, now required sponsorship by the young person's own government and reciprocal arrangements for UK citizens in that country. The remaining Tier 4 is for students.

The PBS is predicated on the value of selecting skilled migrants and admitting the low skilled only where unavoidable, on the grounds that it is those with high skills who complement (rather than displace) the existing workforce, that their fiscal benefits are likely to be greater (contributing more to the public purse and relying less on services or benefits) and that they are more likely to contribute to long-term growth (MAC, 2009a: para 8.4). It has been argued that, for this reason, governments may choose to provide a more generous package of entitlements to those whose skills are in greater demand than to those they are less keen to attract (a 'numbers versus rights trade-off'; see Ruhs, 2010). This was indeed the case when the PBS was established, the most skilled (in Tier 1) having greatest freedom of choice in the labour market for instance and only skilled workers allowed to be accompanied by their families.

Workers who enter under the PBS are not generally entitled to support from public funds but through National Insurance contributions become eligible for contributory benefits. Workers in Tiers 1 and 2 could (with some exceptions) become eligible for permanent residence and citizenship, a link some argued should be severed in order to limit population growth (Balanced Migration, 2010), while those in the other three tiers cannot. A Tier 2 worker who wants to change employer must reapply and the employer must first advertise the post unless it is on the shortage occupation list. Like the restriction on access to benefits, this makes it difficult for the worker to leave an abusive employer: their immigration status, right to work and livelihood are at risk if they resign (Ryan, 2007).

Distinct UK model

In designing the UK model, the government had many examples from which to draw inspiration, but no clear indication that reliance on particular criteria or a balance between employer-led (Tier 2) and migrant-led (Tier 1) entry channels would prove of greatest economic benefit. Nor are lessons from abroad necessarily transferable. Countries that operate variations on points-based systems have differed in the extent to which they have taken into account attributes such as language ability; previous work experience or qualifications obtained in the country; 'ability to settle' (New Zealand); adaptability (as in Denmark, assessed by past experience of education or work in an EEA country); health and police records; and in whether points are given for an existing job offer. Australia, Canada and New Zealand, anticipating that those who enter will remain in the long term, also give points for having close relatives in the country: a crossover to the family migration channel absent in the UK model (MAC, 2009b). Comparative research has found success in attracting migrants is also significantly affected by the way in which schemes are administered and enforced (Cerna, 2008).

Within employer-led schemes (as in Tier 2) there are variations in the process of matching migrants to jobs. While the UK opted for both a shortage list and resident labour market test, Australia uses only the former and Norway the latter. Some countries require employers to obtain a certificate confirming that the requirements of the test have been met, as in Ireland, whereas UK employers have to attest that they have advertised with Jobcentre Plus. Systems vary in whether the permit is issued to the migrant or, as in the UK and US, tied to the job. Some countries have minimum pay thresholds (Sweden, Germany), others allow trade unions to contest the need for recruitment from abroad (Denmark, Iceland). Requirements vary for where jobs must be advertised, for how long and whether local applicants must be interviewed: some requiring employers to explain why they cannot hire local candidates, or precluding any redundancies of local workers. Differing requirements can 'leave a substantial margin for discretion and subjective opinion' and impose significant burdens on employers (MAC, 2009a: para 5.41). Conditions under which intra-company transfers are allowed also vary, with states seeking to allow companies reasonable access to their own staff while avoiding misuse of this entry channel.

There is considerable scope for debate on which approach is most likely to be optimal in matching supply to demand, relative to the burden placed on employers to demonstrate that vacancies cannot be filled from the existing workforce. Migration Watch found the PBS fundamentally flawed in allowing migrants to take up employment without the job always having to be advertised. Insisting that Tier 1 should be suspended, along with the shortage occupation list route, it also argued that graduates and the dependants of labour migrants should have to apply for a work permit and that intra-company transfers should be allowed only if the employee had worked for the company for two years, not six months (Migration Watch, 2008). The British Chambers of Commerce in contrast argued that requiring businesses to advertise jobs for four weeks at Jobcentre Plus is onerous (BCC, 2009), demonstrating the infinite scope for debate on fine-tuning the schemes depending on levels of confidence that the resident labour market will be able to deliver the workers required.

The Liberal Democrats in opposition proposed a regional PBS 'to ensure that migrants can work only where they are needed' (Liberal Democrat Party, 2010). A UK sufficiency of labour may indeed mask significant regional differences as has been recognised in allowing variations in the shortage occupation list in Scotland. The Scottish Government believes that population growth is an economic necessity, reflecting analysis of the GDP growth differential (in 2007) between Scotland and the UK as a whole which found nearly half of the gap to be due to the UK population growing at a higher rate (Cavanagh et al, 2008). The Equality and Human Rights Commission in Scotland fears that Scotland 'will be a retirement home' unless measures are taken to attract and retain new migrants so that the country remains competitive (Adams, 2009). The differing objectives of the UK and Scottish governments in this respect have raised the question whether Scotland needs more direct control over migration or whether its differing needs could receive greater recognition within the existing system, notwithstanding a need to ensure that it did not simply become a gateway to the rest of the UK (Kyambi, 2009).

Differing views on economic impacts

As government brought the PBS into operation in 2008 it remained confident that labour migration was good for the economy, a view shared by the Confederation of British Industry (migrants 'undoubtedly brought economic benefit to the UK'; CBI, 2008) and the Trades Union Congress (migrants make 'a substantial contribution to Britain's economy and some sectors would collapse if they were removed overnight'; TUC, 2007). The evidence had indeed suggested that migration had a positive impact on economic growth without displacing UK workers (Coats, 2008); an overall, small positive effect on wages (but potentially negative for the low paid) (Dustmann et al, 2007); that migrants make a stronger contribution to the public purse than non-migrants (Sriskandarajah et al, 2005) and had not increased unemployment (Wadsworth, 2007; Lemos and Portes, 2008). Migrants had made 'a significant contribution' to the growth of Northern Ireland's economy, one third of employers saying that migrants had helped their organisation to survive. Their presence may nevertheless have discouraged employers from training other staff and potentially slowed a transformation from low-skilled occupations to a higher-value economy (Oxford Economics, 2009).

An inquiry by the House of Lords Economics Committee came, however, to a more sombre conclusion. The claim that migrants had a positive impact on GDP was, it argued, 'irrelevant', the apposite measure being impact on income per capita, which it found to be limited. It was dismissive of the 'small' fiscal benefits and of the argument that migrants are needed to pay for the pensions of an ageing population, arguing that raising the retirement age is the only viable approach to that challenge. While many firms and services made use of migrants, this did not mean that they were indispensable and migrants' contribution must be weighed against broader impacts including demand for housing and the implications for cultural diversity and cohesion. The fact that employing migrants was in the interests of particular employers and of migrants themselves did not mean that it was in the interests of the economy per se, nor indeed of low-paid workers whose wages were depressed (HLSC Economic Affairs, 2008). The government, however, was not deterred, sending a 37-page rebuttal and implementing the PBS which, it argued, would ensure, as the Committee sought, that only those labour migrants with the skills and talents to make a positive contribution were admitted (Home Office, 2008b).

Migration Advisory Committee

In order to be confident that the PBS reflected shifting demand for migrant labour, and sensitive to criticism that its assessment of the economic benefits was inflated, Labour sought access to expert advice on fine-tuning the system and political cover for the hard choices that this would entail. The Migration Advisory Committee (MAC), five senior academics with a remit to advise on sectors and occupations that can 'sensibly' be filled by migration, has advised to a level of detail and on the basis of a more authoritative evidence base than had ever been available before. Moreover, in taking evidence from employers, trades unions and others with a keen interest in extending or shrinking channels of entry, it has served to deflect some of the pressure on government and provide subsequent decisions with greater legitimacy.

As the economy moved from growth to recession in the second quarter of 2008, leading to a rise in unemployment and a fall in job vacancies, the question for government was whether significant adjustments were needed in the PBS model. The number of non-EEA migrants entering on work permits had fallen in 2008, having peaked in 2006 (see Figure 3.1), and National Insurance data also showed a 32% fall in migrants from the EEA (MAC, 2009a: para 3.28). The government nevertheless raised the qualifications threshold for migrants to qualify for Tier 1, extended advertising requirements for jobs in Tier 2 and triggered a skills review of occupations on the shortage list with a view to upskilling existing workers to reduce future dependency on migrant labour (Home Office, 2009b).

Research suggested, however, that the downturn in demand would be temporary (Somerville and Sumption, 2009). The underlying drivers of migration would remain and, as we saw in Chapter 1, migration is not governed only by economic considerations. The MAC advised that the fall in demand for labour through Tier 2 was likely to be short-lived. As this entry channel is employer demand-driven, it could be expected to respond naturally to the UK's changing economic circumstances; thus any refinements such as extending the duration of advertising should apply regardless of the economic cycle (MAC, 2009a: para 4.45). Later in 2009 it similarly advised on Tier 1, examining the pros and cons of 10 potential refinements from closure of this entry channel entirely (advising strongly against) through to changes in qualifications, prior earnings or maintenance capacity. Significantly for our consideration of policy on international students, the MAC had reservations about the extent to which students should be able to stay after their course, 'one of the most generous schemes of its type in the world' (MAC, 2009b: 8) – but hesitated to recommend that it be curtailed:

> This would risk making UK higher education somewhat less attractive to students from abroad. Any reduced financial contribution from overseas students may mean that our universities and colleges cannot afford to train as many British students as they do at present: the flow of new British human capital could be eroded' (MAC, 2009b: 2).

The Coalition government, as we shall see, did not agree.

Annual cap on non-EEA labour migrants

The Conservatives' 2010 manifesto commitment to reduce net migration from 196,000 in 2009 to 'tens of thousands' included a specific commitment to cap labour migration from outside the EEA, thus excluding migrants who 'do jobs that could be carried out by British citizens' (Conservative Party, 2010a, 2010b). The Coalition government took immediate steps to implement an interim cap on Tiers 1 and 2 and to consult on the level and form of a long-term measure from April 2011. The interim cap was modest, demonstrating some hesitancy in saying no to employers before assessing the scale of opposition to a substantial cut at a time when the economy and employment rates might be expected to be growing once again (UKBA, 2010a, 2010c).

The interim cap nevertheless had an impact. Local authorities unable to recruit social workers were among those anticipating a damaging impact on services, and the Mayor of London was critical of the effect on the competitiveness of the capital city (Reid, 2010). The Immigration Minister insisted it was unfair to blame the cap for recruitment difficulties as 'the ability of employers to fill vacancies is affected by a wide range of factors including their own training policies, pay and conditions and corporate reputation' (Green, 2010a). UKBA's Impact Assessment on the interim cap nevertheless concluded that, as fewer migrant workers would be available:

> there may be negative impacts in the short term on businesses and the labour market, particularly in sectors where there are higher volumes of migrant workers. Over the longer term we expect businesses to adapt to the changes by adjusting production. (UKBA, 2010b)

The key question, of course, is whether that expectation – not only for business but for public services at a time of severe expenditure cuts – is justified.

Critics anticipated that a cap would put the objectives of limiting migrant numbers and population growth above that of economic performance; the British Chambers of Commerce, for instance, insisting that shortages remain even in recession, that just under a quarter of all UK businesses employ migrant workers and that they must continue to be able to recruit the people they need (BCC, 2009). The challenge for government was that a cap set high enough to enable the economy to flourish post-recession would not satisfy those who wanted to see a significant fall in migrant numbers. Government could, alternatively, end the right of skilled workers to bring their families but this would affect capacity to compete for their talents. A cap that reduced net migration to the level of the 1990s could have a profound effect on firms, public services and even football teams dependent on people from abroad. Moreover, if job vacancies remained unfilled, the outcome could be to increase irregular migration – people entering lawfully but staying on to work without permission. The government could impose tighter restrictions on settling in the UK, but skilled migrants might then choose to offer their skills to a country like Canada that did provide the option of citizenship. A rigid cap could prove a political own goal if acute skill shortages meant pressure to exceed the cap proved irresistible. No Home Secretary would want to raise the cap, regardless of changing economic and demographic circumstances (Mulley, 2010).

Post-election splits in the cabinet illustrated the competing objectives at stake, the Business Secretary and the Universities Minister concerned that significant restrictions on entry could exclude skilled workers and students which the UK needs. The Prime Minister also found himself obliged to assure India that it would be consulted, its concern reportedly threatening agreement on terms for UK investment in Indian financial services and defence: illustrating the implications of curtailing migration for foreign and trade relations that we saw in relation to Commonwealth immigration four decades earlier (see Chapter 1) (Asthana, 2010; Watt, 2010). These exchanges have demonstrated publicly, in a way that has been too rare in migration policy, that each option to curb migration can have costs attached.

The government nevertheless proceeded to implement a cap from April 2011, limiting Tier 2 to 20,700 places (2011/12) and Tier 1 to entrepreneurs and no more than 1,000 'persons of exceptional talent' (Labour's original intention for its precursor, the HSMP), a study having established that many in Tier 1 were working in low-skilled jobs such as supermarket cashiers (UKBA, 2010d). By contrast, in the year to September 2010, 32, 065 people had been given visas to come through Tier 1 and 68,675 through Tier 2 (ONS, 2010a). Intra-company transfers were also curtailed, notwithstanding concern from foreign-owned firms such as car manufacturers that restrictions would prevent transfer of staff to support the launch of new products (Webb, 2010). 'We need employers to look first', the Home Secretary said, 'to people who are out of work and who are already in this country' (May, 2010).

Hitting a cautionary note, the MAC had advised that Tiers 1 and 2 accounted for only half of the non-EEA migrants who came for work in 2009, and that those who came for work were in turn only one in five of all non-EEA migrants. Even closure of Tiers 1 and 2 entirely would thus be unlikely to achieve the low net migration the government sought. It would need to cut not only student numbers but also family migration if it wanted to achieve that goal (MAC, 2010b: 1). Meanwhile, the Home Affairs Committee also concluded that the cap would make little difference to net migration but could do serious damage to the economy. It was concerned at the impact of any steps that might therefore be taken to cut entry through alternative routes (SC Home Affairs, 2010).

Protection within the labour market

Before turning to international students, we need to consider one further aspect of policy towards labour migrants which is central to any analysis of demand: protection of their rights in the workplace. There has long been evidence that some employers pay below the going rate (including below the minimum wage), require excessive working hours, treat migrants less favourably than other workers and house them in unacceptable living conditions (eg Anderson and Rogaly,

2005). This is not only bad for the migrants concerned but means that they are undercutting the domestic labour market. Moreover, it creates a demand for irregular migrants working without permission (see Chapter 5).

The drowning of 23 Chinese cockle-pickers in Morecombe Bay in February 2004, for whose manslaughter their gangmaster was later convicted (GLA, 2009), provided the political momentum to set up the Gangmasters' Licensing Authority (GLA) to regulate the operation of labour providers in agriculture and food processing (but not to overcome resistance to its extension to other sectors). By summer 2009, the GLA estimated there were some 300 providers still operating unlawfully outside its licensing system (BIS, 2009: para 12). Such moves to address exploitation have been closely related, however, to efforts to tackle illegal working (CLG, 2008). Coupled with the low visibility of employment enforcement agencies, this suggested that government's first priority was not to protect vulnerable workers.

Migrants were nevertheless one focus of a cross-government strategy launched in 2007 to enforce workplace standards and of a Vulnerable Workers Enforcement Forum that reported in 2008. There was now recognition of a need to promote awareness of employment rights and access to enforcement bodies: for better agency coordination; collaboration with business, unions and advice agencies aware of the issues on the ground; and for higher-profile, targeted enforcement (BERR, 2008). There was a 50% increase in the budget for enforcing the minimum wage from 2007/08 and a doubling of the number of Employment Agency Inspectors (Home Office, 2008b: paras 3.6, 4.23). Public expenditure cuts and the Coalition government's ambition to curtail state regulatory activity may now cast doubt, however, on the future impact of this programme.

An inquiry by the Equality and Human Rights Commission (2008–10) found that existing safeguards had not prevented the widespread mistreatment and exploitation of workers in the meat and poultry processing sector where one third of staff are migrants, including physical and verbal abuse, lack of proper health and safety protection, and the treatment of pregnant workers found to be a particular concern.

Workers had little knowledge of their rights and feared complaints would lead to dismissal. There were frequent breaches of the law and of licensing standards. Firms that treated their staff well benefited from retention of well-motivated and increasingly skilled workers. It was not in immigration law that the Commission saw solutions, but action by supermarkets to improve their auditing of suppliers and resourcing of the GLA to extend its reach (EHRC, 2010). The earlier House of Lords inquiry on the economic impact of migration had seen stricter enforcement of employment regulations as the key means to ensure that employers did not give preference to cheap migrant labour over the resident labour force (HLSC Economic Affairs, 2008).

Migration for study

Although opportunities to study bring significantly more people to live in Britain than any other entry channel, policy towards international students only recently became the focus of political and media attention. Nor was government policy a major factor in the early growth of student numbers. In the past decade, however, recruitment has, like that of labour migrants, been actively promoted because of benefits to the UK. Within government, it has at times been marked by the involvement of the Foreign and Commonwealth Office (FCO) and in the direct engagement of the Prime Minister: not, as for asylum, in face of a crisis but here spearheading a global recruitment drive. Blair launched a successful campaign to secure 25% of the English-speaking university student market in 1999 before the philosophy of 'managed migration' had even been articulated. Only later did concern that access channels for study were being abused put students on the political agenda and, coupled with the recession, lead to restrictions which have implications not only for education but for sectors of the labour market in which students work.

In the 1960s–80s many international students were supported by government scholarships or technical assistance schemes, policy towards non-EU students primarily motivated at this stage by international development and relations objectives. International student numbers rose in the 1970s but a sharp rise in tuition fees for non-EEA students to full cost in 1980 led to a fall in those coming to the UK. This prompted the British Council to market the benefits of UK education across the globe during the following decade and the FCO to launch its Chevening Scholarship Scheme: competition had begun. *The Times Higher Education Supplement* urged universities to have the confidence to make a powerful case for international students to government: arguing that they foster an internationalist outlook among British students, make it viable to teach rare subjects, introduce different and challenging intellectual traditions, test the quality of higher education against world standards and contribute to research (cited in UKCISA, 2008a: 19).

As in relation to labour migration, scholars have explored the nature of the demand driving student mobility. Social demand theorists have emphasised the power of social and cultural capital in parental motivations to get places for their children in universities that will enhance their career prospects. Other scholars have focused on the supply-side financial interests of education providers and of states keen to expand human and cultural capital in their knowledge economies. Together, both are 'powerful players in structuring the patterns of student flows' (Findlay, 2010: 5). As with labour migration there are winners and losers: between those education institutions that are successful in attracting international students and the wealth that they bring and those that are not; and for the source countries to which the students may or may not return with the knowledge and skills they have acquired.

European students

In contrast to the competition characterising the market for non-European students, within Europe the arrangement is intended to be one of mutuality. Students from EU countries (extended, as usual, to EEA nationals) are able to take up places to study in any member state and pay the same fees as domestic students. The EU's Erasmus Programme to promote mobility, established in 1987, had an annual budget of more than €440 million by 2009, with 90% of universities in the EU taking part and hosting in excess of 180,000 students a year (European Commission, 2009). For the UK, expansion of the EU in 2004 meant students from 10 additional countries now benefited from lower fees, Cyprus and Poland rising into the top 10 source countries for EU students in higher education by 2008/09 (HESA, 2010). The increase in East European students has benefited the post-1992 universities in particular (Thorp, 2008: 66). It is calculated that the economy also benefits substantially from EU higher education students during and after their education: an estimated £866 million in fees and living expenditure per annum with a further £100 million fiscal gain (2004/05) from those remaining to work after graduation (Vickers and Bekhradnia, 2007).

Campaign to increase the UK's market share

During the 1990s, non-EEA student numbers rose significantly (Home Office, 2001a) but competition intensified, not least from the USA. UK marketing was largely organised by education providers with British Council support. Blair's initiative, launched in June 1999, was overt in its intention to make it 'easier to apply, easier to enter' in order to boost university student numbers by 50,000 and further education numbers by 25,000 by 2005. Removing a requirement on students to get permission to work enabled students to support themselves while studying, a step that made the UK 'a far more attractive destination' (UKCISA, 2008a: 25). 'UK Education' was now marketed with a new brand and streamlined visa procedures. 'More open doors' to students, Blair argued, would increase income for universities and to the public purse and enable UK students to 'gain a window on the world', while helping trade and diplomacy (Blair, 1999). Significantly, there was no intention at this stage that students should remain in the UK to work after studying: they were refused entry if they indicated that this was their aspiration.

Higher education students would nevertheless be in the UK for a number of years and those on shorter courses for months. So it is striking that this initiative was launched without a glance towards the simultaneous development of policy on another group of arrivals who were in some cases from the same countries, asylum seekers, who by 1999 were already the focus of intense political and media debate. In that year, 71,000 people sought asylum compared to the entry of 272,000 non-EEA students (Home Office, 2009a: Table 1.3). For the government, these were entirely distinct categories of entry, one contributing to the exchequer and the other supported by it. As a government special advisor was later to acknowledge, however (Spencer, 2007: 349), and research was to confirm (Lewis, 2005), these distinctions were less apparent to the public.

The campaign, meanwhile, was a success, the British Council reporting in 2004 that the UK had achieved a 25% share of the English-speaking university student market. The top source countries were China, Greece, the USA, Germany and France. Women made up 48% of the students (British Council, 2004). Overseas students as a whole now made up over 13% of students in higher education; non-EU university student numbers having grown by 72% in the five years to 2004 compared to a 19% increase in domestic students. University fee income from non-EU students rose from £672 million to £1,275 million over that five-year period: international fees for undergraduates even then ranged from £7,600 to more than £22,000 per annum (2004/05). There was also a significant rise in the number of British people studying abroad, the UK being just one player in the broader globalisation of education (Findlay, 2006; Universities UK, 2010).

Need to maintain momentum

Global demand for international student places was expected almost to treble by 2020 but so was competition, including from European universities providing courses in English. The UK student 'industry' depended on too few countries and there was a perception among potential students that the quality of education and value of UK qualifications did not always compare well to the offer elsewhere. Analysts suggested that the UK might also compete less favourably in future because of improvements in education in source countries such as China and Malaysia, the expansion of English as the language of instruction in countries with lower living costs and greater access to employment than in the UK, and because of harmonisation of higher education standards across the EU (British Council, 2004; Cemmell and Bekhradnia, 2008).

There was a need to diversify markets, support education providers in expanding their offer and retain contact with alumni to extend the UK's influence. Phase two of the Prime Minister's Initiative for International Education was thus launched in 2006: a £35 million investment to attract a further 70,000 students to higher education and 30,000 to further education by 2011, with the intention of doubling the number of countries sending more than 10,000 students a year. A new focus on improving the quality of students' experiences reflected awareness that, in an expanding international marketplace, students could choose to go elsewhere. Funding from the initiative made it possible to produce the information, guidance and orientation material that has been lacking for other new arrivals (see Chapter 6) (UKCISA, 2008a: 30). Once again it is striking that, in launching the initiative, there was no read-across to parallel developments in migration policy, by now focused on the impacts of migration at the local level. Despite being the largest group of recent migrants in the UK, students were not a focus of that debate (see Chapter 6).

By 2008/09, 10.5% of all students in higher education (251,310) were from non-EU countries. One third came from China and India, followed by Nigeria, the USA and Malaysia. A further 4.9% came from within the EU, so that in total 15% of the UK's university students (including 34% of postgraduates) were now from overseas. The off-campus expenditure of overseas students was estimated to be some £2.3 billion (2007/08), generating 27,600 jobs and contributing £1.51 billion to the UK's GDP. The contribution of non-EU university students is particularly significant because it includes their higher fees, contributing £3.42 billion to the UK balance of trade in that year (Kelly et al, 2009; HESA, 2010). A further 76,785 international students were studying in further education (FE) in 2007/08, a little over half from within the EU (British Council, 2009).

Points-Based System Tier 4

Meanwhile student policy had taken an interesting turn in Scotland where, as we saw, the Scottish Executive wanted international graduates to fill skill shortages and, in 2005, persuaded the Home Office to allow students to remain after completion of their studies as part of its 'Fresh Talent' initiative (Scottish Executive, 2005). A shortage of people with science and engineering skills led to a more limited UK-wide scheme to allow graduates to remain for 12 months, extended to all graduates in 2007. Significantly, universities now used future access to jobs as a selling feature (Findlay, 2010). The rationale for government policy had evolved from its benefit to the education sector 'to being a rich source of global talent' for the UK, contributing to the amassing of human capital for its knowledge-based economy (Findlay, 2006: 24).

Less apparent has been the contribution made by those working part time during their studies. Work not only makes it possible for many students to study but helps to fill low-skill vacancies, as in the care sector (Cangiano et al, 2009). A third of international FE students, for instance, were working part time in 2006, with non-EU students on average working 16 hours a week (UKCOSA, 2006). Taken together with work after graduation, student policy was thus now inextricably linked with the labour market. The government, however, had become concerned that access for study was being used by those whose *primary* intention was access to the labour market, facilitated by 'bogus colleges'. It moved in 2004 to allow only accredited colleges to receive international students, a step the national advisory body for international students, UKCOSA (UK Council for Overseas Student Affairs), had long recommended for students' own protection.

It was only with the advent of the Points-Based System (PBS) that the education and labour dimensions of student policy were formally brought together. In making provision for students within the PBS, the government stressed the contribution that international students

Figure 3.2: Non-EEA students* given leave to enter 2000–2009

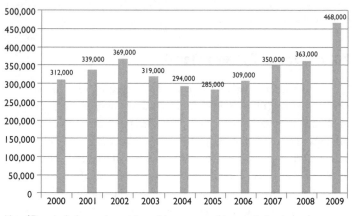

Note: *Data includes student visitors (short courses) but excludes dependants, rounded to the nearest thousand

Source: Home Office Control of Immigraton Statistics (2009, Table 1.4)

make to the economy – £2.5 billion per annum in tuition fees and an estimated £8.5 billion in total (2003/04) – as well as the cultural value of their 'ideas, attitudes and experiences'. Moreover, as students rise to positions of influence in their own countries, they may look to the UK for technology, trade and investment (Lenton, 2007; UKBA, 2008). The rationale for inclusion in the PBS was that the system needed to be 'simpler and more robust', with greater objectivity and transparency on entry decisions and a stronger role for education providers in 'vouching for the students they want us to allow into the UK' (Home Office, 2006a: 31). Tier 4 applicants apply for a Student Visa (or Student Visitor Visa for short courses), for which the fee was raised to £199 in 2010. As with labour migrants, students must pass a points threshold to be accepted (points being awarded for acceptance on a course at a sufficiently advanced level by an approved education provider) and have funds to cover the course fees and living costs. Those on Student Visas were allowed to work part time during term time for up to 20 hours per week and full time during the vacation, and to bring their dependants if they could provide for them without any recourse to public funds. Their spouse could take up almost any form of employment and accompanying children could attend state schools. At the end of a course of a year or longer, the student could, as we have seen, apply for a Post Study Work Visa (part of Tier 1, PBS) enabling them to stay and work for two years. Student Visitors must leave at the end of their short course and may not work during their stay.

Some education providers are heavily dependent on international student income: 50% of students at the London School of Economics (LSE), for instance, were from beyond the EU in 2009, their tuition fees amounting to one third of its income, with a further 20% of its students from EU countries. Non-EU students contribute nearly 8% of all university income (2007/08) and sustain departments which would otherwise struggle to remain financially viable. Courses such as engineering and computer science can be particularly reliant on their contribution. A major snarl-up in the administration of student visas or drop in student numbers for other reasons would thus leave forensic holes in some disciplines (Home Affairs Select Committee, 2009a: para 24; Universities UK, 2009; Kelly et al, 2009).

Critics have challenged the reduction of education to an export market in which students may be valued more for their economic than their academic or cultural contribution (De Vita and Case, 2003; Coate, 2009). A requirement that tutors monitor and report to UKBA on students' attendance, moreover, threatens to damage the relationship of trust between them. There has been some criticism that the PBS system in practice is expensive for users, causes late arrivals through long delays in processing visas and is unpredictable in its refusal of visas (Hartwich, 2010). Migration Watch, from an alternative perspective, argues that the scheme reduced scrutiny of applications by immigration officers, giving too great a say to institutions that have a strong financial interest in attracting students and too little expertise to detect fraudulent applications: 'Student visas have long been a serious loophole in immigration control; the PBS makes a bad situation considerably worse' (Migration Watch, 2009). Yet there are very high rates of refusal of student visas, some 32% in 2008/09. Low refusal rates from the Americas, moreover, mask the 61% of refusals from African countries and from countries such as Pakistan (71%) (UKBA, 2009a).

Rules tightened

Within a year of the roll-out of Tier 4, Labour's Prime Minister announced a review, focusing on courses below degree level deemed most at risk of abuse by colleges and students. Inspection of further and higher education providers had already led to a severe cutback in the number of approved sponsors (Brown, 2009). In January 2010, all applications from India, Nepal and Bangladesh were temporarily suspended pending an investigation of suspected fraudulent applications, bringing criticism from the Indian government and concern from UK universities about the impact on genuine applicants for the coming academic year. By February, the Home Office had announced it would allow only 'highly trusted sponsor' institutions to sponsor students for many courses below degree level. It cut the amount of time a student at that level was able to work in term time to 10 hours per week and removed the right of their dependants to work, on penalty of removal from the UK (see Chapter 5). The stated rationale was to weed out those whose primary aim was not to study but to gain access to work for themselves and their spouse (Home Office, 2010a). It is known, however, that students unable to find a job can have financial difficulties as a result (UKCOSA, 2006). In practice, student working hours are extremely difficult to enforce.

Language testing became compulsory for many of those planning to study below degree level, but English language providers successfully challenged, on procedural grounds, a ban on students with little English coming to take a language course. The High Court agreed that the change should have been laid before Parliament. English UK, representing 440 schools and colleges, argued that the ruling had saved more than 3,000 jobs in language schools and more than £600 million a year in overseas income (Gabbatt, 2010). The Home Office had sought to go further and ban entry of all non-EEA students below degree level but pulled back in face of protests from private education providers and from universities that feared the loss of thousands of students each year who do A-levels or foundation courses before staying on to do degrees (Farthing, 2009; Morgan, 2010).

The year 2009 nevertheless saw the number of non-EEA students admitted up by 25% on 2008,[4] suggesting that fears (or government hopes) that the pre-2010 changes would cut student numbers were unfounded (Home Office, 2010b). The UK's share of the global market for all international students has nevertheless fallen in recent years, while that of competitors such as Australia, New Zealand and Canada has grown (Cemmell and Bekhradnia, 2008). There is some limited evidence to suggest a level of dissatisfaction with the offer in the UK: many students finding the new application process for visas and extensions to be slow, complex and expensive and 10% having to apply more than once before being successful (UKCISA, 2009, 2010). Of non-EU students at universities in England in 2006/07, 30% were dissatisfied with the value for money of their course (Bekhradnia, 2009). Students have also expressed some dissatisfaction with their broader experiences, including lack of social contact with UK students (UKCOSA, 2006). If students are to continue to want to choose to come to the UK, it has been suggested that government should ensure that immigration and employment regulations 'demonstrate the fairness and efficiency for which the UK would want to be known abroad' and that support services (such as pre-departure advice, orientation programmes and assistance with accommodation) should be resourced to keep pace with numbers (UKCOSA, 2006; UKCISA, 2008b).

Prior to being elected, the Conservatives argued that the student visa system was 'the biggest weakness in our border controls' and suggested they would require some students to pay a bond of up to £2,000, repayable after they had left the UK (Conservative Party, 2010b; Wintour, 2010). Post-election it was clear that student numbers would need to be severely cut back if the Coalition government's low net migration target was to be met. This immediately raised the concern not only of education providers but of the Education Secretary and Universities Minister, reportedly arguing within government that severe cuts could both hit the competitiveness of the UK education sector and the UK's reputation among international students (Travis, 2010). At the very time that universities believe they face a funding 'valley of death' (Smith, 2010), their financial lifeline from international students may, to achieve a quite different political objective, be curtailed.

Towards half of students entering through Tier 4 are, however, en route to courses below degree level and it is those providers who are likely to be hardest hit, albeit access for Student Visitors to short courses will remain. It is likely that university students will no longer be allowed to work at all (except on campus) during the week, that dependants will only be able to accompany those on longer courses and will themselves have no access to work. The post-study Tier 1 route into employment will close and students will be expected to leave when they complete their course – bringing policy back full circle to the early days of the Labour government a decade ago: 'This government wants high-calibre students with a genuine desire to study to come to our country for temporary periods', the Coalition Immigration Minister said, 'and then return home' (Green, 2010b; see also UKBA, 2010e).

Conclusion

Tasked with advising on the level at which a cap on non-EEA migration should be set, the MAC articulated the question that now lies at the heart of labour and student migration policy: how should it 'trade off, prioritise, and balance the economic, public service and social impacts of migration' and how should it measure and assess those impacts? (MAC, 2010a: 15). The answer is not straightforward. An essential contribution to an employer, service user or even the public education system may not equate to benefit for the population as a whole. Nor is the evidence base available in many respects on which to make that judgement call.

In this chapter we have looked at the two categories of migrants actively sought by the UK in the past decade because of economic and broader benefits, before the recession, perceptions of abuse and public resistance reversed that trend. In contrast to policy on asylum and family migrants, the pressure on government to resist tighter regulation has been largely economic: articulated by employers in sectors facing skill and labour shortages and by education providers anxious to retain and expand income from international students.

On labour migration, a laissez-faire policy of expansion in the 1990s was transformed into an overt intention to make the UK competitive in the global market for talent: first easing restrictions, then streamlining entry channels into a Points-Based System open to fine-tuning when demand for labour fell. Channels of entry for low-skilled workers, opened up to reduce the incentive to work illegally, could conveniently be cut back when free movement for A8 workers provided an unexpectedly plentiful supply. Having chosen not to restrict their entry in 2004, and despite evidence of a positive economic contribution, the government now found its inability to limit their numbers to be its Achilles heel as labour migration took the place of asylum in the heated politics of immigration control. Labour migration policymaking has been distinct in the impact of membership of the EU; in requiring little primary legislation (thus enabling rules on non-EEA workers to be relaxed without parliamentary debate); in the limited constraints imposed by international agreements or the courts; and, since 2007, in having the MAC to provide a more authoritative evidence base and a forum in which the voices of sectoral interests could be heard at one remove from government itself.

Lack of consensus on the economic benefits of migration were apparent before the recession hit in 2008, but the downturn strengthened the voices of sceptics and those questioning the broader impact of migration on public services, local communities and population growth. For skill and labour shortages, there is little disagreement that the goal should be to upskill the existing workforce and to encourage employers to pursue alternatives to low-skilled migrants from abroad. Given the complex relationship between employer demand and supply, however, it cannot be assumed that cutting off the supply of migrants will see jobs filled by UK or EEA workers.

Even if the door to non-EEA labour migrants were firmly shut, family migrants and refugees would remain in the labour market and vulnerable to exploitation unless employment regulations – quite separately from immigration control – are more effectively enforced.

Where employers' preference is for workers willing to accept pay and conditions below the going rate, we saw that the answer is thus to be found less in immigration controls than in employment policy: in the enforcement of the minimum wage, health and safety rules and broader labour market regulations. Reducing the UK's reliance on migrant labour will primarily require changes to the structural and systemic factors that create that demand, not simply changes to migration policy. We explore this further in Chapter 5.

In relation to students we saw that a policy initially driven by a desire to maximise the UK's share of the global student market, sprinkled with internationalism, took on the additional objective of meeting UK skill shortages: students once told they could not enter if they intended to stay, later encouraged to deploy their skills as graduates in the labour market. Evidence of some abuse by 'bogus' colleges and by students more intent on work than study latterly led to a clampdown on 'rogue' colleges and, in the economic downturn, to more limited access for students to the labour market.

Policy development, during its expansive phase, was distinct in the leadership of the Prime Minister and, as for labour migration, in the limited role of the courts. Despite the significance of student numbers, the lack of read-across to simultaneous policy development on asylum or on the local impact of migrants stands out as a striking example of Whitehall policy silos. The fact that most students eventually leave does not detract from their significance while in the country. The fact that they have not been a focus of the local impact debate (Chapter 6) may suggest that the information and support role played by colleges is a success from which lessons could be applied more broadly. Alternatively, the public and service providers may not be identifying this group of migrants separately from labour migrants or asylum seekers when they express their views.

The value of international students to the education sector, unlike the impact of labour migrants, is largely accepted. Their engagement in employment, during and after their studies, has been more contentious. Here the government is caught in a bind as many students need to work in order to support themselves while studying, and if they cannot work may choose to study in a country where they can. Low-skilled sectors of the labour market are affected, moreover, when work restrictions on students are imposed. The line between entry for study and for work is not an easy one to regulate. It is, moreover, difficult to enforce.

Student numbers have, to date, continued to rise, but the UK has lost ground in the global market and analysts predict competition will become more intense. As the recession has put a premium on jobs for UK residents, the balance for government has tipped in favour of tighter controls, higher visa fees and a fall in student numbers. For education providers facing cutbacks in public expenditure, however, and perhaps for a Foreign Office seeking to retain the UK's global influence, the need to continue to attract international students has never been more important. In labour migration and student policy it is apparent that each policy option carries costs. Policy choice depends on priorities and, knowing the costs, deciding where they should fall.

Notes

[1] Includes first permissions and the Training and Work Experience Scheme but not extensions or changes in employment.

[2] These measures remained throughout the seven-year transition period permitted by the EU, closing on 30 April 2011.

[3] As we have seen in other chapters, policy relating to EU citizens extended to those in the larger European Economic Area (EEA): that is, to include Iceland, Norway and Liechtenstein.

[4] Including Student Visitors.

References

Adams, L. (2009) 'Scotland will be Retirement Home without New Migrants', *Herald Scotland*, 20 January.

Anderson, B. (2010) 'Migration, Immigration Controls and the Fashioning of Precarious Workers', *Work, Employment and Society* 24(2): 300–17.

Anderson, B. and Rogaly, B. (2005) *Forced Labour and Migration to the UK: Study Prepared by COMPAS in Collaboration with the Trades Union Congress*. London: TUC.

Anderson, B. and Ruhs, M. (2010) 'Migrant Workers: Who Needs Them? A Framework for the Analysis of Staff Shortages, Immigration and Public Policy', in M. Ruhs and B. Anderson (eds) *Who Needs Migrant Workers? Labour Shortages, Immigration and Public Policy*. Oxford: OUP.

Anderson, B., Ruhs, M., Spencer, S. and Rogaly, B. (2006) *Fair Enough? Central and East European Migrants in Low Wage Employment in the UK*. York: Joseph Rowntree Foundation.

Asthana, A. (2010) 'Cap on Skilled Immigrants May Hit Recovery, Businesses Warn', *The Observer*, 18 July.

Bach, S. (2003) 'International Migration of Health Workers: Labour and Social Issues', Working Paper, Geneva: International Labour Organisation.

Balanced Migration (2010) 'Our Case'. Available at: http://www.balancedmigration.com/ourcase.php

BCC (British Chambers of Commerce) (2009) 'Migration Policy Brief', London. Availbale at: http://www.britishchambers.org.uk/topics/employment

Bekhradnia, B. (2009) *The Academic Experiences of Students in English Universities, 2009 Report*, Oxford: Higher Education Policy Institute.

BERR (Department for Business, Enterprise and Regulatory Reform) (2008) *Vulnerable Worker Enforcement Forum Final Report and Government Conclusions*, London: BERR.

BIS (Department for Business, Innovation and Skills) (2009) *Gangmasters Licensing Authority: A Hampton Implementation Review Report*. London: BIS.

Blair, T. (1999) 'Attracting More International Students', London, 10 Downing Street, 18 June 1999. Available at: www.britishcouncil.org/eumd-pmi2-history.htm

Blair, T. (2004) 'Speech to the Confederation of British Industry', 27 April, London.

British Council (2004) *Vision 2020: Forecasting International Student Mobility, a UK Perspective*. London: British Council.

British Council (2009) 'Further Education International Student Numbers 2002/2003 to 2007/2008'. London: British Council.

Brown, G. (2009) 'Speech on Immigration', Ealing, 12 November, London: 10 Downing Street.

Cangiano, A., Shutes, I., Spencer, S. and Leeson, G. (2009) *Migrant Care Workers in Ageing Societies: Research Findings in the United Kingdom*. Oxford: COMPAS, University of Oxford.

Cavanagh, L., Eirich, F. and McLaren, J.G. (2008) *Fresh Talent: Working in Scotland Scheme: An Evidence Review*. Edinburgh: Scottish Government Social Research.

CBI (Confederation of British Industry) (2008) *CBI Evidence to House of Lords Economic Affairs Committee: The Economic Impact of Migration*, SC/06-07/EA243. London: CBI.

Cemmell, J. and Bekhradnia, B. (2008) 'The Bologna Process and the UK's International Student Market', Oxford: Higher Education Policy Institute.

Cerna, L. (2008) 'Towards an EU Blue Card? The Delegation of National High Skilled Immigration Policies to the EU Level', Working Paper 65, COMPAS, University of Oxford.

Chappell, L. and Glennie, A. (2009) *Maximising the Development Outcomes of Migration: A Policy Perspective*. London: Institute for Public Policy Research.

CLG (Department for Communities and Local Government) (2008) *Managing the Impacts of Migration: A Cross-Government Approach*. London: CLG.

Coate, K. (2009) 'Exploring the Unknown: Levinas and International Students in UK Higher Education', *Journal of Education Policy* 24(3): 271–82.

Coats, D. (2008) 'Migration Myths: Employment, Wages and Labour Market Performance', London: The Work Foundation.

Conservative Party (2010a) 'Where We Stand: Immigration. Available at: http://www.conservatives.com/Policy/Where_we_stand/Immigration.aspx (accessed 15 February 2010).

Conservative Party (2010b) *Invitation to Join the Government of Britain: The Conservative Manifesto 2010*. London: Conservative Party.

De Vita, G. and Case, P. (2003) 'Rethinking the Internationalisation Agenda in UK Higher Education', *Journal of Further and Higher Education* 27(4): 383–98.

DH (Department of Health) (2000) 'The NHS Plan: A Plan for Investment, A Plan for Reform', Cm 4818-1. London: Department of Health.

DH (2004) *Code of Practice for the International Recruitment of Health Professionals*. London: Department of Health.

Dustmann, C., Frattini, T. and Preston, I. (2007) *A Study of Migrant Workers and the National Minimum Wage and Enforcement Issues that Arise*. London: Low Pay Commission.

EHRC (Equality and Human Rights Commission) (2010) *Inquiry into Recruitment and Employment in the Meat and Poultry Processing Sector: Report of the Findings and Recommendations*. London: Equality and Human Rights Commission.

European Commission (2009) 'Erasmus Programme'. Available at: http://ec.europa.eu/education/lifelong-learning-programme/doc80_en.htm (accessed 12 April 2010).

Farthing, M. (2009) 'New Student Visa Rules Risk Creating "Fortress Britain"', *The Independent*, 10 December.

Findlay, A. (1994) 'An Economic Audit of Contemporary Migration', in S. Spencer (ed) *Strangers and Citizens: A Positive Approach to Migrants and Refugees*. London: Rivers Oram.

Findlay, A. (2006) 'International Student Migration in the UK: Training for the global economy or simply another form of global talent recruitment?', International Competition for S&E Students and Workers, Georgetown University, Washington DC, 30–31 March.

Findlay, A. (2010) 'An Assessment of Supply and Demand-side Theorizations of International Student Mobility', *International Migration*, 49(2): 162-90.

Gabbatt, A. (2010) 'English Language Schools Win Court Battle over Tightening of Visa Rules', *The Guardian*, 9 July.

Gilpin, N., Henty, M., Lemos, S., Portes, J. and Bullen, C. (2006) *The Impact of Free Movement of Workers from Central and Eastern Europe on the UK Labour Market*, Working Paper 29. London: DWP.

GLA (Gangmasters Licensing Authority) (2009) 'Prime Minister and Chairman of the GLA: Morecombe Bay Tragedy', Press release, 5 February. Available at: http://www.gla.gov.uk/embedded_object. asp?id=1013468

Glover, S., Gott, C., Loizillon, A., Portes, J., Price, R., Spencer, S., Srinivasan, V. and Willis, C. (2001) 'Migration: An Economic and Social Analysis', *RDS Occasional Paper 67*. London: Home Office.

Green, D. (2010a) 'Minister Defends Interim Limit on Economic Migrants', UKBA press notice, 4 October.

Green, D. (2010b) 'Government Sets out Proposals for Major Reform of the Student Visa System', UKBA press notice, 7 December.

Hartwich, V. (2010) 'Fortress Academy – The Points-Based Visa System and the Policing of International Students and Academics'. London: Manifesto Club.

HESA (Higher Education Statistics Agency) (2010) 'Students in Higher Education Institutions 2008/09', Press release, 25 March, Cheltenham: Higher Education Statistics Agency.

HLSC Economic Affairs (House of Lords Select Committee on Economic Affairs) (2008) *The Economic Impact of Immigration, Volume 1: Report; Volume 2: Evidence*, First Report Session 2007–08, HL Paper 82-I, London: House of Lords Select Committee on Economic Affairs.

Homeless Link (2009) *Central and East European Rough Sleepers in London: Repeat Survey*. London: Homeless Link.

Home Office (2001a) *Control of Immigration: Statistics United Kingdom 2000*. London: Home Office.

Home Office (2001b) 'Bridging the Information Gaps: A Conference of Research on Asylum and Immigration in the UK (Conference report)', 21 March. London: Home Office.

Home Office (2002) *Secure Borders, Safe Haven: Integration with Diversity in Modern Britain*. Cm 5387. London: Home Office.

Home Office (2005) *Controlling Our Borders: Making Migration Work for Britain – Five Year Strategy for Asylum and Immigration*, Cm 6472. London: Home Office.

Home Office (2006a) *A Points-Based System: Making Migration Work for Britain*, Cm 6741. London: Home Office.

Home Office (2006b) 'Controlled Access to UK Labour Market for New Accession Countries', Press release, 25 October, London: Home Office.

Home Office (2008a) 'Government Response to the Consultation on Visitors'. London: Home Office.

Home Office (2008b) 'The Government Reply to the First Report from the House of Lords Committee on Economic Affairs Session 2007–08 HL Paper 82', Cm 7414. London: Home Office.

Home Office (2009a) *Control of Immigration Statistics 2008*, Home Office Statistical Bulletin 14/09. London: Home Office.

Home Office (2009b) 'Migrant Workers Face Tougher Test to Work in the United Kingdom', Press release, 22 February.

Home Office (2010a) 'Statement of Changes in Immigration Rules', HC 357, London: Home Office.

Home Office (2010b) *Control of Immigration: Statistics United Kingdom 2009*, Home Office Statistical Bulletin 15/10. London: Home Office.

Kelly, U., McLellan, D. and McNicoll, I. (2009) *The Impact of Universities on the UK Economy: Fourth Report*. London: Universities UK.

Kempton, J. (2002) *Migrants in the UK: Their Characteristics and Labour Market Outcomes and Impacts*. London: Home Office.

Kyambi, S. (2009) *Room for Manoeuvre? The Options for Addressing Immigration-Policy Divergence between Holyrood and Westminster*. Glasgow: Equality and Human Rights Commission Scotland.

Lemos, S. and Portes, J. (2008) *New Labour? The Impact of Migration from the New European Member States on the UK Labour Market*. London: Department for Work and Pensions.

Lenton, P. (2007) *Global Value: The Value of UK Education and Training Exports: an Update*. London: British Council.

Lewis, M. (2005) *Asylum – Understanding Public Attitudes*. London: Institute for Public Policy Research.

Liberal Democrat Party (2010) *Manifesto 2010*. London: Liberal Democrat Party.

MAC (2009a) *Analysis of the Points-Based System:Tier 2 and Dependants.* London: Migration Advisory Committee.

MAC (2009b) *Analysis of the Points-Based System: Tier 1.* London: Migration Advisory Committee.

MAC (2010a) *Consultation by the Migration Advisory Committee on the Level of an Annual Limit on Economic Migration to the UK.* London: Migration Advisory Committee.

MAC (2010b) *Limits on Migration: Limits on Tier 1 and Tier 2 for 2011/12 and Supporting Policies.* London: Migration Advisory Committee.

Malmberg, B.,Tamas, K., Bloom, D., Münz, R. and Canning, D. (2006) *Global Population Ageing, Migration and European External Policies.* Stockholm: Institute for Future Studies.

May, T. (2010) 'Government Sets First Annual Limit for Non-European Workers', press notice, London: Home Office, 23 November.

MigrationWatch UK (2008) *Toughening the Points-Based System,* Briefing paper, Employment 3.5.Available at: http://www.migrationwatchuk. org/briefingPaper/document/30 (accessed 10 September 2010).

Migration Watch UK (2009) *Students and the Points-Based System,* Briefing paper, Education 2.3. London: Migration Watch.

MigrationWatch UK (2010) 'What Can Be Done?'. Available at: www. migrationwatchuk.org/WhatCanBeDone

Morgan, J. (2010) 'Relief Greets Revised Student Visa Regulations', *Times Higher Education,* 11 February.

Moriarty, J. (2010) 'Competing with Myths: Migrant Labour in Social Care', in M. Ruhs and B.Anderson (eds) *Who Needs Migrant Workers? Labour Shortages, Immigration and Public Policy.* Oxford: OUP.

Mulley, S. (2010) 'The Limits to Limits: Is a Cap on Immigration a Viable Policy for the UK?', London: Institute for Public Policy Research.

ONS (Office for National Statistics) (2010a) *Migration Statistics Quarterly Report,* No 7, November. London: Office for National Statistics.

ONS (2010b) 'Labour Market Statistics', *Statistical Bulletin,* December, London: Office for National Statistics.

Oxford Economics (2009) *The Economic, Labour Market and Skills Impact of Migrant Workers in Northern Ireland*. Belfast: Department for Employment and Learning, Northern Ireland Executive.

Reid, L. (2010) 'Immigration Cap Stops Councils Hiring Needed Social Workers', *The Guardian*, 27 September.

Roche, B. (2000) 'UK Migration in a Global Economy', Presentation to conference organised by the Institute for Public Policy Research, 11 September, Home Office, London.

Ruhs, M. (2010) 'Migrant Rights, Immigration Policy and Human Development', *Journal of Human Development and Capabilities* 11(2): 259–79.

Ryan, B. (2007) 'Migrant Rights in the Workplace', in D. Flynn and Z. Williams (eds) *Towards a Progressive Immigration Policy*. London: Compass, Migrants Rights Network and Barrow Cadbury Trust.

Salt, J. (2001) *International Migration and the United Kingdom: Recent Patterns and Trends*, RDS Occasional Paper No 75. London: Home Office.

Salt, J. (2009) *International Migration and the United Kingdom: Report of the UK SOPEMI Correspondent to the OECD*. London: University College London.

SC Home Affairs (Select Committee on Home Affairs) (2009a) *Managing Migration: The Points-Based System, Volume I*, Thirteenth Report Session 2008–09, HC 219-1. London: House of Commons.

SC Home Affairs (2009b) *Managing Migration: Points-Based System Volume II Oral and Written Evidence*, House of Commons.

SC Home Affairs (2010) *Immigration Cap*, First Report Session 2010–11, HC 361. London: Select Committee on Home Affairs.

SC International Development (2004) *Migration and Development: How to Make Migration Work for Poverty Reduction. Volume 1*, 6th Report Session 2003–04 HC 79-1. London: House of Commons.

Scottish Executive (2005) 'Graduates – Working in Scotland Scheme'. Available at: http://www.scotland.gov.uk/News/Releases/2005/016102727 (accessed 11 April 2011).

Smith, S. (2010) 'Our Universities are on the Brink of Catastrophe', *The Observer*, 13 June.

Somerville, W. (2007) *Immigration under New Labour*. Bristol: The Policy Press.

Somerville, W. and Sumption, M. (2009) *Immigration in the UK: The Recession and Beyond*. London: Equality and Human Rights Commission.

Spencer, S. (1994a) 'The Implications of Immigration Policy for Race Relations', in S. Spencer (ed) *Strangers and Citizens: A Positive Approach to Migrants and Refugees*. London: Rivers Oram.

Spencer, S. (ed) (1994b) *Immigration as an Economic Asset: The German Experience*. Stoke-on-Trent: Trentham.

Spencer, S. (2007) 'Immigration', in A. Seldon (ed) *Blair's Britain 1997–2007*. Cambridge: Cambridge University Press.

Sriskandarajah, D., Cooley, L. and Reed, H. (2005) *Paying Their Way: The Fiscal Contribution of Immigrants in the UK*. London: Institute for Public Policy Research.

Thorp, A. (ed) (2008) *Impacts of Immigration*, House of Commons Library, Research Paper 08/65. London: House of Commons.

Travis, A. (2008) 'Skilled Migrants Win Right to Stay as Judge Says Rule Change Unlawful', *The Guardian*, 9 April.

Travis, A. (2010) 'May Waters Down Immigration Pledge but Looks to Curb Overseas Student Numbers', *The Guardian*, 29 June, p 4.

TUC (Trades Union Congress) (2007) *The Economics of Migration*. London: Trades Union Congress.

TUC Commission on Vulnerable Employment (2008) *Hard Work, Hidden Lives: The Short Report of the Commission on Vulnerable Employment*. London: Trades Union Congress

UKBA (UK Border Agency) (2008) 'Students under the Points-Based System: Statement of Intent', London: Home Office.

UKBA (2009a) 'Entry Clearance Statistics 2008–09', London: Home Office.

UKBA (2009b) *Accession Monitoring Report May 2004–March 2009*. London: Home Office.

UKBA (2010a) *Limits on Non-EU Economic Migration – A Consultation*. London: Home Office.

UKBA (2010b) *Migration Interim Limits (PBS Tier 1 and Tier 2) Impact Assessment*. London: Home Office.

UKBA (2010c) 'Coalition Commits to Impose Migration Limit', Press notice, 28 June. London: Home Office.

UKBA (2010d) 'Highly Skilled Migrants Should Do Highly Skilled Jobs, Says Immigration Minister', Press notice, 27 October, London: Home Office.

UKBA (2010e) 'The Student Immigration System: A Consultation', December, London: Home Office .

UKCISA (UK Council for International Student Affairs) (2008a) *Mobility Matters, Forty Years of International Students, Forty Years of UKCISA*. London: UKCISA.

UKCISA (2008b) *Benchmarking the Provision of Services for International Students in Further Education*. London: UKCISA.

UKCISA (2009) *Tier 4 Students' Experiences: Applying from Outside the UK*. London: UKCISA.

UKCISA (2010) *Tier 4 Students' Experiences Surveys: Extending their Visas in the UK*. London: UKCISA.

UKCOSA (UK Council for Overseas Student Affairs) (2006) *New Horizons: The Experiences of International Students in UK Further Education Colleges*, Report of the UKCOSA Survey. London: UKCOSA.

UNDP (United Nations Development Report) (2009) 'Overcoming Barriers: Human Mobility and Development', *Human Development Report 2009*. New York: UNDP.

Universities UK (2009) 'Memorandum to the Home Affairs Select Committee', July 2008, in Select Committee on Home Affairs, *Managing Migration: Points-Based System, Volume II Oral and Written Evidence*. London: House of Commons.

Universities UK (2010) 'International Student Tuition Fees Survey Results 2009–2010'. Available at: http://www.universitiesuk.ac.uk/ Newsroom/Facts-and-Figures/International-student-tuition-fees/ Survey-results-2009-2010/Pages/Default.aspx

Vickers, P. and Bekhradnia, B. (2007) *The Economic Costs and Benefits of International Students*, Oxford: Higher Education Policy Institute.

Wadsworth, J. (2007) 'Immigration to the UK: Evidence from Economic Research, Centre for Economic Performance', London: London School of Economics.

Watt, N. (2010) 'David Cameron to Offer India Direct Say on Immigration Policy', *The Guardian*, 28 July.

Webb, T. (2010) 'UK Carmakers Attack Cap on Immigration', *The Guardian*, 28 October.

Wintour, P. (2010) 'Tories Plan to Crack Down on UK Visas for Foreign Students', *The Guardian*, 9 January.

4

Family migration

Family members often come to the UK as a consequence of earlier migrations or by accompanying today's labour migrants, students and asylum seekers. Hence we explore family migration here after chapters on those topics. We should not forget, however, that family members also migrate to join British citizens in the UK, so policy in this area can directly affect those who themselves have no migration background.

In family migration we revisit some themes that have emerged in other chapters including the multiple challenges governments face in trying to regulate entry and the indirect and sometimes covert methods used in attempts to do so. Picking up on the early history in Chapter 1, we see a consistent pattern of reactive initiatives to address 'abuse' rather than a coherent strategy with clear objectives, and the close relationship that has developed between controls on entry and internal controls on access to services and benefits. It is here too that we find perhaps the clearest race and gender dimensions, in policies and practices impacting disproportionately on Black and Asian family members and the divided families and genuine hardship that can be the consequence of their operation. As in relation to asylum policy, we see policy repeatedly challenged by the courts under European human rights law.

We look first at what is meant by family migration and at the changing relationships recognised in migration policy over time. In the UK, as across Europe, some people have the right to be accompanied or joined by family members while others do not. We see that the definition of family members and the conditions that have to be met in order for them to enter the UK have progressively tightened (in most respects) as successive governments have sought to restrict those entitled to come and to stay. Finally, we look at the complex pattern of rights and restrictions attached to family members' conditions of entry and their access (or not) to employment, social housing, services and welfare benefits: conditions that might be thought highly significant to integration processes but are rarely considered in that light (Chapter 6).

Three modes of family migration

Kofman has helpfully categorised family migration into three forms:

- *family reunification*: where an individual is already in the country and is subsequently joined by their partner, children and, more rarely, parents or extended family;
- *family formation* or *marriage migration*: where an individual has chosen a partner from abroad; and
- *whole family migrates together*: as when a skilled labour migrant is allowed to be accompanied by 'dependants', or a refugee family arrive together on a resettlement programme (Kofman, 2004).

The number of non-European (EEA) people coming to the UK for family reunion and formation is low relative to those coming to work or study: a total of 36,500 people in 2009 compared to 161,000 labour migrants (which, however, includes 32,700 dependants) and 270,100 students[1] (including 21,000 dependants) (Home Office, 2010e: Table 1.3). Policy towards family migrants today is thus significant for those coming to study and to work, not only for UK residents hoping to be joined by existing or new family members.

For those interested in the long-term implications of family migration, however, there is a key distinction to be made between permission to enter temporarily and permission to settle. While the number of family members who *enter* is low relative to workers and students, family members are significant among those given the right to settle in the long term. In 2009, 72,000 non-EEA people were granted the right to settle on the basis of family formation or reunion but that rises to 120,000 if we include the dependants of people who first came to work or (in a minority of cases) as refugees (Home

Office, 2010e: Table 4.4). It is in part because of this expansion of those arriving and settling as dependants of labour migrants (who would once have returned home once the work permit had expired), and until recently of asylum-related dependants, that it is not only the numbers of family members settling in the UK that have risen (Figure 1.2) but their diversity in terms of countries of origin, gender and skills (Kofman, 2004).

Capacity to restrict entry

Family migrants have historically been a significant component of long-term migration in Europe and an entry channel that has remained at least partially open when governments have sought to close other doors. In periods of recession, family migration has at times exceeded labour migration, so that migration numbers in total are less sensitive to an economic downturn than might otherwise be expected (OECD, 2009: 47–8). This has been of somewhat less concern to traditional countries of immigration and to Southern European countries which have seen family members as making a positive contribution to social integration; the Canadian Immigration and Refugee Protection Act 2001, for instance, cites among its objectives 'to see that family are reunited in Canada' (Canadian Government, 2001: s 3(d)). Northern European states, in contrast, have tended to view family migration as an unfortunate consequence of the 'primary' immigration of those allowed to enter for other reasons and in some respects as an obstacle to integration and open to abuse. As a result, their governments have made successive attempts to restrict entry, in which the UK is no exception (IOM, 2008).

We saw in Chapter 1 that international human rights obligations, and more broadly the accepted ethics within a liberal democracy, are among the constraints on government's capacity to control migration flows. Here, the wide acceptance that people should be able to choose their marriage partner and that children should be able to live with their parents, values enshrined in international law, do indeed impose some limits on the steps that government can take. Those expecting to find government significantly held back by Article 8 of the European Convention on Human Rights (ECHR) in its protection of the right to respect for private and family life may, however, be disappointed. If a family member is refused entry, that right is largely deemed to be breached only if there are no insurmountable obstacles to the family living together abroad, even if that involves some hardship (Jackson et al, 2008: 162).

In some EU states, as in the UK, the overall number of family members allowed to enter depends on the shifting number of applicants who fulfil the entry criteria. More rarely there is an annual quota, thus excluding even nuclear family members once the quota is met (EMN, 2008). In the UK, a cap on family members was considered in 2005 but rejected because 'a rigid quota would cause considerable hardship and is not acceptable' (Home Office, 2005: 24). At the time of writing, the focus of the Coalition government's cap is on non-EEA labour migrants but we saw in Chapter 3 that the cost of scaling back labour migrants and students makes it difficult to reduce net migration sufficiently if cuts are applied to those categories alone (Home Office, 2010c).

The UK is constrained, as in labour migration, by EU law, here in relation to the entry of family members of EEA nationals. An EU family reunification Directive also set down minimum standards in relation to the families of third-country nationals in 2003 (2003/86/ED). A number of states took the opportunity to downgrade their standards to the minimum allowed while imposing new conditions such as pre-entry language tests and mandatory integration courses (Kraler and Kofman, 2009). The Directive does not directly affect the UK as it chose to opt out, arguing that it could clash with future changes in policy, but UK policies were deemed in 2008 to be 'generally consistent' with its provisions (EMN, 2008; Wright and Larsen, 2008).

One significant feature of UK policymaking in this field is the huge discretion that the Home Office has been granted to change entry criteria, procedural requirements and subsequent entitlements via a constant evolution of Immigration Rules with scant parliamentary scrutiny. It has often done so on the basis of limited evidence either on the practice it was trying to change or subsequently on the impact on the lives of those affected. It is, nevertheless, one area of migration policymaking in which the voices of minority ethnic communities have been raised and, to a limited extent, influenced policy reform.

Limits on who can be joined by family members

The first lever government can use to limit family migration is to say that only some people in the UK, or who are planning to come to the UK, have the right to be accompanied or joined by family members. EU law, binding in this instance on the UK, determines the rights in this respect of EEA nationals, including those whose family members are not themselves European citizens. While the EU right to free movement was granted to facilitate mobility for work it was recognised that allowing families to be together was a necessary corollary. The only exception to this in the UK is for EU citizens from the accession ('A8' and 'A2') countries who initially face restrictions on being joined by family members who are not themselves EEA nationals. Those temporary exceptions are the only ways in which the UK can restrict entry to the family of EEA nationals; a matter that received little political attention until families of A8 nationals began to arrive and their children entered state schools after EU enlargement in 2004.

This right under EU law to be joined by family members can in some respects be *more* generous than the rights Europeans enjoy under their own national laws. One key difference is that parents benefiting from EU rights may bring in children up to the age of 21 rather than only up to 18 as under UK law. This anomaly means that if a UK citizen works in another EU country and is joined there by family members from abroad they can subsequently all come to the UK under EU rules (known as the 'Surinder Singh route' from the test case from which it arose). Otherwise they are subject to the more stringent UK provisions that apply to those who have never worked elsewhere in the EU (Wright and Larsen, 2008: 27).

The area where UK policymakers have most room for manoeuvre is in relation to the family members of non-European migrants who are living in the UK only temporarily or have not yet acquired the right to settle. For those with temporary status, policy has been relatively generous to those whom government wants to attract to Britain – recognising that being allowed to bring family members can be significant in their choice of destination – while denying that right to others. Thus skilled workers have been allowed to be joined by their families, as have international students (except those on short courses), while low-skilled workers and working holidaymakers have not.

For those already living in the UK, the right to be joined by family members or fiancé(e)s depends on their current immigration status, how long they have been resident and the length of their relationship with the individual(s) concerned. UK citizens and those who are 'settled and present' in the UK have the right to be joined by eligible family members where they intend to make the UK their permanent home. Refugees may also be joined by their family immediately, whereas others must wait until they acquire settled status. These highly complex requirements are set out in Chapter 8 of the Immigration Rules (UKBA, 2010a).

Redefining who counts as family

The second means by which governments can change patterns of family migration is by restricting (or extending) who counts as a family member. As a result, the definition does not necessarily coincide with the family's own perception of those relationships, nor match domestic policy. Across Europe, states have increasingly restricted access largely to the nuclear family with little or no flexibility in relation to other family members.

When the UK government first set out to regulate who might enter as a family member in the Commonwealth Immigrants Act 1962 (see Chapter 1), it cannot have foreseen how many times it would return to that definition, first to narrow it down to the core nuclear family, and later to include cohabiting and same-sex partners. In the 1960s, the door was thus quickly closed to nephews and cousins, for instance, and the rules changed again in 1968 to limit eligibility to be joined by children, a move that led to a sharp drop in the number arriving from Pakistan. Rule changes were similarly all that was needed in 1980 to restrict access for elderly parents who now had to show they had no relatives in their own country to support them, that they lived at a standard of living substantially below the average and were mainly dependent on their offspring in the UK (Spencer, 1997). As it now stands, the rules – in exceptional, compassionate, circumstances – do allow the entry of parents below the age of 65 and of more distant relatives such as siblings, aunts and uncles. Nevertheless, of all those granted settlement in 2009, less than 1% were elderly parents and grandparents (Home Office, 2010e).

For those not fortunate enough to benefit from EU law, the entry of unmarried children under the age of 18 is allowed, but only if both parents are in the UK or the UK-based parent has 'sole responsibility' for the child. The latter is one of many instances where the small print of the rules can create numerous hurdles for applicants to overcome. The exclusion of adopted children from a country whose adoption procedure is not recognised by the UK is a further example, however well intended. In the case of polygamous marriages, however, although only one spouse is permitted, the children of another spouse will not always be barred. Notwithstanding that occasional flexibility, the limited conceptualisation of a Eurocentric nuclear family on which the rules are based has been criticised by scholars for taking little account of cultural differences in family relationships, and for limiting the support that families can receive from grandparents, and the care that can be provided to them at a distance (Kofman, 2004).

In relation to spouses, the UK has acknowledged some need to modernise the rules by allowing entry for a long-term cohabiting partner since 1985; a concession that included same-sex couples from 1997 following lobbying by Stonewall and others, until their rights were formally recognised in the Immigration Rules in 2000 and following the Civil Partnership Act 2004. As with heterosexual couples, the rules require that the couple intend to live permanently together and, as we shall explore later, that they have suitable accommodation and can support themselves without help from public funds. Those not in a civil partnership (or marriage) must show that their relationship is of at least two years' standing and that any previous relationship has irrevocably broken down (Wright and Larsen, 2008). It has been argued that these rules are based on a narrow perception of ideal relationships and are intrusive in the proof of intimacy that couples are required to provide (Simmons, 2008). Yet in 2008 there were still three EU states (Greece, Latvia and Romania) that made no provision at all for the entry of same-sex partners (EMN, 2008). In the following year, 725 men and 205 women were allowed to settle in the UK on the basis of a civil partnership or same-sex relationship, just 1.7% of all grants of settlement to non-EEA partners (Home Office, 2010e: Table 4.5).

Curbing entry on the basis of marriage

Particularly contentious have been a succession of measures to prevent not only the fraudulent use of marriage to evade immigration controls but entry of a spouse or fiancé(e) if one motivation for the marriage is deemed to be entry to the UK, even if the marriage is genuine and the couple fully intend to live together. Academic and legal critics have argued that this fails to recognise that prospective couples quite legitimately take many considerations into account when deciding whether to marry, including their financial prospects. The fact that immigration status may add to a potential spouse's attractions should not therefore be a reason to deny entry (Charsley, 2006; Wray, 2006). Baroness Hale argued in a House of Lords case:

> There are many perfectly genuine marriages which may bring some immigration advantage to one or both of the parties depending on where for the time being they wish to make their home. That does not make them 'sham marriages'.[2]

A series of overt attempts were made in the 1960s and 1970s to curb marriage migration from the Commonwealth, including an outright ban on husbands and fiancés from 1969 to 1974 unless there were 'special features' such as cultural differences that made it difficult for the woman to live in her husband's country of origin, an argument with which white women had more success than their Asian counterparts. Bolstered by a Select Committee report hostile to marriage migration (SC Race Relations and Immigration, 1978), the Conservatives were elected in 1979 on a manifesto that included a promise once again to stop the admission of foreign husbands, while continuing to allow the entry of wives. Normal practice in Indian society, the new government argued, was for wives to move to live with their husbands; hence the practice of husbands coming to the UK through arranged marriages was an abuse of immigration control (Sachdeva, 1993: 64). Downing Street papers reveal that the Home Secretary promised the Prime Minister in 1979 that the new restrictions would be 'a kind of steeplechase designed to weed out South Asians in particular' (Travis, 2009). The government's intention was subsequently modified to allow *UK-born* British women to bring in their spouse, thus ensuring that this right became largely the preserve of white women. Successfully challenged as sex discrimination at the European Court of Human Rights in 1985,[3] the government responded by making the rules for wives as tight as those for husbands (Dummett and Nicol, 1990: 230). However, by then the government also had a significant new tool in its arsenal to restrict entry, the 'primary purpose rule'.

Primary purpose rule

The primary purpose rule, introduced in 1980, went far beyond a ban on sham marriages, requiring foreign nationals to prove that the primary purpose of the marriage was *not* to obtain entry and settlement in the UK. Couples found themselves questioned on their sex lives and, in one illustrative case, were refused on the grounds that their letters to each other sounded insufficiently affectionate for the marriage to be genuine. Instructions to immigration officers in 1983 said the applicant 'should not be given the benefit of the doubt'. In that year, 47% of husbands and fiancés from the Indian subcontinent were refused entry, 73% on the basis of the primary purpose rule (Bhabha et al, 1985: 69–70).

The courts intervened to mitigate some of the harshest effects of the rule but it remained the grounds for excluding many thousands of people over the next decade. Critics argued that this was not only unjust, dividing couples or forcing the UK partner to join their spouse abroad, but discriminatory, rarely if ever affecting white couples. Under pressure from ethnic minority constituents, Labour's manifesto in 1997 included a commitment to abolish the rule, which it honoured, reiterating in 2008 that it would never reintroduce a measure 'which did so much to keep loved ones apart' (UKBA, 2008: 4).

The law nevertheless retained provisions that require entry officers to judge, from what they are told of the couple's relationship and such factors as their relative ages, whether there is a genuine intention to live together. Politely put, this is a process in which it is suggested that 'decision-makers sometimes demonstrate an uncertain grasp of the standard of proof' (Wray, 2006: 312). The unpredictability of entry decisions has consequences: the continuing risk that the husband of a British Pakistani wife may not be allowed to enter, for instance, has been found to be a factor in some married couples choosing to delay cohabitation until the husband has obtained entry, thus avoiding the woman having a child without a resident father and, if necessary, enabling the marriage to be annulled (Charsley, 2006).

Arranged and forced marriages

One of the criteria for entry to marry in the UK is that the couple have already met, effectively excluding those arranged marriages in which the couple do not meet until their wedding day. Underlying concerns about arranged marriages involving a partner from abroad are assumptions that young women in particular do not enter such arrangements willingly, but this is not necessarily the case. For women in the UK, a husband from abroad may limit otherwise onerous obligations to his parents (while having less congenial implications for some 'unhappy husbands'; Charsley, 2005) and her level of education and knowledge of the UK may give her the upper hand. For some women abroad, emigration to the UK means a degree of liberation from the constraints in which they have lived in their country of origin. Nevertheless, 'choice' and 'voluntary' are relative words and policy has also been criticised for making a clearer distinction between arranged and forced marriages than can always be justified in practice (Kofman, 2004).

Concern to prevent individuals being forced into marriage (and arguably to contain the growth of Islamic communities) has led some European states to take a series of measures including raising the age at which a spouse or fiancé(e) can enter: in the case of Denmark in 2003 to 24 years, leading some young Danes wanting to marry a foreigner to move elsewhere in the EU (Hedetoft, 2006). In the UK, the age was raised to 18 then 21 in 2008, the legal age of marriage being 16. NGO critics argued that this made it more likely that the forced marriage would take place abroad where victims would have no means of support or redress and that, in seeking to prevent abuse, the age limit also prevents the marriage of two willing parties (JCWI, 2008).

A joint Home Office–FCO Forced Marriage Unit was established to help prevent forced marriage and ensure effective services for victims. In 2009, the unit reported providing advice or support in 1,682 cases, 86% relating to females (FCO, 2010). Legislation in 2007 (the Forced Marriage (Civil Protection) Act) provided additional civil law protection and remedies, following unsuccessful attempts by the government to make forced marriage a criminal offence. While these measures have attracted significant support, some argue that forced marriages should not attract specific offences but be tackled through mainstream legislation in which the focus should equally be on those forced marriages in which both parties are already in the UK (Kofman et al, 2008a). The disproportionate impact of marriage rules on South Asian couples, set against a history of measures to limit entry through marriage rules, prompted some scepticism that government's 'new-found' concern for the plight of South Asian women in forced marriages 'belies a deeper structure of racism' and is in part motivated by a desire to police communities, an approach with colonial roots (Wilson, 2007). The Home Affairs Select Committee, however, concerned by evidence that visas were being approved because reluctant spouses would not give evidence, argued that evidence should therefore be accepted from a third party and that more women should be interviewed before granting a visa to their fiancé; demonstrating the fine line between measures to protect victims and unacceptable intrusion into applicants' private lives (SC Home Affairs, 2008: paras 119–22).

Marriage within the UK

For marriages within the UK, measures in 1999 included instructions to marriage registrars to report any suspicions they might have that the intended marriage is not genuine. The UK is not alone in this approach, Dutch, Austrian and German marriage registrars also being enlisted to assist in detecting the fraudulent use of marriage to obtain entry (EMN, 2008: 15). A subsequent ban in 2002 on switching from a temporary immigration status to a right to remain through marriage was also introduced in part to curb sham marriages. The fact that 50% of those who asked to remain on the basis of marriage did so within six months of entry suggested to the government either that the marriage was 'bogus' or that the couple had 'lied about their intentions to the entry clearance officer' (Home Office, 2002: para 7.11). The possibility that the couple might have needed time together to see how their relationship developed before making that long-term commitment, making work or study in the UK an attractive option meanwhile, is not considered, immigration rules leaving little room for overlapping motivations of that kind. In practice, the 'no switching' rule now requires anyone in these circumstances to return to their country of origin to reapply, a step that can be costly and, in less stable parts of the world, involve personal risk.

Rules were again amended in 2005 to require couples, if either individual does not have permission to be in the UK for more than six months, to get a Home Office 'certificate of approval' to marry or register a civil partnership unless, anomalously, the wedding was to take place in an Anglican church. A certificate cost £295 by 2007 and £590 for a couple both subject to immigration control. In the first 14 months in which the rule was in operation, 1,805 applications were refused.

The High Court found the breadth of the rules to be unlawful in 2006: a disproportionate interference in the right to marry and discriminatory in giving preference to marriages in an Anglican church. This was to prove a telling example not only of the way in which the courts have intervened to curb rules that infringe fundamental human rights but also of government's reluctance to comply when they do so. The Home Office amended the rules to allow couples with shorter leave periods to apply (in so doing requiring proof that the marriage was genuine, such as letters and photographs; UKBA, 2010b). It did not concede without a fight, however, unsuccessfully appealing the ruling through to the House of Lords in July 2008.[4] It was then required to suspend the application fee to which the Law Lords had objected (waiting almost a year to comply). In January 2010, however, the UKBA website still advised those planning to marry in an Anglican church that no certificate of approval was required, noting that:

> the policy of excluding these religious ceremonies from the certificate of approval scheme was declared unlawful by the High Court. The Government has indicated it will change the rules to bring such marriages within the scope of the scheme. The date of this change has not yet been determined. (UKBA, 2010b: 6)

The Coalition government took an early decision to abolish the scheme in 2011 to comply with the court but also, it argued, because the changes had weakened the scheme so that it is 'no longer an effective method of preventing sham marriages' (UKBA, 2010d). It is not yet clear if, and with what, it may be replaced.

Although there continues to be concern expressed by some marriage registrars that many thousands of sham marriages take place each year, evidence substantiating the level of abuse is not available and, in the case of the certificate of approval in 2005, was insufficient to satisfy a parliamentary committee that it was necessary. While 2,251 'suspicious marriages' had been reported by registrars in the first six months of 2004, the committee was not satisfied that this represented a genuine increase on the previous year and questioned why only 37 had led to criminal charges. Taking other factors into account, it concluded that while the prevention of sham marriages was a 'legitimate aim', the government's proposals were 'disproportionate' and hence incompatible with the right to marry protected by the ECHR – one of a number of occasions when the committee has found immigration rules to be wanting (JCHR, 2004: paras 57, 68). The conviction of a Sussex vicar in July 2010 for conducting more than 350 sham marriages over a period of four years (itself not an isolated case) indicates nevertheless that concern that marriage can be used inappropriately to secure residence in the UK and, by its procurers, for profit, is not entirely without foundation (Barkham and Davies, 2010; BBC, 2010a).

Further conditions attached

Whether family members can in practice enter or secure the right to settle in the UK is dependent on fulfilling a further set of entry and post-entry conditions. Here again we find that the goalposts have moved as successive governments have sought to prevent entry for some categories of people and to limit their impact on public expenditure. Ideas for new criteria are never far from the policy agenda.

Across the EU, states require evidence that those who sponsor family members have sufficient income to support them and often that they have health care insurance. The precise terms differ: Germany waives the income requirement for skilled migrants, for instance, and the Netherlands does not specify capacity to accommodate per se. The conditions imposed for those seeking to settle in the UK require the individual who sponsors prospective family migrants to demonstrate that he or she has sufficient income and accommodation to provide for them without 'recourse to public funds'. There is no fixed minimum income, officials having discretion to decide whether the income available will be sufficient (although minima are set for the dependants of students and labour migrants). The conditions apply equally to elderly relatives who may not access benefits or local authority housing for five years unless the relative who brought them to the UK dies.

This requirement that the sponsor be able to support and accommodate their relatives can effectively exclude those on low incomes from the right to family reunion. No statistics are published, however, on the number of applications turned down on those grounds. Directions to immigration staff say that rejection of spouses on these grounds will be rare (UKBA, 2009: para 4.6) but advice agencies have suggested in the past that families are divided on this basis (Citizens Advice Bureau, 1996).

Applicants also have to be able to afford the application fee, no small matter. A dependent relative applying to enter the UK paid £585 for that privilege in 2009/10, raised to a staggering £1,680 for 2010/11. Meanwhile the fee for an application for settlement made within the UK was to be raised to £1,930, although the cost of administering it is estimated to be only £256. Justifying this discrepancy when laying the fees before Parliament, Labour's Immigration Minister said that setting fees above the cost of the service generates revenue that is used to fund broader objectives, including the roll-out of ID cards for foreign nationals (see Chapter 5) and the Migration Impacts Fund (abolished in 2010) (Home Office, 2010a).

A family member of long standing may be given the right to settle as soon as they arrive but most get initial permission to stay for two years before being eligible to apply for Indefinite Leave to Remain. Access to that status has, since 2007, also been subject to a level of proficiency in English (or Welsh or Scottish Gaelic) and knowledge of life in the UK, except for those under 16 or over 65. Again, the UK has not been alone in adding these additional conditions: Germany, for instance, requires those over 16 to have a command of German unless their previous education and way of life suggest they will nevertheless be able to integrate successfully. The UK government argued that its intention was 'to ensure that migrants have an understanding of life in the UK and the requisite skills to allow them to play a full and active part in society' (Wright and Larsen, 2008: 29). EEA nationals and their family do not need to demonstrate that knowledge unless they go one stage further and apply for British citizenship (see Chapter 6).

From November 2010, another hurdle was introduced: non-Europeans applying to come to join a partner in the UK have to provide evidence with their visa application that they have already passed a basic spoken English language test (by an approved test provider) to 'help promote integration, remove cultural barriers and protect public services' (UKBA, 2010c) (see Chapter 6). A legal Opinion sought by Liberty found this pre-entry test likely to breach Article 8 of the ECHR in keeping families apart, as well as discriminatory in its effect on a number of grounds (Singh and McColgan, 2010). It may, therefore, yet be challenged in the courts.

Procedural barriers to entry

Even if family members and their sponsors fulfil all of the entry criteria they can face procedural barriers that delay or prevent entry to the UK. In the 1970s and 1980s, extended delays in processing applications for family members in the Indian subcontinent became so contentious that they were recorded separately in the immigration statistics. Refusals, nearing 50% in the early 1980s, reportedly relied in many cases on discrepancies between answers given by family members on details of the marriage or family life in the country of origin, such as the colour of the bride's dress or where the family drew their water (Wray, 2006). By 2002, those applying in the subcontinent for settlement could still wait up to nine months for their first interview, with intermittent 'fast-track' arrangements to clear the backlog (Home Office, 2003: Table 2.6). More recently, the Public Accounts Committee found that applications to remain on the basis of marriage had in some cases been outstanding for a period of over four years or more and urged UKBA to eradicate this backlog 'with the same degree of effort and in the same timescales as the legacy asylum cases' (PAC, 2009: 14).

Checks on the identity of those seeking entry have also proved highly intrusive, including examinations at ports of entry in the 1970s to establish if Asian women and girls were virgins and thus (in the eyes of policymakers) genuine prospective brides or dependent children (Dummett and Nicol, 1990). DNA tests are carried out now on children to establish their parentage, the UK being one of five EU states to do so (EMN, 2008). In 1997, 1,400 DNA tests were carried out in the subcontinent. In around 90% of cases the child was found to be related to both parents (Home Office, 1998), no doubt with serious implications for the mother, aside from immigration control, in the 10% of cases where this was found not to be the case.

Impact of restrictive conditions of stay

Those who fulfil the entry criteria and overcome the procedural hurdles are then subject to varying restrictions within the UK on access to jobs, social housing and benefits for varying periods of time. The resulting pattern of restrictions in each case reflects a classic trade-off in migration policy, albeit not often spelt out in policy debates. Exclusion from jobs, services and benefits protects access to scarce resources for existing residents, limits public expenditure and reassures or appeases public opinion (depending on your point of view). On the other hand, access to jobs and services may be granted to dependants in order to attract those migrants whom the country wants, to meet humanitarian needs, to protect public health (eg by ensuring access to health care for transferable diseases) and to promote integration. Underlying the political debates that periodically surface in the UK in relation to social housing in particular is a tension grounded in differing views on the basis of entitlement (explored further in Chapter 6).

Thus, fiancés and fiancées may not work or have access to public funds for the first six months, for instance, during which time they are expected to marry; while many spouses are subject to a two-year probation period during which they may work but not have recourse to public funds. The impact of the 'no recourse to public funds' rule can be profound but it does not cover all services or benefits. While it has barred those affected from a growing list of welfare benefits in the past decade, those who are working may be able to access benefits based on National Insurance contributions; while all migrant children are, for instance, entitled to free education in state schools (Wright and Larsen, 2008: 34).

Asylum applicants and their families are in most cases excluded from work, mainstream benefits and social housing but may use the National Health Service (NHS). EEA nationals, in contrast, have greater access to benefits and social housing, with the exception of A2 nationals in their first year after arrival. Immigrants who are 'habitually resident', including British emigrants who have returned to the UK after many years, can use the NHS. This is a hugely complex picture; hence service providers, employers and migrants alike are often confused as to what their entitlements are (Audit Commission, 2007: 10). In most cases, moreover, there is surprisingly little evidence on the impact of this pattern of entitlements and restrictions to inform policymaking.

As we saw in Chapter 3, the spouses of skilled workers and of students in the UK for more than 12 months have in the past been allowed to work largely without restrictions to ensure that the primary migrant is not deterred from coming to the UK. The Migration Advisory Committee (MAC), which advises the government on some of the labour market dimensions of immigration policy, was asked to review this approach, a task it found difficult in the absence of almost any evidence on the jobs that these partners are doing, their labour market impact or the significance of access to work for the individuals concerned. It found that around half of spouses and partners are in employment but that, even though a significant proportion are highly qualified, the majority were in unskilled occupations. It had no reason to conclude that greater restrictions on working rights for dependants would be better for UK workers or for the UK economy but could form only a tentative conclusion due to the very limited evidence base, deeming this an area 'ripe for further data collection and research' (MAC, 2009: para 8.16).

Impact on victims of domestic violence

One outcome of the 'no recourse to public funds' rule on which there is evidence is the impact of the two-year probationary period before a marriage or civil partner is entitled to remain in the UK in their own right. The threat of losing their right to stay if the relationship fails ties women (in most cases) to the marital home and the lack of welfare support should they leave prevents many from using refuges, which cannot accommodate them without reimbursement. Research and the work of support groups have revealed the genuine hardship to which this has led (eg Sundari et al, 2008). As a result, rules were modified in 2002 to enable victims to remain in the UK if they can provide evidence of the abuse: 745 people were given the right to stay on this basis in 2009, of whom 35 were men (Home Office, 2010e).

Critics have argued that the length of the probationary period, the nature of the evidence required to establish abuse and the exclusion from the concession of the spouses of students and children who have experienced violence also need to be addressed (Kofman et al, 2008a). Moreover, in the 7–12 months that the UKBA takes to make a decision, women still 'face a stark "choice" between living with life-threatening ongoing violence or facing destitution'. Case law under the National Assistance Act 1948, Human Rights Act 1998 and Children Act 1989 has established that children and adults may be entitled to support if otherwise destitute or they have community care needs but local authorities have no obligation to provide support in other cases and practice is inconsistent (Anitha, 2008). The Coalition government has committed itself to finding a long-term funding solution to ensure protection for victims of domestic violence in these circumstances, within a broader commitment to end violence against women (Home Office, 2010d).

Costs incurred in providing such support are currently not reimbursed by central government. Nevertheless, the local authority No Recourse to Public Funds (NRPF) network found that, in 2007–08, 48 local authorities were providing support to 3,910 individuals with no recourse to public funds, costing £33.4 million, an increase in expenditure of 8% over the previous year. While the majority of those supported appear to be asylum seekers whose claim has been rejected (see Chapter 2), the expenditure includes support to spouses and children who came for family union and reunion. Local authorities were concerned that this increase in demand meant funds being diverted from core services but that the alternative was destitution and its social consequences (Price and Fellas, 2008: 6).

Family visitors

Many family members are not seeking to settle in the UK but merely to visit for holidays, weddings and funerals on a family visitor visa that allows entry for up to six months. Refusal of visas on suspicion that the visitor might remain in the country has long been a source of frustration to ethnic minority families and a right of appeal for family visitors was reinstated by the Labour government in 1999. Migration Watch, critical of the number and cost of appeals, argues that the range of eligible family members is far too widely drawn, that only British citizens should be able to sponsor family visitors and that access to an appeal should be subject to a fee: 'There is no reason why the British tax payer should pay the costs of appeals by foreign visitors' (Migration Watch, 2010).

A proposal that families might be required to pay a bond, returnable when the visitor left the country, 'proved controversial and highly unpopular with ethnic minorities' and was dropped (Home Office, 2002: para 7.15). Labour later considered a formal sponsorship scheme, limited to British citizens and those with settled status, with stiff penalties for the sponsor if visitors failed to leave. Residents would face checks on their finances, criminal record and immigration status before being allowed to sponsor family members and be subject to a fine of up to £5,000 if the visitor failed to leave, or up to 14 years in prison if they were deemed to have facilitated the visitor remaining illegally. The government anticipated that the new arrangement, if implemented, would lead to a fall in the number of family visitors (Home Office, 2008: 25–6).

Conclusion

Family migration policies have evolved in reaction to historical flows and to perceptions of abuse rather than as a coherent strategy to achieve clear objectives. Within a series of constraints, including European and domestic law and the values placed in a liberal democracy on allowing individuals to marry or live with whom they choose, successive governments have sought to limit entry numbers and the impact of family members on the public purse. Parliament has granted huge discretion to the Home Office to change the rules on who can enter and on what conditions, policy reform often relying on a severely limited evidence base. Definitions of family have been narrowed for the purposes of immigration control (while extended to same-sex and cohabiting partners), and the conditions with which family members must comply have been progressively tightened. The measures used to regulate entry and establish identity have at times been highly intrusive, discriminatory on grounds of race and gender, and consistently challenged in the courts. Family members have nevertheless remained a significant component of those given the right to settle. In this trajectory, UK policy reform has in recent years largely mirrored that of other EU states and the requirements of the EU Directive on family reunification, notwithstanding the UK's decision to opt out of its provisions.

Concern that family migrants do not always speak English has recently translated into a requirement that they should be required to demonstrate 'a basic command' of spoken English before being granted a visa to enter on the basis of marriage or civil partnership, in effect keeping partners apart where this condition is not met, potentially in breach of the ECHR. Officials have indeed estimated that it will lead to 10% fewer successful applications (mostly from the Indian subcontinent). The government argues that this pre-entry requirement will 'help promote integration, remove cultural barriers and protect public services' (BBC, 2010b; Home Office, 2010b). As we shall see in Chapter 6, however, there has been no broader discussion of any need for an integration policy for family members.

We saw that across the EU states apply rules designed to limit the impact of family migrants on the public purse by restricting the entry of those who might be reliant on benefits, and precluding 'recourse to public funds' by those allowed to come. A highly complex pattern of rights and restrictions attached to conditions of stay, limiting access to work, social housing and welfare benefits (while more generous to the families of migrants whom the UK wants to attract), illustrates the kind of trade-offs that we have found throughout this book. In the response from those local authorities that support victims of domestic violence despite receiving no recompense, we see conflicting priorities within the state, as we shall when we look at responses to irregular migration in Chapter 5.

Despite the significance of family members among those allowed to settle, and notwithstanding the extent of the measures taken to limit their access to services and benefits, we know almost nothing about the impact of family members on the labour market, their civic engagement for instance, or (with the exception of victims of domestic violence) a great deal about the impact of post-entry controls on their well-being. Without that evidence we cannot know whether what government achieves by curtailing access to benefits and services is outweighed by the impact it has on individuals and on integration. The UK is not alone in relying on a thin evidence base for policymaking in this field, a recent European review concluding that 'Little attention is paid to the consequences policies have on the persons affected by them. Nor is enough made of whether policies and measures actually attain their objectives' (Kraler and Kofman, 2009: 1). In relation to the former, some of the evidence is there but 'buried in casework records' of those concerned (Kofman et al, 2008b).

The economic and social significance of this area of policy and its implications for the individuals concerned suggests that it is long overdue for review. Policy on entry and on post-entry access to services and benefits does require difficult choices on which reasoned, evidence-based decisions must be taken, underpinned by compliance with the letter and the spirit of the UK's international human rights obligations. The right to be joined by family members will not be without limits in immigration law but could nevertheless be directed towards positive goals, as in the Canadian Act cited (Canadian Government, 2001). As I shall argue for migration policy as a whole, identifying the strategic goals to which it is directed is one essential step towards public ownership of the multiple and sometimes competing objectives that any migration policy has to fulfil.

Notes

[1] Not including the further 198,000 shorter-stay 'Student Visitors'.

[2] *R (Baiai and Others) v Secretary of State for the Home Department* [2008] UKHL 53 (Admin).

[3] European Court of Human Rights, *Abdulaziz, Cabales and Balkandali v UK*, decision of 28 May 1985 (1985) 7 EHRR 471.

[4] *R (Baiai and Others) v Secretary of State for the Home Department* [2008] UKHL 53 (Admin).

References

Anitha, S. (2008) 'No Recourse, No Support: State Policy and Practice towards South Asian Women Facing Domestic Violence in the UK', *British Journal of Social Work* 40 (2): 462-79.

Audit Commission (2007) *Crossing Borders: Responding to the Local Challenges of Migrant Workers*. London: Audit Commission.

Barkham, P. and Davies, C. (2010) 'Vicar Convicted over Fake Marriage Scam That Allowed Hundreds to Stay in Britain', *The Guardian*, 30 July.

BBC (British Broadcasting Association) (2010a) 'Rise in Sham Marriages to Beat UK Immigration Laws', 7 January. Available at: http://news.bbc.co.uk/1/hi/uk/8444360.stm

BBC (2010b) 'English Rules Tightened for Immigrant Partners', 9 June. Available at: http://news.bbc.co.uk/1/hi/uk/10270797.stm (accessed 9 June 2010).

Bhabha, J., Klug, F. and Shutter, S. (1985) *Worlds Apart: Women under Immigration and Nationality Law*. London: Pluto Press.

Canadian Government (2001) 'Immigration and Refugee Protection Act', Ottawa.

Charsley, K. (2005) 'Unhappy Husbands: Masculinity and Migration in Transnational Pakistani Marriages', *Journal of the Royal Anthropological Institute* 11: 85–105.

Charsley, K. (2006) 'Risk and Ritual: The Protection of British Pakistani Women in Transnational Marriage', *Journal of Ethnic and Migration Studies* 32(7): 1169–87.

Citizens Advice Bureau (1996) 'A Right to Family Life: CAB Clients' Experiences of Immigration and Asylum', CAB evidence, London.

Dummett, A. and Nicol, A. (1990) *Subjects, Citizens, Aliens and Others: Nationality and Immigration Law*. London: Weidenfeld and Nicolson.

EMN (European Migration Network) (2008) *Family Reunification*. Brussels: European Commission.

FCO (Foreign and Commonwealth Office) (2010) 'Victims of Forced Marriage: Forced Marriage Unit'. Available at: http://www.fco.gov.uk/en/travel-and-living-abroad/when-things-go-wrong/forced-marriage (accessed 15 February 2010).

Hedetoft, U. (2006) 'Denmark: Integrating Immigrants into a Homogenous Welfare State', *Country Profiles*. Available at: http://www.migrationinformation.org/Profiles/display.cfm?ID=485 (accessed 31 August 2010).

Home Office (1998) *Control of Immigration: Statistics United Kingdom 1997*, London: Home Office.

Home Office (2002) *Secure Borders, Safe Haven: Integration with Diversity in Modern Britain*. Cm 5387. London: Home Office.

Home Office (2003) *Control of Immigration: Statistics United Kingdom 2002*, London: Home Office.

Home Office (2005) *Controlling Our Borders: Making Migration Work for Britain – Five Year Strategy for Asylum and Immigration*, Cm 6472. London: Home Office.

Home Office (2008) 'Government Response to the Consultation on Visitors', London: Home Office.

Home Office (2010a) Written Ministerial Statement Announcing Proposed Fees for FY 2010/11. London: Home Office.

Home Office (2010b) 'Migrants Marrying UK Citizens Must Now Learn English', Press notice, 9 June. London: Home Office.

Home Office (2010c) 'Coalition Commits to Impose Immigration Limit', Press notice, 28 June. London: Home Office.

Home Office (2010d) 'Home Secretary Commits to Ending Violence against Women', Press notice, 16 July. London: Home Office.

Home Office (2010e) *Control of Immigration: Statistics United Kingdom 2009,* Home Office Statistical Bulletin 15/10, London: Home Office.

IOM (International Organisation for Migration) (2008) *Family Migration. World Migration Report.* Geneva: IOM.

Jackson, D., Warr, G., Onslow-Cole, J. and Middleton, J. (2008) *Immigration Law and Practice,* 4th edn. Haywards Heath: Tottel Publishing.

JCHR (Joint Committee on Human Rights) (2004) *Asylum and Immigration (Treatment of Claimants etc) Bill: New Clauses,* Fourteenth Report Session 2003–04, London: Houses of Parliament.

JCWI (Joint Council for the Welfare of Immigrants) (2008) 'JCWI's Briefing on the Statement of Changes in the Immigration Rules HC1113'. London: JCWI.

Kofman, E. (2004) 'Family-Related Migration: A Critical Review of European Studies', *Journal of Ethnic and Migration Studies* 30(2): 243–62.

Kofman, E., Lukes, S., Meeto, V. and Aaron, P. (2008a) *Family Migration to United Kingdom: Trends, Statistics and Policies,* Vienna: International Centre for Migration Policy Development.

Kofman, E., Lukes, S. and Aaron, P. (2008b) *Family Migration Policies in the United Kingdom: Actors, Practices and Concerns,* Vienna: International Centre for Migration Policy Development.

Kraler, A. and Kofman, E. (2009) 'Family Migration in Europe: Policies vs. Reality', *IMISCOE Policy Brief 16.* Amsterdam: IMISCOE.

MAC (Migration Advisory Committee) (2009) *Analysis of the Points Based System: Tier 2 and Dependants.* London: Migration Advisory Committee.

Migration Watch UK (2010) 'Family Visitor Appeals', *Policy, Amnesty and Voting 11.19.* Available at: http://www.migrationwatchuk.org/briefingPaper/document/177 (accessed 20 August 2010).

OECD (Organisation for Economic Cooperation and Development) (ed) (2009) *International Migration Outlook: Sopemi 2009 Special Focus: Managing Labour Migration Beyond the Crisis*. Sopemi. Paris: OECD.

PAC (Public Accounts Commiteee) (2009) 'Management of Asylum Applications', 28th Report Session 2008–09, London: Public Accounts Committee.

Price, J. and Fellas, O. (2008) 'No Recourse to Public Funds: Financial Implications for Local Authorities'. London: NRPF Network.

Sachdeva, S. (1993) *The Primary Purpose Rule in British Immigration Law*. Stoke-on-Trent: Trentham.

SC Home Affairs (Select Committee on Home Affairs) (2008) *Domestic Violence, Forced Marriage and "Honour"-Based Violence, Volume 1*, Sixth Report Session 2007–08, House of Commons.

SC Race Relations and Immigration (Select Committee on Race Relations and Immigration) (1978) *Immigration*, First Report Session 1977–78, HC 303, Cmnd 7287.

Simmons, T. (2008) 'Sexuality and Immigration: UK Family Reunion Policy and the Regulation of Sexual Citizens in the European Union', *Political Geography* 27: 213–30.

Singh, R. and McColgan, A. (2010) *Advice: In the Matter of Pre-entry English Language Requirements*. London: Liberty.

Spencer, I. R. G. (1997) *British Immigration Policy Since 1939: The Making of Multi-Racial Britain*. London: Routledge.

Sundari, A., Chopra, P., Farouk, W., Haq, Q. and Khan, S. (2008) *Forgotten Women: Domestic Violence, Poverty and South Asian Women with No Recourse to Public Funds*. Manchester: Saheli.

Travis, A. (2009) 'Margaret Thatcher Reluctant to Give Boat People Refuge in Britain: PM Warned of Riots on Streets if Vietnamese Were Given Council Housing, Downing Street Papers Reveal', *The Guardian*, 30 December.

UKBA (UK Border Agency) (2008) *Marriage Visas: The Way Forward*. London: Home Office.

UKBA (2009) 'Immigration Directorate Instructions'. London: Home Office.

UKBA (2010a) 'Immigration Rules Part 8 (Family members)', consolidated version updated January 2010. London: Home Office.

UKBA (2010b) 'What documents do I need to get married or register a civil partnership?'. Available at: http://www.ukba.homeoffice.gov.uk/while-in-uk/marriageandcivilpartnership/documents/ (accessed 30 January 2010). London: Home Office.

UKBA (2010c) 'Migrants marrying UK citizens must now learn English', Press notice, 9 June, UK Border Agency.

UKBA (2010d) 'Changes to certificate of approval scheme', Press release, 17 December, Home Office.

Wilson, A. (2007) 'The Forced Marriage Debate and the British State', *Race and Class* 49(1): 25–38.

Wray, H. (2006) 'An Ideal Husband? Marriages of Convenience, Moral Gate-Keeping and Immigration to the UK', *European Journal of Migration and Law* 8: 303–20.

Wright, L. and Larsen, C. (2008) *EMN Family Reunification Report*. London: Home Office.

5

Irregular migration

In this chapter we turn to irregular migration: why and how migrants acquire irregular status, the consequences and the strategies deployed to address it. 'Illegal' migrants were thrust high onto the UK political and policy agenda by a series of tragic incidents including the death of 58 Chinese migrants smuggled into the UK in June 2000 and later through association with organised crime (Geddes, 2005). Nevertheless, the extent of irregularity and the challenges it poses are both far broader and in many respects less severe than those associations suggest.

Contrary to popular perception, there is no single category of 'illegal immigrant' but differing modes of irregular status, from the person who evades passport control by hiding in the back of a lorry through to the university student working more than their permitted hours per week. Key to identifying appropriate policy levers is to understand that complexity and the contexts in which irregularity occurs.

No less than in other chapters, we find that for policymakers at central and local level there are conflicting interests at play, not least an economy that relies on rapid transit across borders of people and freight. At the core of the contradictions is a labour market that selects workers by price and skill and a welfare system for which the criteria for inclusion is need, each militating against exclusion on the basis of immigration status. Thus economic and social spheres can be accessible to migrants whether their stay is authorised or not (Boswell, 2008). An international comparative analysis of migration policies concluded that when policymakers cannot effectively address the structural factors driving migration, they redouble their efforts to impose controls by investing more heavily in border enforcement and pursue initiatives that restore the appearance of control (Cornelius et al, 2004: 5). In that experience, the UK has been no exception.

Why 'irregular'?

European states often use the term 'illegal' but the literature abounds with alternatives: undocumented, clandestine, unauthorised, sans papiers and trafficked. 'Irregular' is popular because it is not associated with any particular policy position. It helpfully connotes that there may be differing modes of irregularity and differing degrees of departure from legal status. Those involved, as we shall see, may or may not have acted in a clandestine manner. 'Undocumented' emphasises the vulnerability of those without legal status but can be a misnomer if the migrant has partial legal status or documentation that is borrowed, stolen or forged. 'Illegal' firmly suggests that the law has been broken, whereas irregular status may be associated with breaking lesser rules. Likewise, illegality may suggest that solutions are to be found in stricter enforcement of the law, where irregularity implies that a wider panoply of approaches may be needed. Finally, illegality reinforces a public perception of threat that, if accurate for those of criminal intent, does not match the full spectrum of migrants living outside the rules. 'Irregular' is the term used by the principal international agencies in the field, the International Organisation for Migration (IOM) and the UN High Commissioner for Refugees (UNHCR) (Koser, 2005; Carens, 2008).

Causes: understanding the context

A popular perception of 'illegal migrants' attributes causality to migrants themselves: rule-breakers intent on living and working in Britain without permission. Others see them as victims of exploitation by traffickers and unscrupulous employers and landlords. The reality is more complex. Explaining irregular migration (as we saw for all migration in Chapter 1) requires an understanding of the structural factors in sending *and* receiving countries that drive and shape this persistent global phenomenon: the role of the intermediaries who facilitate it; the role of individual and family decision-making; and the impacts of policy intervention (Koser, 2010).

From the literature, there are four key points on causality we should note. First, the context in which irregular migration persists globally on a significant scale is that of the broader dynamics of migration: the demographic, democratic and economic disparities that provide powerful reasons to move (Duvell, 2008). For those trapped in poverty or displaced by conflict who are unable to secure legal entry to another country, migration through irregular channels may seem their only option, entailing law-breaking where the mobility itself had no criminal intent (Lee, 2005). Within UK policy there has indeed been recognition in this context of the need, through the Department for International Development, to support the efforts of developing countries to promote economic growth and social development, eliminate poverty, improve governance and reduce conflict (Home Office, 2002: para 5.46). Challenging conditions in source countries may nevertheless have little in common with the reasoning of the young overstayers from rich countries who decide to continue working after their visa has expired. Understanding the causes of irregular migration as the basis of appropriate policy interventions needs to extend across its many differing forms.

Second, it is states that set the terms on which an individual's entry, residence and employment is lawful, creating a plethora of differing statuses characterised by varying restrictions and entitlements. States can increase or reduce the propensity for irregularity through their design of entry channels and the conditions attached (De Genova, 2002). Those working with migrants in the UK, for instance, report that the high cost of renewing a visa and the requirement to provide evidence of savings has now priced some migrants out of the market. Curtailing channels of legal entry, meanwhile, with no commensurate reduction in demand for migrant labour, increases the incentive to enter or stay without permission and the demand for the services of those who facilitate it (MRN, 2009: 5). A countermeasure is the extension of legal channels with the overt intention to 'undercut the people smugglers', as Labour did in its second term, recognising that 'the apparent availability of illicit work ... acts as a pull factor for more would-be migrants' (Home Office, 2002: para 5.7; see also

Chapter 3). Where demand is met by legal workers from within the European Economic Area (EEA), demand for irregular workers will increasingly be confined to employers operating outside of the rules; but if a cap is set on legal migration without simultaneously meeting demand in other ways, the demand for migrants to work without permission will be enhanced (Koser, 2010).

Third, irregular migration serves an economic function: there is a demand for low-skilled labour employed under precarious conditions (see Chapter 3). Irregular migrants provide a cheap source of labour offering 'dependency, invisibility and availability' (Morice, 2004). They can also be more compliant and easier to lay off in an economic downturn (Gibney, 2009). In the UK, research has shown how semi-compliance (migrants working in violation of the restrictions attached to their immigration status) can equally serve a function for both employers and migrants: allowing each to maximise economic benefits from employment while minimising the risk of sanction, as semi-compliance is difficult for the state to control. Such irregular employment can be a strategic choice of both employers and migrants, but the complicity of each party varies. The employer may not know the migrant is not allowed to work or choose not to know. Alternatively, the employer can be fully aware but think, as can migrants, that this is 'bending' rather than 'breaking' the rules. Understanding the functions that illegality serves and how it operates helps to explain its persistence. Unless its economic rationale is properly understood, efforts to manage irregular migration are unlikely to succeed (Ruhs and Anderson, 2009).

Finally, it is not only employers and migrants who benefit. There is a highly lucrative global business of facilitating irregular migration which exists because of the market for its services (Salt and Stein, 1997). Evidence compiled for the Home Office found demand for cheap and malleable labour to be a key driver, for instance, of trafficking to the UK (Dowling et al, 2007) and trafficking to Europe for sexual exploitation alone is estimated to be worth €2.5 billion each year (UNODC, 2010: 49). Policymakers draw a distinction between people smuggling, the procuring of illegal entry for material gain and trafficking involving coercion or deception. That distinction is helpful in reminding us that a migrant may choose to use the services of a people smuggler as a travel agent; but the extent to which migrants exercise consent or become the victim of exploitation during or after their journey is less clear-cut in practice. Smugglers and traffickers range from large, bureaucratic, criminal organisations to small kinship groups. Illegal entrants have been found to have paid as much as £22,000 to facilitate a journey from China, a loan to be repaid on arrival. Paying for false documents without transport was considerably cheaper (Black et al, 2006). It is thought that within the 'hierarchies of mobility', more men are able to pay smugglers while women may be more vulnerable to traffickers (Lee, 2005).

Is irregular migration a problem?

States cannot be complacent about irregular migration. There is, first, a significant political cost: the perception that there are people in the country without permission reinforces concern that migration is out of control. Moreover, if irregular migration is extensive, it is not unreasonable for voters to ask why more migration is required (Koser, 2010: 190).

Second, lack of legal status makes adults and children vulnerable to poverty, social exclusion and exploitation both in and beyond the workplace (MRN, 2009). While irregular migrants are still entitled to fundamental human rights, their need to avoid detection and removal means they cannot easily exercise those rights in practice. Their status excludes them from access to most services and welfare benefits with not only individual but social costs. It is necessary to recognise, however, that not all irregular migrants live on the margins of society. Among overstayers and the semi-compliant are people in regular jobs who may continue largely as before. Irregular migrants can feel a greater need to conceal themselves in some countries and contexts than others; with some able to make themselves known to some authorities while avoiding contact with others, and living 'a relatively normal, even "quasi-legal" life' (Duvell, 2008: 490).

The third reason states cannot ignore a significant presence of irregular migrants is that capacity to curtail criminal activity and protect national security is undermined. In practice, there is no indication that irregular migrants in the UK have any greater propensity to criminal activity and evidence from the Netherlands for instance has found little crime among those embedded in the labour market (Engbersen and van der Leun, 2001). While some of those engaged in terrorism may have irregular status, there is no causal connection, and some of the principal actors have indeed been British-born. Measures to detect irregularity may overlap with those related to terrorism, but it would be a mistake to allow perceptions of irregularity and its solutions to be coloured by that association, not least if the support of migrant communities is to be secured in detecting those of ill intent (Papademetriou, 2005).

Finally, there is an economic cost for the state and for displaced workers. Where migrants work without permission and are willing to work for less than the going rate for the job, they may undercut and displace other workers. This can lead to resentment and negative fallout for legal migrants. For the state, there is a loss of tax and National Insurance revenue, although there is evidence that some irregular migrants do pay these in the normal way (Anderson et al, 2006). Estimates of the additional revenue to be gained if irregular migrants were to be granted legal status ('in excess of £1 billion per annum'; ippr, 2009) may therefore be inflated.

For these reasons, governments cannot ignore irregularity; nor, however, should they allow the response to be disproportionate. Irregular migrants in the UK are a small proportion of the population and, as we shall see, most entered lawfully but have overstayed. The threat to personal security would seem to be substantially greater for the migrants themselves than for the rest of the population.

Irregular migrants in the UK

There are four means of acquiring irregular status:

- *Illegal entry:* those who enter the country without permission, whether by evading immigration control or by deception (use of false documents, for instance, or not telling the truth about reasons for coming). We can include here those who obtain a new legal status by deception once in the country, for instance through a sham marriage.
- *Overstay:* a diverse category of those who enter legally as a visitor, labour migrant or asylum seeker, for instance, but remain after their permission to stay has expired.
- *Semi-compliance:* those who enter and remain legally, but who are acting in breach of the conditions attached to their immigration status, working without permission or for longer hours than permitted, for example (Ruhs and Anderson, 2009), or accessing welfare support to which they are not entitled.
- *A child born in the UK to parents who are not in the country legally:* thereby having irregular immigration status without having crossed any border (Duvell, 2008).

Irregular status for adults and children may be a conscious decision, unintentional (through ignorance of complex rules), involuntary as the victim of trafficking or the result of administrative inefficiency if an application to stay is lost in the system (MRN, 2009: 6). Irregularity may not be a permanent status but subsequently change if the rules are amended, a refusal of permission to remain is rescinded or the migrant's country joins the EU: for accession nationals working in the UK without permission in 2004, enlargement of the EU was in effect an amnesty. 'Illegality' can thus be one of a shifting range of statuses that non-citizens move through, rather than an end state (Bloch et al, 2009; Koser, 2010; Anderson and Ruhs, 2010).

These differing forms of irregular status compound the difficulty of estimating numbers and understanding their economic and social significance. The Home Office found itself caught between unwillingness to estimate the size of the irregular population, given the impossibility of collecting verifiable data, and the need to avoid the ignominy of admitting it did not know. After much reluctance, it commissioned a study that concluded that the number in 2001 was within the range of 310,000 to 570,000 (midpoint 430,000, some 0.7% of the then UK population of 59 million), but warned 'over-reliance must not be placed on the results' (Woodbridge, 2005). A more recent study (Gordon et al, 2009), this time including children, estimated that there were between 417,000 and 863,000 irregular migrants in 2007 (midpoint 618,000), of whom 412,000 had been in the UK for more than five years. More than two thirds were thought to be in London. Significantly, neither estimate included the third category of irregular migrants: those in the UK legally but living in breach of their conditions of stay. This has been estimated at an additional 165,000 people (ippr, 2009), based only on students working full time and nationals from the eight EU accession countries (A8) not registered under the Worker Registration Scheme.

Among irregular migrants are 85,000 young people under 18 (Gordon et al, 2009). Policy has tended to assume that those in the UK without their parents are the victims of trafficking, overlooking the agency of young people for whom migration can bring benefits (O'Connell Davidson and Farrow, 2007). Children with irregular status create a tension between two policy agendas: child protection on the one hand and enforcing immigration control on the other (Sigona and Hughes, 2010).

The evidence suggests that most irregular migrants in the UK enter the country legally, but overstay. Among overstayers, the Home Office itself reports 'many are thought to be young and from countries with reasonably high GDP per capita and perhaps with high levels of education' (Home Office, 2007a: 10). In the year to March 2010, around 700 'victims of trafficking' were identified by agencies in the UK of whom 74% were female and a quarter were minors. China, Nigeria, Vietnam and Slovakia figure prominently among their many countries of origin (UKHTC, 2010a). Notwithstanding the seriousness of this practice, claims that it is 'behind three-quarters of illegal immigration to this country' (Home Office, 2007a) are thus grossly exaggerated.

In the EU as a whole, it is estimated that there are some 4–8 million irregular migrants, half of whom are overstayers, with some migrants remaining long term but others seeking only to work for a temporary period. Some countries (such as France) have more irregular residents than others (such as Sweden), in some cases dominated by certain nationalities (eg Albanians in Greece) in contrast to the diversity in the UK (Duvell, 2008).

Inflexible legal framework

UKBA has been explicit that some forms of illegality have more harmful consequences than others and should be prioritised. Overstaying a visa and working illegally are categorised as 'local-level crime', with some people overstaying 'inadvertently' and harm deemed to lie principally in 'undermining the integrity of the system' (Home Office, 2007a: 10–13; UKBA, 2010a). Smuggling, manufacture of false documents, operation of bogus colleges and arranging sham marriages are more serious at level 2, and are a priority for regional Immigration Crime Teams staffed by UKBA and the police; while trafficking, at level 3, is considered the most serious, requiring a high level of international and internal agency cooperation.

The legal framework set 40 years ago in the Immigration Act 1971 fails, however, to reflect these differing forms of irregularity. Unlike many other EU countries where lesser breaches of immigration rules are not criminal offences, UK law does not differentiate between illegal entry, overstaying and breaches of conditions of stay. Categorised in each case as 'illegal entry' (on the grounds that those not complying with conditions have breached the terms of their entry), they attract up to six months imprisonment or a heavy fine and are subject to removal from the UK (UKBA, 2010a: 30). Nor is this an idle threat: UKBA's now daily press reports on 'illegal workers' detected include recent cases of a student 'detained pending removal' for working longer hours in a care home than permitted, for instance, and another for working 'in breach of a working holiday maker visa' (UKBA, 2010c, 2010d). Categorising serious criminal offences alongside such rule-breaking of significantly less import has distorted the lens through which irregular migrants are viewed and made it more difficult to focus debate on a wider array of solutions than reliance on law enforcement.

Policy drivers

While the legal framework was set in 1971, tackling irregular migration became a major focus of activity only in the past decade. The call to arms was the determination to deter asylum seekers reaching the UK and to remove those refused refugee status, the latter deemed irregular migrants and emblematic of government failure to manage migration effectively (see Chapter 2). Individuals facing persecution often use the same channels of transport and entry as others who lack a visa to travel through legal channels. Thus policy measures have targeted asylum seekers alongside irregular migrants and these categories have been elided in public and political debate (Geddes, 2005). Further drivers of the heightened focus on enforcement were concern that sham marriages were being used to secure entry (see Chapter 4), evidence of irregular working and of the vulnerability of some irregular migrants in the workplace, and abuse of the student entry channel (see Chapter 3).

Labour's period in office thus saw the extension of powers and penalties in relation to illegal entry including offences related to destroying travel documents; an increased focus on people trafficking; expansion of the 'detention estate' and greater efforts to remove those detected. It also saw a step-change in reliance on new technology and 'identity management' in border and internal controls and a strengthening of penalties for employing migrants not permitted to work. Many of these changes, announced in a constant stream of White Papers and enforcement strategies, could be introduced merely by changing the Immigration Rules. Others were authorised by legislation including the Immigration, Asylum and Nationality Act 2006, UK Borders Act 2007 and Borders, Citizenship and Immigration Act 2009. Resources for enforcement staff, technology and data-sharing were substantially increased and high-profile raids were carried out on businesses suspected of employing irregular workers in order to ensure the visibility of enforcement activity (Home Office, 1998, 2002, 2005, 2006, 2007a, 2007b; Thorp, 2007; UKBA, 2008a, 2008b, 2010a).

Inter-agency focus on enforcement

The need to demonstrate a visible force at the border saw immigration staff issued with new uniforms and the Immigration and Nationality Department transformed into the firmer sounding 'Border and Immigration Agency' in 2007. Overt in the strategy was communication via the media to build public confidence that effective enforcement action was being taken (Home Office, 2007a). There was no mention of any pre-testing or subsequent evaluation on whether these messages served to reassure as intended or, in emphasising the need to counter a threat, had the opposite effect.

In 2008, responsibility for migration, visas and customs' border staff was brought together as the UK Border Agency (UKBA) whose staff now had powers to address each dimension. A Select Committee had earlier been highly critical of poor levels of coordination (SC Home Affairs, 2006: para 127). UKBA then had 25,000 staff of whom 9,000 were the 'border force', some based abroad in 135 countries (UKBA, 2009b). Exchange of data with external agencies, in particular the police, customs, tax and the Driving and Vehicle Licensing Agency (DVLA), has been enhanced, as has cooperation with local authorities and health care providers (with training for vicars to spot sham marriages; see UKBA, 2010b). The private sector is involved in the design and provision of technology, in checking passengers' right to travel and in providing data on passenger movements.

Notwithstanding its inclination to opt out of EU agreements, this is one area of policy (as with asylum) where the UK has been keen to cooperate with its EU partners bilaterally (as recently re-endorsed with France; see UKBA, 2010e) and under the auspices of the EU: in strengthening external borders, sharing data and fingerprints (2000 Eurodac regulation), and signing readmission agreements with source countries. Although not a full member, it has taken part in the activities of the EU Borders Agency, FRONTEX, charged with enhancing the integration of border security through coordination of operations, shared intelligence, technical cooperation and training. FRONTEX's operational role has expanded since 2007 with the establishment of Rapid Border Intervention Teams, albeit without its own operational staff (HL Select Committee on the EU, 2008).

One effect of this inter-agency collaboration has been to consolidate irregular migration firmly within a criminal law-enforcement paradigm. Labour's 2010 strategy, *Protecting Our Border, Protecting the Public*, argued that the UK 'faces a complex and constantly evolving array of threats from terrorism, organised crime and illegal immigration which left unchecked can cause untold harm'. It positioned UKBA as a 'law enforcement partner', 'our first line of defence against the smuggling of drugs, weapons and people into the UK' (UKBA, 2010a: 4). There was no mention in this strategy, even in passing, of enforcement of the minimum wage or broader employment standards to reduce demand for irregular workers. Rather, impact was to be enhanced by more effective partnership working, sharing intelligence, developing more robust identity management systems and 'biometric storage and matching capability' (UKBA, 2010a: 16–17). The early months of the Coalition government have seen a high public profile given to such enforcement activity (a 'UK-wide crackdown'), with press notices providing a day-by-day account of numbers detected and detained.

E-borders and 'identity management'

As the Labour government felt the pressure to step up controls, considerable emphasis was placed on new technology. A 2005 commitment to fully integrated pre-entry, border and in-country controls was to be delivered by fingerprinting all visa applicants, checked against UK police, immigration and security databases, and by biometric residence permits for (non-EEA) foreign nationals living in the UK. An 'E-borders' programme would provide an audit trail on all passengers, checking and recording the entry and exit of each person against a watch list and their conditions of entry. By December 2010, 95% of passenger movements were expected to be covered by E-borders with 100% covered by 2014.

Between 2005 and 2010, the audit trail had already collected details on 141 million passengers and crew movements and resulted in 4,800 arrests, including for offences unrelated to immigration, and in more than 950 people being refused entry (UKBA, 2010a: 9). UK and EEA citizens can, through registering for iris recognition, bypass the queues at passport control when arriving at airports equipped with that facility. A key benefit of exit controls is that UKBA will know if an individual does not leave when their visa expires, and the number of overstayers in the UK at any one time; but that information in itself will have no impact unless there are resources and the political will to detect and sanction those concerned.

In its haste to implement the system, UKBA was criticised for giving insufficient weight to the costs and practical difficulties it imposes on private carriers, for being slow to recognise the data protection implications of the transfer of personal information and the possibility that, in impeding the mobility of EU citizens, it could breach EU law (SC Home Affairs, 2009: 49; 2010a). The privacy implications of enhanced surveillance are broader, moreover, than those of data transfer. The Equality and Human Rights Commission is among those who consider that high-definition body-scanning, a 'virtual strip-search' trialled at UK airports from 2009, may be unlawful under the Human Rights Act (BBC, 2010). A draft EU regulation authorising their use was withdrawn after protest by the European Parliament in 2008 (Gregory, 2009).

Requiring foreign nationals to have biometric identity cards is intended to facilitate internal controls on access to jobs and services (see later), making it harder to live in the UK without legal status. While ID cards for UK citizens have been cancelled by the Coalition government, those for foreign nationals will remain. Critics argue that any benefits must be set against social costs including the danger that it will exacerbate risks of racial profiling and a culture of suspicion towards those visibly perceived to be from a minority ethnic background

(NIHRC, 2010), while warning that the surveillance capacity of the national register of personal data will increasingly reach across national borders as databases are harmonised and integrated (Lyon, 2007). Failure to replace a card if lost or circumstances change can lead to a fine of up to £1,000 or the curtailment of length of stay. It is unclear how effective identity cards will be as a means of detecting irregular migrants when only they are required to have them.

Trafficking

Within enforcement, we saw that trafficking has been accorded the highest level of priority, the aim being to target and penalise more severely the organised criminal gangs responsible, with multi-agency operations to develop intelligence and detect and detain traffickers in the UK and abroad. In 2006, the UK Human Trafficking Centre was established to improve coordination. Trafficking is criminalised under the Sexual Offences Act 2003 and successive Immigration Acts and carries a sentence of up to 14 years' imprisonment. Internationally, the UN Convention against Transnational Organised Crime (2000) promotes cooperation between states, with a focus on law enforcement. The UK later ratified the Council of Europe's Convention against Trafficking in Human Beings, underpinned by a clearer human rights focus. It encourages awareness-raising among potential victims, who must be offered a minimum of 30 days' support (UKHTC, 2010b). In the UK, each victim is entitled to 45 days of support, including accommodation and health care, and will not be removed during that period, while some are given longer residence to give evidence as a witness in court. Victims nevertheless remain fearful of reporting crimes in case it leads to enforcement action against them. The Crown Prosecution Service argues that it needs more victims to testify if it is to secure convictions (MRN, 2009: 11; CPS, 2010).

Academic analysis of the evidence has suggested a 'moral panic' on trafficking is diverting attention from the actual structural and systemic causes of abuse, obscuring the need for a broader range of policy solutions and justifying increases in police powers and surveillance of migrant workers. The exploitation by traffickers is not always distinct from that experienced by low-wage workers in legally tolerated employment contracts, or in abusive relationships in the sex trade or domestic work, unrelated to migration. It is the existence of those spaces that makes it possible for individuals to exploit the labour of people who have been trafficked (or not), and tackling their continued existence would address the market for trafficked migrants. There is, however, no consensus that these areas of the labour market should be subject to more regulation (Anderson and O'Connell Davidson, 2002; O'Connell Davidson, 2006; Anderson, 2007: 11; 2008; Mai, 2009). States' reluctance to address the structural demand for irregular labour lays them open to the accusation that, despite the rhetoric, they informally tolerate it in order to ensure a continued supply of cheap labour, using enforcement action only to address 'excess supply' (Taran, 2004).

The vulnerability of irregular migrants at work has been found across Europe to be exacerbated by their fear of detection, making them unwilling to report abuse or an employer's failure to pay what is owed (McKay and Wright, 2008; MRN, 2008). Workers thus need to be able to access their employment rights without fear of enforcement action against them. To deny that security is to give priority to immigration control over the need to protect the victims of forced labour. A review of practice across Europe shows that some countries do provide irregular migrants with legal rights to redress, for instance, for payment of wages due, but the extent to which they can exercise those rights in practice is less clear (Le Voy et al, 2004; Carens, 2008).

Notwithstanding greater resources attached to enforcement of employment standards in the later years of the Labour government (see Chapter 3), the weakest link in the strategy to address irregular migration is the continuing capacity of unscrupulous employers to avoid compliance with employment law. The UK model of enforcement is largely to rely on workers making a complaint to a tribunal, problematic for those whose status is vulnerable. Were there a greater reliance on inspections and intelligence-led investigations, including a broader remit and more resources for the Gangmasters

Licensing Authority (Chapter 3), information from third parties such as unions and NGOs could be used to greater effect (Anderson and Rogaly, 2005).

Employer sanctions

Concern about illegal working did lead to the imposition of sanctions on employers of irregular migrants in 1996 (the Asylum and Immigration Act), the UK being one of the last EU countries to do so. Concerned to minimise the burden on employers, the law required only that checks on eligibility were seen to have been made and enforcement was limited (Ryan, 2008). Substantially tougher penalties were introduced a decade later (in the Immigration, Asylum and Nationality Act 2006, in force from 2008): a 'civil penalty regime' imposing on-the-spot fines of up to £10,000 per employee or, for knowingly employing someone lacking permission to work, imprisonment for up to two years. Employees have to provide verifiable documents establishing their right to work and employers are expected to check each year on their continuing eligibility.

The civil penalty scheme 'vastly increased' the pressure on employers to ensure that employees are entitled to work and has the advantage for UKBA of enabling action against employers without recourse to the courts (Jackson et al, 2008: 1051). The Home Office estimated it would cost businesses £27 million to prepare for compliance. To avoid targeting ethnic minority employees inappropriately, employers are advised to check all staff. Businesses nevertheless remained concerned that if they act too hastily and dismiss an employee they may be accused of race discrimination, but if they give the employee the benefit of the doubt they risk being fined by UKBA (Garcia, 2007). The British Chambers of Commerce resented the implication that businesses were responsible for irregular working. It argued that the real issue was a shortage of sufficient skilled people within the UK, requiring resort to migrant labour (Frost, 2006).

In 2008, 7,460 operations to detect illegal working were carried out (compared to 1,600 in 2004), leading to 6,050 arrests. In the first

10 months after the measures came into force, 1,100 fines (totalling some £11 million) were issued to employers (Home Office, 2005; UKBA, 2009b). Only 37 employers had been found guilty under the previous legislation in the decade from 1997 to 2006. The tougher regime now in force has led employers to deny jobs to people in case their status is later found to be irregular, making it more difficult for legal migrants to find jobs and marginalising irregular migrants into the further reaches of the informal economy (McKay and Wright, 2008). Yet the Chief Inspector of Immigration says UKBA has only collected a small proportion of fines due, being 'too accommodating' towards employers willing to cooperate to reduce penalties (ICIUKBA, 2010). While migrants have felt the impact of the tougher rules, it does not necessarily make them more likely to leave the UK (ippr, 2009).

As in the US, enforcement falls to the immigration service and not to the agency responsible for compliance with National Insurance and the minimum wage, HM Revenue and Customs. This contrasts with the system in France where enforcement is integrated into the wider work of labour inspectors; in effect treating employer sanctions as a dimension of labour market regulation. That approach is said to enjoy broader acceptance than that in the UK and US where it is perceived as part of immigration control (Ryan, 2008).

The introduction of licensing for employers and education providers prior to their sponsoring migrant workers or students to enter under the Points-Based System (see Chapter 3) provides a further means to ensure that only those operating appropriately continue to participate. This form of regulation will only have an impact, however, if UKBA is resourced to make sufficient checks; and the system will retain support only if due process ensures sponsor status is not withdrawn unfairly.

Controls on access to services

Although there is limited evidence that access to services has been a factor in irregular migration, government has faced criticism that the 'absence of effective controls' on access to the NHS and on the immigration status of children applying for school places is an incentive that must be addressed (Migration Watch, 2006b). The government does expect some service providers to check the status of service users, the intention being to deter health tourism, to make it difficult for irregular migrants to live in the UK and to detect those who do. Those not prioritised for enforcement, UKBA argues, 'should be denied the benefits and privileges of life in the UK and experience an increasingly uncomfortable environment so that they elect to leave' (Home Office, 2007a: 17).

Arrangements for the NHS to charge 'overseas visitors' for hospital care were set up in 2004 but excluded key services on public health grounds: treatment for most highly infectious diseases, emergency treatment and treatment that is 'immediately necessary'. General Practitioners, meanwhile, have discretion as to whether to register overseas visitors and treat them without charge. It can in practice be difficult to collect charges due, particularly where the individual has left the country, and the government has considered making health insurance obligatory for some migrants and visitors. Significantly for a key theme of this book, the Department of Health is explicit in acknowledging the competing objectives at stake: 'maintaining a policy that balances cost, public health, migration and humanitarian principles is challenging' (DH, 2010: 1). Health professionals argue that some irregular migrants are denied care that they should be given and that others are deterred from seeking it (Cole, 2009; Medact, 2009).

In contrast, the Education Act 1996 requires local education authorities to provide free education to all school-age children regardless of immigration status. There is nevertheless an exchange of data between schools and UKBA on the ostensible grounds that children of parents seeking to avoid immigration controls may need support. It is not known to what extent this deters parents from sending their children to school (as has been found to be the case abroad; see Sigona and Hughes, 2010). UKBA also trains local authority staff to identify false documents, reporting that this has resulted in the denial of access to council services, prosecution and enforced removal (UKBA, 2010a: 18).

The introduction of identity cards for foreign nationals is intended to make it easier for service providers to know if they are entitled to the service. Foreign nationals can be required to provide biometric information such as fingerprints to establish if they are the rightful owner of the card (Thorp, 2007). Parliament's Joint Committee on Human Rights considers it 'highly likely' that members of Black and minority ethnic communities will be disproportionately required to prove their immigration status and hence that the effect of the checks will be racially discriminatory (JCHR, 2007: para 1.26).

Those working with migrants argue from experience that the consequence of internal controls will not be that people leave the UK:

> It is more likely that they will cause irregular migrants to reduce their contact with mainstream structures and systems. By moving further out of the public eye, the vulnerability of irregular migrants to exploitation, forced labour or criminal activity would be increased. (MRN, 2009: 18)

Barring access to services is perhaps the most controversial dimension of policy; devolving responsibility for immigration control to those whose primary responsibility is to provide services to those in need. Some health and education professionals have indeed proved reluctant, doctors arguing that: 'A refusal of treatment could lead to serious public health consequences, as well as significant knock-on costs where conditions deteriorate to such an extent that they require expensive emergency interventions' (Hamm et al, 2008). Denying access to services may also have broader consequences if failure to take up vaccinations puts public health at risk, children are kept out of school or witnesses feel unable to report a crime (Carens, 2008). Enforcement action against pupils in the UK has led teachers, for whom pupils are children first and migrants second, into implicit or overt opposition to immigration policy (NCADC, 2003; Arnot et al, 2009).

Critics argue on human rights grounds that it is wrong to deny essential services to any individual, regardless of their immigration status, if to do so means that their basic needs are not met. Requiring health and education providers to pass on information 'has the effect of taking away with one hand what was granted with the other, reducing the legal protection of the basic human rights of irregular migrants to a nominal entitlement stripped of any substantive effect' (Carens, 2008: 168). To prevent this, states need to put up a firewall, preventing the transfer of information collected by those responsible for human rights protection to those responsible for immigration control. Where fundamental rights are not at stake, however, Carens argues that the balance of argument may lie the other way, in favour of immigration control.

Detention and removal

We saw in Chapter 2 that criticism of the failure to remove refused asylum seekers drove significant expansion of capacity to detain (including at Harmondsworth, now Europe's largest removal centre) and steps to facilitate removal. Many other migrants are also detained before being removed or deported. While deportation remains the procedure for those foreign (and dual) nationals whose presence is 'not conducive to the public good', usually as a result of criminal activity or a threat to national security, irregular migrants have since 2000 been subject to administrative removal, carrying fewer procedural safeguards.

While most EU countries set a time limit on detention, from 32 days in France to 18 months in Germany, there is no limit in the UK. It opted out of the EU Returns Directive that imposes an 18-month upper limit. Of those detained on 30 September 2010, 130 people had been held for more than 18 months (Home Office, 2010d). Critics have questioned the ethics of this use of detention, a sanction normally used only for those convicted of a crime; have argued that detainees include people who are de facto stateless and cannot be returned; and have questioned whether the central role of private companies in running many of the centres gives them a commercial interest in opposing any reduction in the use of detention (Bacon, 2005; HL Select Committee on the EU, 2006: 60; ERT, 2010).

Inspections of removal centres have found both good practice ('an essentially safe place, with good relationships between staff and detainees, plenty of activity') and 'wholly unacceptable' conditions (HMI Prisons, 2010a, 2010b). Evidence suggests that the impact of detention on children can be particularly detrimental for their mental and physical health, education and access to legal advice – concerns endorsed by the Scottish and English Commissioners for Children. In 2009, 1,120 children were detained, of whom many were not subsequently removed from the UK (Home Office, 2010c). The Royal College of General Practitioners argued that the evidence on physical and mental health consequences made the detention of young people unacceptable and that it 'should cease without delay' (RCGP et al, 2009). The Labour government insisted that children were detained to avoid separating them from their parents for whom detention was essential for removal to be enforced (Home Office, 2010a). The Coalition government made an early commitment to end this practice but at the time of writing it is unclear with what it will be replaced.

There are alternatives to detention used to good effect in other countries. A study for UNHCR found provision of competent legal advice and concerned case management (serving as non-intrusive monitoring) to be among options more cost-effective in reducing absconding than detention; while for children guardianship and specialised group homes run by NGOs were among the successful alternatives (Field, 2006). Others have highlighted 'incentivised compliance' schemes used in Sweden and the USA combining advice, representation and information from the beginning of the determination process with supervision and risk assessment as well as information on opportunities for voluntary return (Crawley and Lester, 2005). The Home Affairs Select Committee advocated use of electronic tags, reporting requirements and residence restrictions, arguing that a low risk of absconding was 'a price worth paying to prevent the long-term, indeterminate detention of small children' (SC Home Affairs, 2010b).

Removal

Removal is beset with difficulties leading to a gap in Western countries between those eligible to be deported and actual removals. Globally, states attribute this to cost, public resistance to surveillance and removals, human rights constraints and an unwillingness of source countries to accept returnees (Koser, 2005). In 2009, 67,215 people were removed from the UK or left 'voluntarily', of whom almost half were refused at a port of entry. A further 11,000 were asylum cases so it would appear that fewer than 28,000 other irregular migrants were detected in-country and removed in that year (Home Office, 2010c), low relative to the 618,000 irregular migrants we saw estimated to be living in the UK but on a par with recent years (see Figure 5.1).

Figure 5.1: Removals and voluntary departures from the UK 2000–09

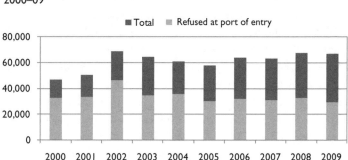

Source: Home Office Control of Immigration Statistics 2009, Table 3.1

Gibney finds three explanations for the deportation gap: that the individual has become socially integrated, 'lost' or 'unreturnable' (Gibney, 2008). Where social relationships have been formed, removal may be vocally opposed, with a public eager for more removals resisting implementation when faced with its human cost (Ellerman, 2006). Others become 'lost' when they go underground to avoid removal, during or after receiving a decision (whether because the original purpose was to secure access to the labour market or for fear that their genuine need for protection will not be recognised). Tracking them down is expensive and time-consuming.

Return also requires the cooperation of another state, which may be reluctant, Gibney explains, because of the loss of remittances, the undesirability of a particular individual or the lack of evidence demonstrating their citizenship. To overcome that resistance Labour pursued a rash of readmission agreements, insisting that 'we will leave our partners in no doubt that accepting return of their nationals is a duty and failure to do so will have implications for our wider relationship' (Home Office, 2005: 30). Readmission agreements, as successfully concluded with China, Vietnam, Pakistan, India and Turkey for instance, in particular help to resolve situations where travel documents have expired or been lost or destroyed (Home Office, 2007a). The UK has also benefited from EU readmission agreements.

A further constraint has been a bar imposed by the courts on return to countries where the individual may be subject to torture (eg *Chahal v UK* in 1997[1]) in breach of Article 3 of the European Convention on Human Rights (ECHR). The Labour government sought to overcome this in relation to terrorist suspects through indefinite detention, which was also ruled unlawful, and subsequently through control orders under the Prevention of Terrorism Act 2005. Memoranda of Agreement with governments that torture would not be used were criticised as unreliable, while suspects could still pose a threat to UK citizens and interests abroad (Thorp, 2007). There are further cases where government and those representing irregular migrants disagree as to whether the country is safe for return. EU states have themselves taken opposing views on whether Iraq, for instance, has been a safe destination (HL Select Committee on the EU, 2006: para 35). The Coalition government quickly found itself under fire from the UNHCR for returning refused asylum seekers to Iraq, given prevailing violence and human rights violations (Jones, 2010).

Voluntary return

The National Audit Office has calculated that the cost of an enforced removal is between £7,900 and £17,000 for a single adult (NAO, 2009b: Table 3), on the basis of which it is estimated that it would cost up to £12 billion to remove all irregular migrants from the UK and take at least 25 years to achieve at the current rate of departures (ippr, 2009).

Cost has been one factor encouraging government since 1999 to fund schemes for voluntary return. They also avoid the controversy of the use of force. Globally, take-up of such opportunities is often low: migrants have reasons not to want to return or may be unaware of the scheme. There are differing views on what kind of package to offer, whom to target and whether a generous scheme would simply encourage others to come illegally to benefit from it (Koser, 2005). In the UK, separate schemes have been run for irregular migrants and asylum seekers, managed by the International Organisation for Migration (IOM). The latter scheme includes financial assistance with reintegration (for business start-up, education or training; see Home Office, 2010b). After the war in the former Yugoslavia, a 'look and see' scheme enabled refugees to judge whether their area was safe to return to. It has been argued that the only way of truly judging whether precarious residence is a choice is by offering genuine options for return that enable successful reintegration, hence the UK is ill advised in making this option available only to those who have sought asylum (and to victims of trafficking), perhaps those least likely to feel able to return (Gibney, 2009). The NAO finds voluntary removal to cost up to £3,400 less than forced removal for a single person and £14,600 less for a family (NAO, 2009a: para 2.33). A financial incentive to return could thus be an investment well spent.

Foreign prisoners

The year 2006 saw the explosion of an issue that has no relation to immigration offences per se but has nevertheless become one plank of the enforcement agenda: the deportation of foreign nationals. Disclosure that, through administrative error, over a thousand foreign national prisoners had been released over the previous seven years after serving sentences for serious offences without any consideration given to deportation prompted the resignation of the Home Secretary, Charles Clarke. The incident led to a rapid rise in deportations and, by changing the law (the UK Borders Act 2007), to automatic deportation of any foreign national who has been sentenced to 12 months in prison. EEA nationals are largely excluded, as are refugees.

Deportation in these circumstances breaches the principle that no one should suffer a second punishment for the same offence, severing people from their homes, families and livelihoods. Nevertheless, some thought the government should go further: that for a second conviction the 'trigger' should be a six-month sentence, that the courts should be able to make deportation part of the sentence itself and that proceedings should commence at the beginning of a sentence to avoid any delay (Thorp, 2007).

Reality check

Notwithstanding the stepping up of enforcement over the past decade, it would be 'naive' to assume that government aims to eliminate or even significantly reduce all forms of illegality given competing pressures that include the economic necessity of facilitating cross-border traffic of people and freight, the cost of enforcing immigration and employment law, public resistance to intrusive surveillance, and the barriers to removing those found in breach of the law (Ruhs and Anderson, 2009).

Border security is in essence a risk management process: 100% effective controls are not practical because of the volume of passenger journeys and the economic benefits from that movement. Each year 30 million international tourists bring more than £16 billion to the tourism industry, our third-largest export earner. The Coalition government intends to attract an additional 4 million visitors over the next four years, generating £2 billion in additional spending and 50,000 jobs (Hunt, 2010; HM Treasury, 2011: para 2.310). In 2006, it was estimated that a 10-minute rise in UK passport clearance could represent an opportunity cost of £400 million a year. Government cannot afford to jeopardise that income and the livelihood of many small businesses. In 2008, Home Office plans to cut the time limit on a visitor visa from six to three months were reportedly dropped on those grounds (Travis, 2008). In its agreements with private-sector carriers, government has been explicit in seeking 'to balance the potentially conflicting demands of rapid transit systems with the need for risk minimising measures' (Gregory, 2009: 5; see also Cabinet Office, 2007).

Within the UK there is a direct tension between the level of regulation and inspection of the labour market necessary to limit spaces for illegality and the preference of successive governments for a light-touch approach. Intrusive border and internal controls, moreover, have the potential to infringe privacy, alienate employers, disrupt business and service provision, deter students from choosing the UK, and damage relationships between tutors and students (Chapter 3). In excluding irregular migrants from services, we saw that controls risk not only their well-being but also that of the public. Such considerations have influenced both the direction of policy and the extent to which it is enforced.

Data on enforcement suggests, moreover, that despite the plethora of new powers, initiatives, inter-agency cooperation and greater resources deployed over the past decade, government is not highly successful in preventing, detecting or removing irregular migrants. In that experience, the UK is not alone. Much has been written on the limited effectiveness of enforcement action in the US and in other parts of Europe and on its unintended consequences: encouraging those already in the country to stay rather than risk being unable to return; diverting migrants into more hazardous means of entry; fuelling demand for the services of smugglers; and marginalising irregular workers into the least regulated sectors of the labour market. Control policies do not change the structural causes of irregular migration and thus cannot alone address it.

Restoration of legal status

Even if it were possible to detect all irregular migrants they could not all be removed because of the cost of removal and the disruption it would cause in workplaces, schools and communities. It is therefore sensible to consider whether more could be returned to legal status. Across the EU, only five of the 27 member states have no practice of regularisation (Baldwin-Edwards and Kraler, 2009).

The heated reaction to the Liberal Democrat proposal during the 2010 general election that irregular migrants resident in the UK for 10 years should be able to access legal status might suggest this was an exceptional proposal. Yet there is already a well-used provision of this kind. In 2003, the government brought within the Immigration Rules an existing 'Long Residence Concession' granting indefinite leave to remain to irregular migrants after 14 years unless there were serious grounds not to do so. The rule had reportedly been applied to some 2,000–3,000 cases a year in the 1990s (ippr, 2006). Guidance to UKBA staff sets out in some detail the factors that should be taken into account including strength of family connections in the UK, employment, criminal record, compassionate circumstances and positive contributions to society (Garton Grimwood, 2009; UKBA, 2009a: ch 18). Case law suggests the rule has been applied after 10 years' residence (Vollmer, 2008).

There has also been a series of occasions on which successive governments have deemed it necessary to regularise the status of some thousands of migrants, including a scheme for seasonal agricultural workers (1986) and resident domestic workers (1998) and likewise for refused asylum seekers and those whose cases had not been resolved, in 1993–94, 1999–2000 and again in 2003–05. The UK was not alone in finding it necessary to regularise asylum seekers remaining in the country, Germany doing so in 2007 for those resident for eight years, reportedly benefiting at least 50,000 people (Papademetriou and Somerville, 2008: 32).

Experience abroad

The UK has never initiated an amnesty for a broader canvas of migrants of the kind regularly deployed abroad: a review in 2005 found 22 such programmes since 1980 in the US and Europe. Those eligible were narrowly or broadly defined and what they were offered varied from a one-year work permit to permanent residence. Governments had been prompted to act in some cases by protests at the treatment of the 'sans papièrs', but underlying drivers had been the need to curb the economic and social consequences of a growing irregular underclass and the failure of enforcement measures to do so. Where temporary status was offered, many subsequently again became irregular. Weaknesses in programme design and administration and the unwillingness of employers to pay higher wages for legalised workers have proved to be barriers to positive outcomes, while well-organised permanent programmes have a positive impact on wages and occupational mobility (Levinson, 2005). The terms of the offer, documentation required, cost and the way it is administered have a major impact on whether it is successful in encouraging people to apply (Anderson, 2004).

Evidence from the US and from Southern Europe has been that regularisation can lead to increased migration due to the extension of networks and family ties. US experience, however, is dominated by its long land border with Mexico, and Southern Europe by its extensive coastline and proximity to North Africa. Experience in Spain, for instance, has been influenced by its geographical location, colonial history and linguistic ties, and by its high level of demand for unskilled labour and narrow front-door for regular migration (Greenway, 2007). Experience abroad has nevertheless been taken as an indication that any kind of regularisation would be an incentive to migrants to try their luck in the UK.

A House of Lords inquiry nevertheless concluded that some form of regularisation is 'unavoidable' if a growing underclass of people, vulnerable to exploitation, is not to be created. It is in the interests of society that long-term residents should not remain in an irregular position but should pay their taxes and have access to public services. Any regularisation would, however, need to be handled carefully to minimise the 'pull factor', dealing with cases on an individual basis rather than a large-scale amnesty. It should also be monitored carefully, providing a rare opportunity to obtain reliable information on the size and nature of the irregular population (HL Select Committee on the EU, 2002: para 86).

Options for the UK

The option of legal status being restored selectively could focus on categories of people (pensioners or family units in which one member is unauthorised, for instance) or broader criteria, as in proposals for 'earned regularisation'. Temporary permits could be issued initially on the basis of length of residence, past record, presence of family members, humanitarian considerations, contribution to the economy and sponsorship by a reputable organisation, with subsequent eligibility to earn longer-term legal status if certain conditions apply, such as English language proficiency and no criminal conviction (ippr, 2006, 2009; JCWI, 2006; MRN, 2009). A modest step could be to adopt the 'bridging visa' proposed by the Irish government to enable those who have become irregular through no fault of their own to return to legal status.

The head of the Roman Catholic Church in England and Wales, the UNITE union and the Conservative Mayor of London, Boris Johnson, are among those who have argued for a regularisation programme in some form, the Mayor suggesting migrants could be eligible after five years if they could demonstrate a commitment to the UK economy and society (BBC, 2008). A regularisation scheme could contribute £3 billion per annum to GDP and a further £846 million to the public purse, cost £419 million per annum to public services; and potentially increase social tensions if there were perceptions of 'queue-jumping' (Gordon et al, 2009: paras 48–51).

Regularisation should, it is suggested, only be implemented as part of a package of reforms designed to reduce future irregularity. To succeed it must reflect an understanding of the behaviour and needs of both migrants and employers and learn lessons from earlier programmes. A well-planned regularisation policy, as part of a broader package of reforms to address the causes of irregularity, has the potential, Papademetriou and Somerville argue, 'to enhance public safety, cement the rule of law, increase tax revenues, create more orderly labour markets, cut down on exploitation and foster greater social stability' (Papademetriou and Somerville, 2008). It would reduce the number of people unknown to the authorities, enable enforcement to focus on those who pose a threat, encourage cooperation with the authorities by those who currently shun contact and reduce the financial burden on local authorities for which they are not reimbursed (see Chapters 2 and 4). Moreover, they argue, there is no practical alternative solution on the table. A fee paid by the migrant could also offset the cost of running the programme (Papademetriou and Somerville, 2008).

That view has not been supported by the Conservative or Labour parties. Migration Watch argues that regularisation would reward illegal behaviour, that those granted an amnesty would be replaced by others and that it would be a cost to the public purse because the migrants would gain access to the welfare state, albeit offset to an extent by their contribution to the economy (Migration Watch, 2006; Garton Grimwood, 2009). The actual impacts of regularisation would depend on the current economic and social position of irregular migrants, their position after regularisation, the effect that removing constraints has on their life choices and consequent impacts on the labour and housing markets. Those factors depend not only on the design of any regularisation scheme but also on the extent to which the migrant has been, and subsequently is, integrated into the workforce and society (Gordon et al, 2009).

Conclusion

The best available estimate is that there were 618,000 irregular migrants in the UK in 2007, just over 1% of the population. The majority came legally and overstayed. There is a further semi-compliant group working in breach of their conditions of stay. This chapter explored the causes of irregularity including the economic functions it serves, the extent to which it is shaped by migration and employment policies and how it is oiled by a lucrative global industry that exists because of the demand for its services. Yet the conditions that lead some migrants to risk all to reach the UK may be far removed from those leading young people from rich countries to remain after their visa has expired. Understanding irregularity in all its forms is a necessary basis for appropriate policy intervention.

The consequences of irregularity mean that government cannot be complacent yet its response should be proportionate, reflecting the modest levels of harm acknowledged to arise in most cases. A legal framework set 40 years ago, defining all breaches of the rules as criminal offences subject to removal from the UK, has however narrowed the scope for policy solutions beyond law enforcement. Redefining the less serious breaches so that they attract civil penalties could facilitate proportional enforcement and sanctions, the object being future compliance not removal from the UK.

The enforcement paradigm has been reinforced by UKBA's location within the Home Office alongside responsibility for policing and national security, and its position within an inter-agency partnership addressing border control issues relating to drugs, organised crime and terrorism. The past decade has seen a constant stream of new offences and resources invested in detection, detention and removal. Yet just 67,000 people were removed in 2009 or left 'voluntarily', nearly half of whom were detected at ports of entry. That figure, relative to the size of the irregular population, suggests that a greater focus is needed on prevention, addressing causes within the migration system itself and in the labour market.

Where demand for labour is not met from within the EEA, lack of legal migration channels encourages irregular working. Notwithstanding the impact of the recession, we saw in Chapter 3 that there remain sectors where pay and conditions are insufficient to attract local staff. The government needs to be clear how these jobs will be filled by UK or EEA workers if this situation is not to lead 'overstayers' to take up this employment. Demand for irregular migrants is also shaped by poor working conditions being allowed to continue within the labour market. The weakest link in the strategy to address irregular migration is the continuing capacity of unscrupulous employers to avoid compliance with employment standards. Experience abroad suggests that inspection relating to employment standards rather than separately as part of immigration control has greater levels of acceptance among employers.

If employers are to know whether an individual is entitled to work and to check without discriminating on any grounds, all prospective employees must have reliable documentation. A secure system of verifiable National Insurance numbers for that purpose would have been more appropriate than ID cards for foreign nationals. If issued solely for employment, there would have been less danger of further personal data being added and of cards being demanded for unrelated purposes. As in any ID system, it would be effective only to the extent that fraudulent manufacture and use is prevented and employers have the technology to check the information the card contains. To ensure that migrants do not inadvertently fall outside the rules they need clear information on their conditions of stay, not simply 'No recourse to public funds' stamped in their passport. While government recognises that it should 'make it as straightforward as possible for migrants to stay compliant' (Home Office, 2007a: 16) it has a long way to go to achieve that objective. Strengthening the evidence base on the full range of pathways to irregular status could provide the basis for a systematic review of rules and procedures to reduce the rate at which this is happening.

Extending identity checks to prevent access to services is highly problematic. Although access to some essential services is provided regardless of immigration status, the effect of the rules and transfer of data to UKBA is denying some individuals health care and potentially schooling – to what extent, we do not know. Beyond the implications for the individuals concerned, their exclusion from the institutions of mainstream society may pose risks to other members of the community. One necessary solution is a firewall that enables an individual to use an essential service, and report abuse by their employer or that they have been a victim of crime, without their personal details being transferred: a firm legal principle that no information gathered by those responsible for protecting basic human rights can be used for immigration enforcement. That would not only protect the individuals concerned but secure their cooperation for the wider public good. Enabling exploited employees to report their employer would also, in curtailing opportunities for abuse, limit the demand for irregular workers.

Notwithstanding the heavy focus of rhetoric on enforcement, we saw that UKBA cannot eliminate or even severely reduce the extent of irregularity. There are a series of counter-pressures, not least the economic necessity of facilitating passenger movements across UK borders, the cost of detection and removal, and constraints imposed by the courts. This suggests that government should not over-promise what cannot be delivered. It might also reconsider its assumption that focusing public attention on enforcement activity does reassure: in reinforcing misconceptions on the scale of irregularity and the threat it poses, it may have the opposite effect.

The limited efficacy of enforcement further reinforces the need to look for complementary strategies to address the vulnerability of those who remain in the UK and identify pathways for some to return to legal status. If the argument for extending regularisation is accepted (acknowledging that limited pathways already exist), it is necessary to address the concern that it should not reward those who have broken the law more than those who abided by it and should minimise encouragement to future migrants to overstay. Setting conditions for regularisation that require the applicant to cover costs and to demonstrate a contribution to the UK (while not so onerous that few apply), and setting regularisation alongside preventative measures, coupled with proportional enforcement and voluntary return packages, could go some way towards meeting those concerns. Reducing the threshold for eligibility for automatic consideration well below the current residence threshold of 14 years could be a first pragmatic step, leading perhaps to consecutive reductions over a period of years to deliver a manageable programme from which lessons could be learnt. In this way addressing irregularity would be mainstreamed across migration, employment and development policy: regular policies for irregular migration.

At the same time, it is important to be realistic. It is possible to reduce irregular migration but with the volume of mobility through the UK it will continue:

> Instead of seeking perfection, with its predictable disappointments, controlling illegal immigration might proceed from the twin premises that uncertainty and imperfection will be a way of life, and policies will always be partly an exercise in the inexact. (Papademetriou, 2005)

Note
[1] *Chahal v the UK* (1997) 23 EHRR 413.

References

Anderson, B. (2004) 'The Devil is in the Detail: Lessons to be Drawn from the UK's Recent Exercise in Regularising Undocumented Workers', in M. LeVoy, N.Verbruggen and J.Wets (eds) *Undocumented Migrant Workers in Europe*. Brussels: PICUM.

Anderson, B. (2007) 'Motherhood, Apple Pie and Slavery: Reflections on Trafficking Debates', Working Paper 07-48. Oxford: COMPAS, University of Oxford.

Anderson, B. (2008) '"Illegal Immigrant":Victim orVillain?', Working Paper 08-64. Oxford: COMPAS, University of Oxford.

Anderson, B. and O'Connell Davidson, J. (2002) *Trafficking: A Demand Led Problem? A Multi-Country Pilot Study*. Sweden: Save the Children.

Anderson, B. and Rogaly, B. (2005) *Forced Labour and Migration to the UK: Study Prepared by COMPAS in Collaboration with the Trades Union Congress*. London: TUC.

Anderson, B. and Ruhs, M. (2010) 'Guest Editorial: Researching Illegality and Labour Migration', *Population, Space and Place*, 16(3): 175-9.

Anderson, B., Ruhs, M., Spencer, S. and Rogaly, B. (2006) *Fair Enough? Central and East European Migrants in Low-wage Employment in the UK*. York: Joseph Rowntree Foundation.

Arnot, M., Pinson, H. and Candappa, M. (2009) 'Compassion, Caring and Justice: Teachers' Strategies to Maintain Moral Integrity in the Face of National Hostility to the "Non-Citizen"', *Educational Review* 61(3): 249–64.

Bacon, C. (2005) 'The Evolution of Immigration Detention in the UK: The Involvement of Private Prison Companies', RSC Working Paper No 27. Oxford: Refugee Studies Centre.

Baldwin-Edwards, M. and Kraler, A. (2009) *REGINE: Regularisation in Europe. Study on Practices in the Area of Regularisation of Illegally Staying Third-Country Nationals in the Member States of the EU, Final Report*. Vienna: ICMPD.

BBC (British Broadcasting Association) (2008) 'Johnson Ponders Immigrant Amnesty', 22 November. Available at: http://news.bbc.co.uk/l/hi/uk/7743081.stm

BBC (2010) 'Airport Body Scanners "May Be Unlawful"'. Available at: http: //news.bbc.co.uk/1/hi/uk/8516574.stm (accessed 13 June 2010).

Black, R., Collyer, M., Skeldon, R. and Waddington, C. (2006) 'Routes to Illegal Residence: A Case Study of Immigration Detainees in the United Kingdom', *Geoforum* 37: 552–64.

Bloch, A., Sigona, N. and Zetter, R. (2009) *No Right to Dream: The Social and Economic Lives of Young Undocumented Migrants in Britain*. London: Paul Hamlyn Foundation.

Boswell, C. (2008) 'The Elusive Rights of an Invisible Population', *Ethics and International Affairs* 22(2): 187–92.

Cabinet Office (2007) *Security in a Global Hub: Establishing the UK's New Border Arrangements*. London: Cabinet Office.

Carens, J.H. (2008) 'The Rights of Irregular Migrants', *Ethics and International Affairs* 22(2): 163–86.

Cole, P. (2009) 'Migration and the Human Right to Health', *Cambridge Quarterly of Healthcare Ethics* 18(1): 70–7.

Cornelius, W., Martin, P. and Hollifield, J. (2004) 'Introduction: The Ambivalent Quest for Immigration Control', in W. Cornelius, T. Takeyuki et al (eds) *Controlling Immigration: A Global Perspective*, 2nd edn. Stanford: Stanford University Press.

CPS (Crown Prosecution Service) (2010) 'CPS launches consultation on human trafficking public policy', Press notice, 29 July, London: Crown Prosecution Service.

Crawley, H. and Lester, T. (2005) *No Place for a Child: Children in UK Immigration Detention: Impacts, Alternatives and Safeguards*. London: Save the Children.

De Genova, N. P. (2002) 'Migrant "Illegality" and Deportability in Everyday Life', *Annual Review of Anthropology* 31: 419–47.

DH (Department of Health) (2010) *Review of Access to the NHS by Foreign Nationals: Consultation on Proposals*. London: Department of Health.

Dowling, S., Moreton, K. and Wright, L. (2007) 'Trafficking for the Purposes of Labour Exploitation: A Literature Review', Online Report 10/07. London: Home Office.

Duvell, F. (2008) 'Clandestine Migration in Europe', *Social Science Information* 47(4): 479-97.

Ellerman, A. (2006) 'Street-Level Democracy: How Immigration Bureaucrats Manage Public Opposition', *West European Politics* 29(2): 293–309.

Engbersen, G. and van der Leun, J. (2001) 'The Social Construction of Illegality and Criminality', *European Journal on Criminal Policy and Research* 9(1): 51–70.

ERT (Equal Rights Trust) (2010) *Unravelling Anomaly: Detention, Discrimination and the Protection Needs of Stateless Persons*, London.

Field, O. (2006) 'Alternatives to Detention of Asylum Seekers and Refugees', *UNHCR Legal and Protection Policy Research Series POLAS/2006/03*. Geneva: UNHCR.

Frost, D. (2006) 'Employers Are Not the Villains in the Battle over Immigration', *Financial Times*, 24 July.

Garcia, K. (2007) 'Illegal Workers: How Much Responsibility Should Fall on Employers?' *Personnel Today*, 3 September.

Garton Grimwood, G. (2009) 'Immigration: An Amnesty for Undocumented Migrants?', Standard Note, SN/HA/4080. London: House of Commons Library.

Geddes, A. (2005) 'Chronicle of a Crisis Foretold: The Politics of Irregular Migration, Human Trafficking and People Smuggling in the UK', *British Journal of Politics and International Relations* 7: 324–39.

Gibney, M. J. (2008) 'Asylum and the Expansion of Deportation in the United Kingdom', *Government and Opposition* 43(2): 146–67.

Gibney, M. (2009) *Precarious Residents: Migration Control, Membership and the Rights of Non-Citizens*, Human Development Research Paper, United Nations Development Programme. New York: UNDP.

Gordon, I., Scanlon, K., Travers, T. and Whitehead, C. (2009) *Economic Impact on the London and UK Economy of an Earned Regularisation of Irregular Migrants to the UK*. London: Greater London Authority.

Greenway, J. (2007) 'Regularisation Programmes for Irregular Migrants: Report to the Committee on Migration, Refugees and Population', Doc 11350 6 July. Strasbourg: Council of Europe Parliamentary Assembly.

Gregory, F. (2009) *UK Border Security: Issues, Systems and Recent Reforms: a Submission to the Ippr Commission on National Security for the 21st Century*. London: Institute for Public Policy Research.

Hamm, C., Harrison, C., Mussel, R., Sheather, J., Sommerville, A. and Tizzard, J. (2008) 'Ethics Briefings', *Journal of Medical Ethics* 34: 125–6.

HL Select Committee on the EU (House of Lords Select Committee on the European Union) (2002) *A Common Policy on Illegal Immigration*, 37th Report Session 2001–02, HL 187. London: House of Lords.

HL Select Committee on the EU (2006) *Illegal Migrants: Proposals for a Common EU Returns Policy*, 32nd Report Session 2005–06, HL 166. London: House of Lords.

HL Select Committee on the EU (2008) *Frontex: The EU External Borders Agency*, 9th Report Session 2007–08, HL 60. London: House of Lords.

HMI Prisons (2010a) *Report of an Announced Inspection of Campsfield House Immigration Removal Centre 5–9 October 2009*. London: HM Inspectorate of Prisons.

HMI Prisons (2010b) 'Tinsley House IRC: "Wholly Unacceptable" Conditions for Women and Children', Press release, 18 December, HM Inspectorate of Prisons.

HM Treasury (2011) *The Plan for Growth*. London: HM Treasury and Department for Business.

Home Office (1998) *Fairer, Faster, and Firmer: A Modern Approach to Immigration and Asylum*, Cm 4018. London: Home Office.

Home Office (2002) *Secure Borders, Safe Haven: Integration with Diversity in Modern Britain*, Cm 5387. London: Home Office.

Home Office (2005) *Controlling Our Borders: Making Migration Work for Britain – Five Year Strategy for Asylum and Immigration*, Cm 6472. London: Home Office.

Home Office (2006) *Fair, Effective, Transparent and Trusted: Rebuilding Confidence in our Immigration System*. London: Home Office.

Home Office (2007a) *Enforcing the Rules: A Strategy to Ensure and Enforce Compliance With Our Immigration Laws*. London: Home Office.

Home Office (2007b) *Securing the UK Border: Our Vision and Strategy for the Future*. London: Home Office.

Home Office (2010a) 'Government Response to Childrens' Commissioner Report on Yarl's Wood', Press release, 17 February, UKBA.

Home Office (2010b) *The Detention of Children in the Immigration System: The Government Reply to the First Report from the Home Affairs Committee Session 2009–10 HC 73*. London: Home Office.

Home Office (2010c) *Control of Immigration: Statistics United Kingdom 2009*, Home Office Statistical Bulletin 15/10. London: Home Office.

Home Office (2010d) *Control of Immigration Quarterly Statistical Summary United Kingdom July–September 2010*. London: Home Office.

Hunt, J. (2010) 'Secretary of State's Speech on Tourism to Weymouth and Portland National Sailing Academy, Weymouth', 11 June, London, Department of Culture Media and Sport.

ICIUKBA (Independent Chief Inspector of the United Kingdom Border Agency) (2010) 'Asylum: Getting the Balance Right? A Thematic Inspection, July–November 2009', Home Office, Independent Chief Inspector of the UKBA.

ippr (2006) *Irregular Migration in the UK: An ippr FactFile*. London: Institute for Public Policy Research.

ippr (2009) *Irregular Migration in the UK: An ippr Update*. London: Institute for Public Policy Research.

Jackson, D., Warr, G., Onslow, J. and Middleton, J. (2008) *Immigration Law and Practice*, 4th edn. Haywards Heath: Tottel Publishing.

JCHR (Joint Committee on Human Rights) (2007) *Legislative Scrutiny: Sixth Progress Report*, 13th Report Session 2006–07, HL 105/HC 538. London: Joint Committee on Human Rights.

JCWI (Joint Council for the Welfare of Immigrants) (2006) *Recognising Rights, Recognising Political Realities: The Case for Regularising Irregular Migrants*. London: Joint Council for the Welfare of Immigrants.

Jones, S. (2010) 'UN Criticises Britain over Forced Return of Iraqi Refugees', *The Guardian*, 17 June.

Koser, K. (2005) *Irregular Migration, State Security and Human Security, a Paper Prepared for the Policy Analysis and Research Programme of the Global Commission on International Migration*. Geneva: GCIM.

Koser, K. (2010) 'Dimensions and Dynamics of Irregular Migration', *Population, Space and Place* 16: 181–93.

Lee, M. (2005) 'Human Trade and the Criminalisation of Irregular Migration', *International Journal of the Sociology of Law* 33: 1–15.

Levinson, A. (2005) 'Why Countries Continue to Consider Regularization'. Available at: http://www.unityblueprint. net/_documents/research-and-policy/legalization-in-other-countries/2.%20AmandaLevinson-MigrationPolicyInstitute.pdf (accessed 31 May 2010).

Le Voy, M., Verbruggen, N. and Wets, J. (eds) (2004) *Undocumented Migrant Workers in Europe*. Brussels: PICUM.

Lyon, D. (2007) 'National ID Cards: Crime Control, Citizenship and Social Sorting', *Policing* 1(1): 111–18.

Mai, N. (2009) *Migrant Workers in the UK Sex Industry Policy – Relevant Findings*. London: ISET, London Metropolitan University.

McKay, S. and Wright, T. (2008) 'Tightening Immigration Policies and Labour Market Impacts', *Transfer: European Review of Labour and Research* 14: 653–64.

Medact (2009) *Memorandum Submitted to the JCHR Scrutiny of the Borders, Citizenship and Immigration Bill*. London: Parliamentary Joint Committee on Human Rights.

Migration Watch UK (2006) *An Amnesty for Illegal Immigrants?* Briefing paper. Available at: http: //www.migrationwatchuk.com/ briefingPaper/document/131 (accessed 31 May 2010).

Morice, A. (2004) 'Migratory Policies and the Evolution of Work in the European Union: Where Undocumented Migrants Fit into this System', in M. Le Voy, N. Verbruggen and J. Wets (eds) *Undocumented Migrant Workers in Europe*. Brussels: PICUM.

MRN (Migrants Rights Network) (2008) *Papers Please*. London: Migrants Rights Network.

MRN (2009) *Irregular Migrants: The Urgent Need for a New Approach*. London: Migrants Rights Network.

NAO (National Audit Office) (2009a) *Management of Asylum Applications by the UK Border Agency*, Session 2008–09, HC 124. London: National Audit Office.

NAO (2009b) 'Management of Asylum Applications by the UK Border Agency: Costing Workstream', Session 2008–09, HC 124. London: National Audit Office.

NCADC (National Coalition of Anti Deportation Campaigns) (2003) 'Reality of Deportation', *Newszine 36*. Available at: http://www.ncadc.org.uk/news/index.html (accessed 18 June 2010).

NIHRC (Northern Ireland Human Rights Commission) (2010) *Identity Documents Bill: Written Evidence to the House of Lords (October 2010)*. Belfast: Northern Ireland Human Rights Commission.

O'Connell Davidson, J. (2006) 'Will the Real Sex Slave Please Stand Up?' *Feminist Review* 83: 4–22.

O'Connell Davidson, J. and Farrow, C. (2007) *Child Migration and the Construction of Vulnerability*. Sweden: Save the Children.

Papademetriou, D. (2005) 'The Global Struggle with Illegal Immigration: No End in Sight'. Available at: http: //www. migrationinformation.org/feature/display.cfm?ID=336

Papademetriou, D. and Somerville, W. (2008) *Earned Amnesty: Bringing Illegal Workers out of the Shadows*. London: Centre Forum.

RCGP (Royal College of General Practitioners), Royal College of Paediatrics and Child Health, Royal College of Psychiatrists, and others (2009) 'Intercollegiate Briefing Paper: Significant Harm – The Effects of Administrative Detention on the Health of Children, Young People and Their Families', Royal College of General Practitioners et al.

Ruhs, M. and Anderson, B. (2009) 'Semi-Compliance and Illegality in Migrant Labour Markets: An Analysis of Migrants, Employers and the State in the UK', *Population, Space and Place,* 16 (3): 195-211.

Ryan, B. (2008) *Innovations in Employer Sanctions in the United States and Europe*. Washington DC: ISIM.

Salt, J. and J. Stein (1997) 'Migration as a Business: The Case of Trafficking', *International Migration* 35(4): 467–94.

SC Home Affairs (Home Affairs Select Committee) (2006) *Immigration Control*, 5th Report, Session 2005–06, HC 775. London: House of Commons.

SC Home Affairs (2009) *The E-Borders Programme*, 3rd Report, Session 2009–10, HC 56. London: House of Commons.

SC Home Affairs (2010a) *UK Border Agency: Follow-up on Asylum Cases and E-Borders Programme*, 12th Report, Session 2009–10, HC 406. London: House of Commons.

SC Home Affairs (2010b) *The Detention of Children in the Immigration System*, Session 2009–10, HC 73. London: House of Commons.

Sigona, N. and Hughes, V. (2010) *Being Children and Undocumented: Review of Legal, Policy and Academic Literature on Undocumented Migrant Children in the UK. Background paper*. Oxford: COMPAS, University of Oxford.

Taran, P.A. (2004) 'Globalization, Migration and Exploitation: Irregular Migrants and Fundamental Rights at Work', in M. Le Voy, N. Verbruggen and J.Wets (eds) *Undocumented Migrant Workers in Europe*. Brussels: PICUM.

Thorp, A. (2007) 'UK Borders Bill', Research Paper 07/11. London: House of Commons Library.

Travis, A. (2008) 'Britons May Be Jailed if Relatives from Abroad Overstay', *The Guardian*, 26 June.

UKBA (United Kingdom Border Agency) (2008a) *A Strong New Force at the Border*. London: Home Office.

UKBA (2008b) *Enforcing the Deal: Our Plans for Enforcing the Immigration Laws in the United Kingdom's Communities*. London: Home Office.

UKBA (2009a) 'Immigration Directorate Instructions', Home Office, UKBA.

UKBA (2009b) *Business Plan April 2009–March 2012*, London: Home Office.

UKBA (2010a) *Protecting Our Border, Protecting the Public: The UKBA's Five Year Strategy for Enforcing Our Immigration Rules and Addressing Immigration and Cross Border Crime*. London: Home Office.

UKBA (2010b) 'Vicars Are Taught How to Spot Sham Marriages', Press notice, 17 September, Home Office, London.

UKBA (2010c) 'Liverpool Company Facing Fine for Illegal Worker', Press notice, 20 May, Home Office, London.

UKBA (2010d) 'Immigration Arrest at Eastbourne Care Home', Press notice, 17 November, Home Office, London.

UKBA (2010e) 'Joint Declaration on Immigration at UK–France Summit', Press notice, 2 November, Home Office, London.

UKHTC (UK Human Trafficking Centre) (2010a) 'NRM Annual Data April 2009–March 2010'. London: UK Human Trafficking Centre.

UKHTC (2010b) 'Council of Europe Convention Against Trafficking in Human Beings'. Available at: http://www.soca.gov.uk/about-soca/about-the-ukhtc/council-of-europe-convention (accessed 29 June 2010, no longer available).

UNODC (UN Office on Drugs and Crime) (2010) *Globalization of Crime: A Transnational Organized Crime Threat Assessment.* Vienna: UN Office on Drugs and Crime.

Vollmer, B. (2008) *Undocumented Migration, Counting the Uncountable. Data and Trends across Europe: Country Report UK (revised July 2009).* Oxford: COMPAS. Available at: http://clandestino.eliamep.gr

Woodbridge, J. (2005) *Sizing the Unauthorised (Illegal) Migrant Population in the United Kingdom in 2001,* Online Report 29/05. London: Home Office.

6

Integration and citizenship

In previous chapters we looked at policy relating to migrants' entry into the UK. It was evident that people come for different (if overlapping) reasons and stay for differing lengths of time. Here we look at policy relating to the 1,500 people who on average arrive each day and plan to stay for at least a year (Home Office, 2010). The intense political debates on migrant numbers are fuelled by perceptions of their impacts after arrival. Yet policy relating to what happens to those who come to work, study or join family in the UK has been neglected and marginal to those debates. That requires some explanation.

More than in any other chapter we find a lack of coherence on policy across government and, crucial on this topic, between government at national and local level. In part, I shall argue, this is because of a lack of clarity on what is meant by 'integration' and hence the aims of policy intervention; and in part because the policy paradigm had its origins in the post-war era and has not adjusted to the migration patterns of modern times. More recently, integration was conveniently buried within the cohesion agenda. We shall see that EU policy and funding has only impinged in limited respects and that there has been some convergence with, but also departures from, policies in other EU countries. Each, in effect, faces the same questions: what are the aims of policy intervention, which policy levers could be used and which tier of government should be responsible? Should policy target only some of those who come and to what extent should the public, employers and civil society be valued partners in delivery?

In Chapter 1, we looked briefly at some of the insights from migration theory relevant to developing appropriate policy levers. It is equally worth taking a moment to see what we can learn from analyses of the integration processes in which migrants are engaged before turning to policy at EU level and then to national policy in the

UK. Although local strategies are also crucial in this field it is on the national policy framework that I necessarily focus here.

Why 'integration'?

The evolving relationship between migrants and the 'host society' is most commonly conceptualised in European academic and policy literature as 'integration'. That term is less accepted in the UK, carrying connotations of 'assimilation': an expectation that migrants will become culturally similar to the host population and, as a policy objective, that they should (Brubaker, 2001). In policy debates it is also not uncommon to find 'integration' used to refer to a characteristic of a group or individual, as in 'they are not well integrated'. Used in this way, the term implies that the onus is solely on migrants, overlooking any responsibility that the receiving society might have to address the barriers they may face, like discrimination. Integration is also sometimes used to refer to a characteristic of a society, as in 'Britain is one of the most integrated countries in the Western world' (Alibhai Brown, 2006).

Civil society and academic critics have often avoided using 'integration' because of this emphasis on race relations, cultural change and the agency of migrants rather than on the systemic barriers to participation that minorities can experience. That scepticism was reinforced when critics of multiculturalism, following terrorist attacks in London in 2005, advocated 'integration' as the antidote, encapsulated by Prime Minister Blair in a speech entitled 'The Duty to Integrate: Shared British Values' (Blair, 2006; Kundani, 2007: 123). Critics have struggled, however, to find an alternative term. Inclusion, for instance, has sometimes been used at the local level because it chimed with the mainstream social exclusion agenda (WMSMP, 2009: 3). Inclusion, however, implies enclosure within – not the two-way process of mutual change in which migrants are engaged.

I use integration here because of a lack of an acceptable alternative and because, as used by scholars in continental Europe, it does not focus exclusively on cultural change or community relations; nor solely on the migrant's role. Rather, integration is understood as a process engaging not only migrants but also the institutions and people among whom they live. It is the nature of the interaction between the migrant and society that has been found to determine the outcome of the process, but the two players are unequal in terms of power and resources: 'The receiving society, its institutional structure and its reactions to newcomers are consequently far more decisive for the outcome of the process than the immigrants themselves' (Penninx and Martiniello, 2004: 142).

Equally significant for policy intervention is the analysis that integration is not a single process but takes place across economic, social, cultural and political domains (Entzinger, 2000; Heckman et al, 2006). In broad terms we can define these as:

- *Structural:* participation in the labour and housing markets and in social institutions such as education and health care. Here organisations, from public agencies to small employers, are key players and the opportunities they provide or barriers they erect are influential in integration outcomes.
- *Social:* processes of interaction between migrants and non-migrants within and beyond the workplace and social institutions.
- *Cultural:* changes in values and behaviour; including attitudes and behaviour *towards* migrants.
- *Civic and political:* participation in community life and the democratic process.
- *Identity:* the process that enables individuals, notwithstanding differing cultural backgrounds, beliefs and identities, to feel at some level that they can identify with the neighbourhood or country in which, and people among whom, they are living.

In this chapter, I therefore use the term integration to mean: processes of interaction between migrants and the individuals and institutions of the receiving society that facilitate economic, social, cultural, and civic participation and an inclusive sense of belonging at the national and local level.

Underpinning participation in each domain are migrants' legal rights: whether they are permitted to work, to access public services and to vote, for instance, and their responsibilities. Whether the legal framework is inclusive or exclusive thus has significant implications for integration outcomes (Spencer, 2006a).

Integration processes: what do we know?

Comparative studies in Europe reveal similarities in the experiences of migrants from different countries of origin but also differences between and within migrant groups, not least between men and women: there is no single integration experience (Kofman and Phizacklea, 2000; Vermeulen and Penninx, 2000). Significantly, a positive experience in one domain is not necessarily mirrored in another. An individual may be securely employed for instance but have little social interaction, nor identify with their local area (Spencer and Cooper, 2006; Rutter et al, 2008).

In designing policy levers, it is helpful to clarify that there are three sets of factors known to facilitate or impede integration processes:

- *Factors relating to the migrant:* including reasons for migration; education; skill level and previous work experience; proficiency in English; age; knowledge of the ways in which the labour market and services operate; and motivation. Migrants' social and community networks also play a role in access to jobs and services (Castles, 2001; Kloosterman and Rath, 2003). Evidence on the relative importance of these factors is an essential foundation for policy intervention. We know for instance that language proficiency is strongly associated with the probability of being employed (Dustmann et al, 2003) and that migrants with poor English are least likely to have the practical information they need on arrival, to feel well treated by British people or to mix with them socially (Spencer et al, 2007).
- *Factors relating to the society:* determining whether there are opportunities open to migrants in relation to the labour market, accommodation, social and civic participation. At different points

in the economic cycle and in differing localities there may or may not be jobs that match their skills. Accommodation and other resources may be scarce; local institutions may be more or less open to participation by newcomers; and neighbours may be welcoming, distant or hostile. The history of migration into a neighbourhood, its current ethnic profile and lack of experience of migrants among local service providers have been found among the relevant factors at the local level (Waters and Jimenez, 2005; Robinson and Reeve, 2006; SC Communities and Local Government, 2008: 13).

• *Policy interventions:* including generic policies covering all residents and targeted measures such as language tuition, specialist health care and local information packs; measures to address discrimination and public hostility; dispersal to areas ill equipped to meet migrants' needs (Phillimore and Goodson, 2008a); and rules that allow or restrict migrants' access to work and services.

Looking at migrant inequality in the employment domain in particular, we find 10 causal factors identified, including language proficiency, discrimination, length of residence, lack of knowledge of job-seeking processes, poor health and immigration status. Migrants found the service at Jobcentre Plus poorly tailored to their needs (Rutter et al, 2008). An earlier study of barriers to refugees' labour market participation found language, lack of UK work experience, lack of qualifications and employer discrimination to be the principal factors (Bloch, 2004). The overall employment rate of the foreign-born is 67%, not far short of 73.5% for the UK-born (data for the first quarter of 2010; ONS, 2010); but the far lower employment rates of those born in countries such as Bangladesh and Somalia can be masked by the high rates of white migrants (Dustmann and Fabbri, 2005; Cangiano, 2007: Table 1).

It is striking that, beyond employment, evidence on outcomes for migrants, as opposed to ethnic minorities, is not routinely monitored. Even within employment there are significant gaps in knowledge essential for any integration strategy, such as the impacts of those labour market programmes for which migrants are eligible (Cangiano, 2007).

The most comprehensive review of inequality ever commissioned by government was not asked to include the foreign-born within its focus (NEP, 2010). There is an active debate on the way in which indicators can be used to measure integration, their limitations (eg in regularly omitting measures of adaptation by the host society) and the paucity of data available in practice to conduct the analysis (Entzinger and Biezeveld, 2003; Ager and Strang, 2004; Carrera, 2008; Phillimore and Goodson, 2008b; Niessen et al, 2009).

Models of policy intervention

Integration processes take place regardless of policy intervention. Migrants may find jobs, access public services and develop a sense of attachment to their neighbourhood without the benefit of any targeted policy measures, but policy may facilitate (or hinder) that process. The question is what forms of intervention are most likely to foster that participation and what level of resources should be invested, by and for whom. We might expect that some aspects of integration will be more susceptible to policy intervention than others.

There is a whole body of literature exploring why countries have different 'philosophies of integration', including differing traditions in the roles of public bodies and of welfare states (Favell, 2001b). Typologies often characterise countries as having clearly defined models: the French as 'assimilationist', for instance, and the UK as 'multicultural'. Evidence suggests that there may have been strengths and weaknesses in the differing approaches across integration domains: France more successful in encouraging migrant youth to identify as French, for instance, but weak on labour market integration, Germany stronger on access to jobs and training, but weak on identification (Heckman et al, 2001).

In recent times, interventions have nevertheless been more similar than those dichotomies suggest (Ireland, 2004). Policies are responding to similar pressures and interventions have shown some convergence at the national and local level: in narrowing the gap between rights enjoyed by citizens and long-term residents, for instance, and in combating discrimination (Niessen, 2001: 31). A common feature has been policy shifts in reaction to events and to address what are perceived to be failures of earlier approaches (Doormernik, 2003). It is also common to find a gap between national policies and those at the local level where the social and economic situation may be different from that in the capital and local politicians develop their own approach (Castles et al, 2002; Ireland, 2004; Penninx and Martiniello, 2004).

Nevertheless, there remain four differences in emphasis across Europe that are reflected in recent policy shifts in the UK:

• whether policy focuses on individuals or minority communities;
• whether the priority is economic, social or cultural integration;
• which categories of migrant are the target of policy intervention; and
• whether participation in language and civic courses is voluntary or required.

Focus on individuals or minority communities?

Some European governments have, to an extent, pursued multicultural policies that see value in diverse cultural traditions, recognise ethnic (and recently faith) communities and give this recognition some institutional form (Vertovec and Wessendorf, 2010: 3). Arrangements are made to consult minority communities and minor adjustments made in law to accommodate cultural or religious differences, in relation to burial arrangements for instance. Legislation to tackle discrimination does so on the basis of an individual's membership of a group defined by race, religion or belief and data is collected on that basis to provide an evidence base.

Advocates of this approach argue that valuing cultural heritage provides a positive identity and community support to individuals who are making their way in a sometimes hostile environment. It recognises that group membership is a factor in the way an individual is treated; while collecting data according to group membership makes it possible to implement effective anti-discrimination legislation. The rights of communities can be balanced against the right not to be part of that community (Commission on the Future of Multi-Ethnic Britain, 2000: para 3.26), and respect for cultural traditions is not to be hidebound by them:

> Multicultural integration policies support neither the crossing of boundaries from one culture to another, as do assimilation policies, nor the preservation of those boundaries, as does segregation, but aim to foster their permeability. (Spencer and Rudiger, 2003)

Critics counter that a multicultural approach can nevertheless overemphasise group differences, create vested interests in local ethnic political groupings, give too much power to patriarchal community leaders and reinforce what divides rather than what we have in common. It can ossify cultural practices that would otherwise adapt over time, pigeonhole individuals into an identity that may play a small part in their lives and encourage solidarity around ethnicity rather than political ideals. To some critics, its raison d'etre is less the protection of rights, than the maintenance of public order through managing relations between majority and minority populations (Favell, 2001a, 2001b; Ireland, 2004; Malik, 2005).

These concerns contributed to a serious questioning of multiculturalism in the UK in the past decade (Alibhai Brown, 2000; Goodhart, 2004; Phillips, 2005), reflected in Labour's community cohesion agenda and, in reform of access to citizenship, in its emphasis on strengthening the direct relationship between the individual and the state.

Priority for intervention: economic, social or cultural integration?

Across Europe, policy prioritises some domains of integration more than others. States operating temporary labour schemes, for instance, may place little emphasis on migrants' social integration, even though the migrants live within the community and may in practice remain long term (Entzinger, 2000). Equally, a focus on integration in the labour market may neglect public attitudes towards migrants; or a focus on cultural integration may neglect access to jobs and services. Within the cultural domain, the degree to which shared norms are in fact necessary may be overemphasised (Bader, 2001) and the extent to which it is appropriate for the state to intervene to secure that goal is open to challenge. Policies relating to separate domains can also be uncoordinated or contradictory. In part this happens because strategies lack clear goals or are subject to competing departmental objectives (Zetter et al, 2002).

Which migrants?

On the first day that a migrant arrives, he or she is embarking on a process of integration into the UK's economic, social and cultural life. If the visit is a short one, it is a process that will not proceed far. If it is a permanent stay, it may continue until they participate across all domains. A key question is whether all these new migrants should be the focus of integration policies and, if not, to whom intervention should be directed.

Across Europe, it is common to find a strong focus on refugees and/ or family migrants (though not the latter in the UK), while those who have come for work may also receive some support in improving their language and job skills. Mobile EU citizens are not seen as 'migrants', however (and cannot, therefore, be beneficiaries of EU-supported integration initiatives), despite facing many of the same challenges. The focus of EU and UK integration measures is invariably limited to legal migrants, although some European cities provide services to those with irregular status or fund non-governmental organisations (NGOs) to do so (CLIP, 2008) and the integration processes in which they are effectively engaged cannot be ignored (see Chapter 5). UK interventions have focused on those remaining in the long term, while EU debates increasingly recognise that temporary residents may face some of the greatest challenges.

Voluntary or compulsory?

A number of European states have recently required non-European migrants to demonstrate language skills and civic knowledge and/or to engage in integration programmes, some with compulsory testing. EU law and policy does not preclude this approach, including pre-entry testing as a condition of entry. Compulsion was first evident in relation to language and civic orientation courses for new arrivals (Spencer and Di Mattia, 2004). The Netherlands was the first EU country to expect migrants to start the integration process *before* departure, basic knowledge of the Dutch language and society being required as a condition of entry for family migrants from 2006. The test and substantial accompanying fee, it is argued, also has the implicit aim of reducing the number who enter (Carrera and Wiesbrock, 2009). Denmark is among those that have followed suit and, in relation to language proficiency, Germany and the UK (see later). We should bear in mind these differing approaches as we explore the development of integration policies first at EU level and then within the UK.

EU policy framework

Integration *per se* was not within the competency of the EU until the 2009 Lisbon Treaty. A limited role was nevertheless agreed from 2003 on the grounds that failure of one member state to implement a successful integration policy could have adverse implications elsewhere. A modest programme of activity has been underpinned by agreement on Common Basic Principles on Integration (CEU, 2004), significant despite having no legal force because they reflect a level of consensus on what is meant by integration and the shared responsibility of migrants, the state, employers and civil society to facilitate it. The 11 principles take as their premise that 'immigration is a permanent feature of European society' and that the successful integration of migrants is an essential part of managing migration effectively, but that member state policies and their target groups will differ. Integration is seen as 'a dynamic, long-term and continuous two way process of mutual accommodation' demanding the participation not only of immigrants but of 'every resident', and the onus is on states to create opportunities for immigrants' full economic, social, cultural and political participation (CEU, 2004).

Implementation of EU policy has been through sharing evidence on good practice, including handbooks focusing on key areas such as civic participation and a dedicated website launched in 2009 (European Commission, 2010). More significantly for the UK, a fund for the integration of third-country nationals (2007–2013, following an earlier Refugee Integration Fund) has supported a modest grant programme, while allowing most of it to be allocated to funding English language tuition (UKBA, 2008: 18). The Lisbon Treaty (Art 63a.4) now provides a mandate for measures 'to provide incentives and support' for integration but still only for third-country nationals. In a debate with resonance in the UK, it has been argued that responsibility for integration should be moved from the European Commission's (then) Justice, Freedom and Security directorate, where it sits alongside immigration and security issues, to directorates with more relevant competencies and resources, such as Employment and Social Affairs (Collett, 2009).

Aspects of earlier EU policy were already relevant to integration, notably those relating to employment and social inclusion. Most significant were the Race and Employment Directives in 2000 that required member states to make discrimination unlawful in relation to employment and, to an extent, in services. EU law thus provided a framework for addressing one of the significant barriers migrants can face. Discrimination was, however, the one dimension of integration policy that was already well developed in the UK.

UK policy development

Research across Europe has found that differences between national and local contexts, the short timescale in which politicians need to see 'results' and a political climate of hostility to migrants are among factors that limit integration policy options (Penninx and Martiniello, 2004).

National policy frameworks can be slow to adapt because institutional arrangements are anchored in a particular national ideology, leading to 'pathological' policy problems on which the political system finds it hard to think afresh (Favell, 2001a: 50).

We saw in Chapter 1 how racism marred the 1964 general election and that stark evidence of discrimination led the government to outlaw discrimination in public places and incitement to racial hatred in the first Race Relations Act of 1965. Citing the goal as 'integration', Home Secretary Roy Jenkins famously defined it as 'not a flattening process of assimilation but as equal opportunity accompanied by cultural diversity, in an atmosphere of mutual tolerance' (Rose et al, 1969: 25). The policy model that emerged, including rights to stand and vote in elections, ready access to citizenship and mechanisms for managing race relations through 'community leaders', was designed for a migrant population from a limited number of countries with historical links to the UK, expected to remain in the long term. It proved slow to adapt to the 'superdiversity' and greater mobility of migrants in recent years (Vertovec, 2007). The arrival of white migrants from Eastern Europe, in particular, revealed the 'conceptual emptiness of the old policy framework' (Favell, 2001a: 55).

Significantly, while the initial target of intervention was those who had arrived from abroad, it soon shifted to the second and subsequent generations. The necessity of separating policy relating to these British citizens from that relating to 'immigrants' has meant that policy towards ethnic minorities has been divorced from, and in Whitehall institutionally quite separate from, any policy relating to new arrivals. Moreover, while policy towards minorities retained a high political profile, policy relating to new migrants did not. With the partial exception of refugees, new migrants have been marginal to the policy agenda.

From anti-discrimination to a duty to advance equality

The early Race Relations Acts were, despite their limitations, path-breaking measures to address discrimination. From the first Act in 1965, the law was strengthened over time to cover direct and indirect discrimination in relation to jobs, goods, facilities and services; and from 2000 to require the 43,000 public bodies in Britain, from government departments through to schools and hospitals, to promote equality and good race relations, a duty subsequently extended to disability and gender.

In practice, the 'race equality duty', like the earlier anti-discrimination measures, has largely been used to address issues relating to ethnic minorities rather than recent migrants (McCarvill, 2011). Although the term 'racial' in the Race Relations Act means 'colour, race, nationality, ethnic or national origins', its relevance to people from abroad facing discrimination on the basis of nationality or national origins has received little attention. The Commission for Racial Equality (CRE), established to promote and enforce the Act, had the power to investigate the operation of immigration control but migrants were never central to its agenda (Dummett and Nicol, 1990: 252). The CRE's successor, the Equality and Human Rights Commission, has shown greater interest in embracing them within its remit.

An EU Directive and pressure from Muslim communities prompted government to extend the law to discrimination on grounds of religion or belief. The Equality Act 2010 subsequently went further in providing a single duty on public bodies to advance equality on all grounds and to promote good community relations. That duty is potentially a powerful means to ensure that public bodies, in their employment and service provision, advance equality for all residents, including migrants. Yet the intentional exclusion of some migrants from full access to jobs and services, on the basis of their immigration status, may leave public bodies unsure as to whether the duty to advance equality should embrace this section of the community or not.

Equality for whom? Legal restrictions on access to jobs and services

While new migrants are entitled to civil rights such as freedom of speech as soon as they arrive, for many – as we have seen – the law restricts access to jobs, services, social housing, welfare benefits and voting: a pattern of restrictions that has developed ad hoc with no clear rationale. Migrant children can nevertheless attend state schools and there are no restrictions on using services such as public libraries or emergency health care. The result is complex, different categories of migrant having differing entitlements depending on their immigration status, country of origin and length of residence in the UK (Spencer and Pobjoy, 2011).

This pattern of inclusion and exclusion reflects a tension between the benefits to individuals, the economy and society of allowing access, and competing political and fiscal pressures to restrict it. Services such as English language tuition contribute to employability, and exclusion from a service can prove counterproductive: for instance, use of hospital emergency services when treatment by a GP would have been more cost-effective. Human rights obligations have constrained attempts to limit access in some cases (see Chapter 2); and government has seen a strong public health rationale for allowing all migrants to have access to treatment for communicable diseases (see Chapter 5). Nevertheless, provision incurs costs, not least if migrants have particular needs such as for an interpreter.

Underlying the tension between inclusion and exclusion can also be a difference of view as to whether entitlement should be on the basis of need or long-term residence or 'belonging'. Social housing is the service that, rationed for all residents, most acutely highlights the implications of that choice. Where long-term residents wait long periods to access suitable accommodation, ill feeling may be generated if migrants are perceived to 'jump the queue' (Dench et al, 2006). Yet assessment of entitlement solely at the local level is not possible when migration contributes disproportionately to the national public purse, while having social costs that are concentrated among residents competing in a 'scarcity auction' for social housing at the local level (Keith, 2008). Government estimates that only 6% of social housing lettings to new tenants went to foreign nationals in 2006/07. Nevertheless, 'people feel very strongly about these issues, which go to the heart of their sense of fairness' (CLG, 2008b: 24). The fact that most new migrants are ineligible for social housing and that there is evidence of extreme housing need has not resolved that tension for which the underlying cause is the shortage of accommodation (SC Communities and Local Government, 2008: 18; Robinson, 2010a).

Despite the significance of health, education and housing services in particular to integration processes, and the emphasis on advancing equality for ethnic minorities, government has not developed an evidence base on the impact of excluding migrants from these key services. Evidence on their implications should be part of any review of the efficacy of the current policy framework.

Targeted integration strategy: refugees only

Recognition of the importance of jobs and services to new migrants has indeed been the rationale for the only targeted integration strategy that the UK has seen: for refugees. Reflecting the rise in refugee numbers and evidence of poor education, health and employment outcomes, the catalyst for *Full and Equal Citizens* (Home Office, 2000) was the availability of a new EU funding stream, the Refugee Integration Fund. Politically, it also served as a positive counterweight to the increasingly negative measures being taken to deter asylum seekers (Spencer, 2007). The aim was to help refugees secure access to jobs, accommodation, benefits, health, education and language services and to encourage community participation, all cited as key factors in 'the integration process'. But there was no question of extending it to other migrants: "The assumption was that if coming to the UK is planned then you would be better prepared. But at the time it wasn't discussed if it should be a broader strategy".[1]

A National Refugee Integration Forum with strong NGO participation was set up to identify barriers to integration and practical solutions (with a parallel arrangement in Scotland). Its work on employability was instrumental in the Department for Work and Pensions' own strategy, *Working to Rebuild Lives* (2003, revised in 2005), targeting practical assistance on refugees seeking to enter the labour market, including access to National Insurance numbers, employment training and adaptation of professional qualifications obtained abroad. Significantly, this labour market focus in particular has never been replicated for other migrants (Cangiano, 2007).

The emphasis in the strategy was on opportunities for refugees to develop their potential, moving to self-sufficiency through work and inclusion in community life, with assurance that 'inclusion in our society does not mean that a refugee is required to assimilate' (Home Office, 1999: para 2.3). Revised in 2005, at the end of a decade in which more than 250,000 people had been granted refugee status or exceptional leave to remain (Home Office, 2005) it was sold to the press as a strategy to ensure that refugees contribute to the UK. It nevertheless remained focused on opportunity not compulsion and, significantly, defined integration as:

> the process that takes place when refugees are empowered to achieve their full potential as members of British society, to contribute to the community, and to become fully able to exercise the rights and responsibilities that they share with other residents. (Home Office, 2005: 6)

Noting barriers such as lack of access to training, the aim was a personalised service in which refugees' needs were assessed so that they could be signposted to relevant services. From 2008, a Refugee Integration and Employment Service was established to provide a 12-month advice, employment support and mentoring service but the level of support provided, including that given to refugees on the Gateway programme (see Chapter 2), has never proved sufficient to address the disproportionate unemployment or broader challenges they experience (Phillimore and Goodson, 2008a; Evans and Murray, 2009).

Government insistence on the exclusion of asylum seekers from the strategy has also been a significant concern. NGO critics insist that the integration process starts when the claim for asylum is made and that access to language support, decent housing and health care is critical to the longer term: a difference of view that reflects the tension between the Home Office's overarching concern to limit asylum numbers and competing integration objectives (Refugee Council, 2009).

It is not only asylum seekers that have been excluded, however, but migrants who come to work, for family reasons or to study. There has thus been no review of the evidence on the barriers they experience, or consultation on how they might similarly be empowered to achieve their full potential as members of British society. A government review of the language requirements for accessing citizenship in 2003 did argue that more should be done to foster the integration of new migrants (Life in the UK Advisory Group, 2002, 2003). Ministers, however, had no appetite for a broader strategy: "There was no money to do something for new arrivals. Ministerial level discussion agreed that we would start with those applying for citizenship and work back from there".[2]

English language proficiency

In the absence of a broader strategy for newcomers, expansion of English language tuition – through increased demand rather than strategic intention – is the principal means through which integration can be said to have been fostered. The central government budget contributing directly to integration in 2008 was estimated to be £350 million, of which more than £250 million was for English language courses (UKBA, 2008: 16–17). A level of English language proficiency is widely recognised as critical for those supporting families, accessing services, employability and communicating with the wider community (DIUS, 2009: 7). The cost of provision, however, raises the question of who should pay, whether learning English should be voluntary or required (before or after arrival), whether it should be a priority for those whose residence is only temporary, and whether translation of information into migrant languages reduces the incentive to learn English (Audit Commission, 2007; SC Communities and Local Government, 2008: 42).

Access to education for children has been the service in which the importance of universal access has effectively outweighed counter-pressures. The principal challenge for schools is language support for the rising number of children for whom English is an additional language and the range of first languages spoken. From the 1960s, additional resources have been provided, latterly through an Ethnic Minority Achievement Grant (CLG, 2008b: 7). Schools can also be affected by unanticipated increases in pupil numbers and 'churn' during the school year and by the needs of parents unfamiliar with the UK school system (Audit Commission, 2007).

For adults there is no separate introductory language programme for newcomers as in some European countries. Migrants may attend mainstream English for Speakers of Other Languages (ESOL) classes, or a combined 'language with civic content' course. The increased demand for tuition following EU enlargement in 2004, coupled with requirements on applicants for citizenship to pass a language test (see later), led to increased provision and expenditure more than tripled between 2001 and 2008/09 while still failing to meet demand. To cut costs, asylum seekers in the UK for less than six months were excluded from fee remission from 2007 as were those on 'no recourse to public funds' (Phillimore and Goodson, 2008a).

Women from low-income families and low-paid workers were among those most affected (NIACE, 2008; SC Communities and Local Government, 2008: 39). Critics argued that the cutbacks would make it more difficult for those no longer eligible to become self-sufficient and to qualify for citizenship. Those who have entered the UK as spouses do not qualify for free language tuition in their first year, for instance, yet may have started a family or entered work during that period, reducing their subsequent availability for classes. Moreover, the earlier tuition starts, the quicker English is learnt and delay leads to additional costs if translation and interpreters are needed. The expert agency on adult education, the National Institute of Adult and Continuing Education (NIACE), argues that all those with language skills below ESOL level 1 should at least be entitled to free provision until they reach that level (NIACE, 2008).

There has been a long-term concern that those working shifts or anti-social hours find it difficult to access tuition. More than two thirds of those who speak little English on arrival do not take English classes (Bloch, 2002: Table 4.3; Spencer et al, 2007). An inquiry in 2006 found the quality of some teaching to be substandard and a lack of qualified teachers in parts of the country (Grover, 2006). Research also found provision to be insufficiently vocational and to offer little opportunity for the highly skilled to attain a necessary level of English to work in their profession. Failure to employ learning as a tool for integration means migrants have limited opportunities to develop their employability (Phillimore and Goodson, 2008a: 112). At the time of writing, it is unclear what impact further public expenditure cuts in 2011 may have on the capacity of ESOL provision to meet demand.

Sharing the cost: employers

The cost of tuition raises the question whether employers who benefit from migrant labour should contribute. Labour argued that they bear some responsibility but was reluctant to insist:

> Where employers fail to support English language training they are effectively externalizing the costs of employing migrant workers onto local services in their area. Businesses clearly benefit from a well integrated work-force that can speak English. Employers should look to include English language training as a part of creating a successful long-term sustainable business which adds value to the community. (CLG, 2008b: 33)

Some employers do take steps to facilitate integration, encouraged to do so by a Business in the Community Code of Practice on 'how they can make migrant workers feel welcome and ... integrate more effectively into their workplace and the community' (BIC,

2008: 2). Nevertheless, many are unable or unwilling to provide language training: 'Widespread employer buy-in has not been secured through the prevailing system of voluntarism and exhortation' (NIACE, 2008: para 45).

Pre-entry English requirements

Concern that migrants should have sufficient English on arrival led to a requirement that labour migrants have a level of proficiency in speaking, reading and writing English before coming to the UK. More controversially those coming on the basis of marriage or civil partnership are now also required to speak some English before arrival (UKBA, 2009). The level required is said to need 40–50 hours of tuition and is justified in terms of future employability and savings to the taxpayer of translation services. The UK is not alone in taking this route, Denmark, Germany and the Netherlands, for instance, all having done so. Nevertheless, there is limited access to English classes in some regions of the world and those who are not literate in their own language or cannot afford classes may struggle to reach the level required. Hence they will not be able to join their families in the UK (see Chapter 4).

Community cohesion agenda

The absence of a broader strategy to promote integration can in part be explained by Labour's heavy focus after 2001 on community cohesion, notwithstanding that its target group only latterly included migrants. The driver of cohesion policy was disturbances in northern towns in the summer of 2001. A subsequent inquiry was:

> struck by the depth of polarisation in our towns and cities....
> Separate educational arrangements, community and voluntary
> bodies, employment, places of worship, language, social and
> cultural networks, mean that many communities operate on

the basis of a series of parallel lives. (Cantle and Community Cohesion Review Team, 2001)

The target of concern was second-generation ethnic minority youth, not newcomers to the UK. The agenda that emerged, resonating with critiques of multiculturalism, emphasised contact across community divides, civic participation and a shared sense of belonging based on common goals and shared values (Home Office, 2001). The focus was on addressing ethnic divides rather than the economic inequalities that underlay them (Flint and Robinson, 2008). Within weeks of the disturbances, the events of 9/11 in New York had added a security dimension to the agenda, reinforced by the London bombings of July 2005, but the focus was the radicalisation of British-born people. When the Department for Communities and Local Government (CLG), now responsible for the cohesion agenda, published its 152-page progress report the following year, reference to migrants merited less than a page (CLG, 2006). There was by then a lively debate on whether the diversity brought by migration undermined social solidarity and support for the welfare state, a 'progressive dilemma' that meant supporters of the welfare state could not simultaneously support high levels of migration (Goodhart, 2004). Nevertheless, the thrust of the argument was for less migration, not for measures to promote the integration of those already in the UK. Empirical evidence also cast doubt on the underlying claim (Banting and Kymlicka, 2006; Evans, 2006).

The relevance of migration to the cohesion agenda was however brought to the fore by the Commission on Integration and Cohesion (CIC), established to explore ways in which empowerment of local communities could build capacity to prevent and address community tensions (CIC, 2007a). The timing, following a major terrorist attack in London in 2005, was no coincidence. Nevertheless, the CIC struck a new tone in taking as its starting point that 80% of the public think people in their area get on well together, and challenged claims that Britain was 'sleepwalking to segregation' (see also Finney and Simpson, 2009). It also questioned the narrow focus of the cohesion agenda on the 'parallel lives' scenario, arguing that the causes of community tension differ. Competition for limited public resources could, for instance, create community divides if there was a perception that migrants were receiving special treatment to which longer-term residents were denied.

The CIC saw integration as a process running in parallel to cohesion, defining it as 'the process that ensures new residents and existing residents adapt to one another' (CIC, 2007b: 9). Nevertheless, and to that end, it argued that it was in the UK's interests for migrants – whether temporary or permanent – to be able to participate fully in the labour market and in their local communities. Identifying a series of 'barriers to integration', from lack of information and advice through non-recognition of qualifications to public hostility, it noted that there was no single place in Government responsible for helping to address those barriers. Support of migrants was falling by default to local areas, leading to ad hoc local initiatives and some duplication of effort with no central guidance. All levels of government should do more, supported by an independent agency with a remit to foster economic, social and political participation: a source of evidence and guidance on good practice that could support local practitioners, 'secure buy-in' from Whitehall and the third sector, and act as a catalyst for policy development. Alongside action to address the concerns of settled communities, it advocated local contracts, in which new migrants would register at their local town hall and be given information and advice, there being a need to find creative ways to provide 'cultural briefing' on the norms and expectations particular to local areas (CIC, 2007b: paras 5.24–5.45).

'Integration' subsumed within cohesion

In its response, however, the government rejected the call for a broad integration agenda, subsuming 'integration' within the good relations parameters of cohesion:

> Community cohesion is what must happen in all communities
> to enable different groups of people to get on well together. A

key contributor to community cohesion is integration which is what must happen to enable new residents and existing residents to adjust to one another. (CLG, 2008a: para 1.3)

That definition of integration bears little resemblance to that we saw in the Home Office's Refugee Integration Strategy, with its emphasis on the empowerment of refugees to achieve their full potential, a distinction recognised by UKBA:

"There is a much narrower definition of integration in CLG. It is seen as people getting on, as a subset of cohesion. It is a slightly different focus from the UKBA perspective. We recognise that integration takes place at different levels. We have a sharp focus on language and on knowledge of life in the UK, and a stronger focus on support for the individual whereas CLG are looking at the big picture, and the big picture is cohesion."[3]

Defining integration in this way enabled CLG to fit the language of integration within its existing agendas, not only cohesion but a related issue that hit the radar of CLG after enlargement of the EU in 2004: the impacts of migration on local services:

"CLG ministers were not trying to make a grab for migration policy. They didn't want to take on the responsibilities of other departments. But there were two things that were not covered – community impacts and coordination. So CLG took that on. The implicit assumption was that someone else was dealing with support for newcomers. It wasn't their job."[4]

Focus on impacts of migration at the local level

The government had not anticipated the significant number of 'A8' migrants that would come to the UK following enlargement of the EU. No consideration was given to the implications for services or to wider steps to facilitate integration. Yet EU citizens can experience many of the same challenges as other migrants (Markova and Black, 2007; Spencer et al, 2007a).

Local service providers complained that they had insufficient resources to address the additional demands placed on them, in part because data on local population numbers (on which eligibility for funding is based) did not take account of recent changes. Had there been any overarching strategy for migration it might have been anticipated that investment in public services would need to keep pace, but there was no mechanism for forward planning of that kind. The Audit Commission found unanticipated numbers of East European children in schools, overcrowded housing posing health and safety risks, community tensions (for instance, in relation to rubbish disposal), and service providers facing communication barriers in meeting the needs of newcomers (Audit Commission, 2007).

Guidance was provided for local authorities on good practice (IDEA, 2010) and a fund resourced by visa fees was established to support service providers. However, it was deemed a 'drop in the ocean' by a parliamentary Select Committee which heard that Westminster City Council, one of those most affected, would receive a maximum of £120,000 a year and some authorities less than the amount needed to fund one full-time post (SC Communities and Local Government, 2008: 110, 129). A Migrants Impacts Forum brought local government, police and other stakeholders together "to get grass roots evidence and so that government could be seen to be listening",[5] but it was a less substantial initiative than the Migration Advisory Committee advising on labour migration (see Chapter 3) and, in the event, short-lived.

Fragmented responsibility in Whitehall

CLG's new interest in migration meant that there were now two loci of responsibility for migrants: its own focus on cohesion and the impacts of migration at the local level and the Home Office responsibility for refugee integration and for citizenship. A small Migration Directorate was established in CLG which, following an internal review, rejected the CIC's view that an external integration agency was needed. While it found that there was no strategy drawing together relevant activity across government, it was confident that it could now ensure 'a stronger narrative and greater coherence of government policy around migrant integration' if resourced to do so (CLG, 2008c: 8). At the time, the Migration Directorate had just 15 staff. Within the year it had been absorbed into the Cohesion Directorate.

A Select Committee inquiry on the impact of migration on cohesion in 2008 noted the lack of any policy or guidance on what action is needed for the integration of short-term economic migrants. It reflected on the 'myriad' of departments involved, the Audit Commission's view that local authorities did not always know where to go for information and that there was evidence of conflicting approaches within government. However, if any national strategy emerged:

> Central Government should not dictate to local authorities what practice should be adopted locally. Rather, the role of central government should be to set a national policy framework for action on integration and community cohesion, and provide guidance and support to others, particularly local government. (SC Communities and Local Government, 2008: 33–43)

The Select Committee's remit was the impact of migration on communities and integration was considered through that prism. Had the starting point been integration across socio-economic, cultural and civic domains, the barriers to integration they explored and the range of interventions identified to address them would necessarily have been much broader. In the absence of that analysis, the government resolved with the Select Committee's blessing that leadership on 'integration' should be split between CLG and the Home Office but gave neither the mandate or the resources to fulfil that role.

Citizenship and civic participation

Back at the Home Office, policy had been developed for migrants intending to remain in the long term: on access to British citizenship and to the permanent residence status that preceded it, Indefinite Leave to Remain (ILR). Until 2004, the UK had had a laissez-faire policy towards citizenship, the Nationality Act 1981 allowing those with long-term residence rights to apply after five years in the UK and to retain the citizenship of another country (dual citizenship): 'A low-key, private and bureaucratic process' (UKBA, 2008: 13). Access to citizenship was not used instrumentally to foster integration: applications were not encouraged, nor were new citizens provided with any symbolic acknowledgement of their new status, in contrast to the citizenship ceremonies popular in Canada, the US and Australia.

Home Secretary David Blunkett saw that as a wasted opportunity: access to citizenship was a lever that could be used to encourage civic participation and a sense of belonging to the wider community. He proposed that acquisition of citizenship should be celebrated in civic citizenship ceremonies but should also be a little harder to achieve: applicants required to provide, from 2004, evidence of a level of English language proficiency. Applicants would also (from 2005) be expected to demonstrate some knowledge about life in the UK in order to 'develop a sense of civic identity and shared values' (Home Office, 2002). An Advisory Board on Naturalisation and Integration (ABNI) provided guidance on the tests and on citizenship ceremonies. It argued that its integration remit should be extended to cover those newly arrived in the UK but was abolished in 2008 (ABNI, 2008).

While the threshold for access to citizenship had been raised, the intention was not to limit the numbers achieving that goal. It was desirable that long-term residents eligible to apply for citizenship should do so, the incentive of citizenship status thus being used to lever some improvement in English and knowledge of life in the UK. Those requirements were extended to applicants for settlement in 2007. More failed the test than anticipated in the early years, an average pass rate until 2007 of 67% (UKBA, 2008: 14). Moreover, pass rates near or below 50% for a dozen countries, including Iraq, Bangladesh and Turkey, were masked by the success of those from English-speaking countries; thus the consequences for family migrants and refugees may have been greater than for labour migrants (Ryan, 2008).

Figure 6.1: Grants of British citizenship (1990–2009)

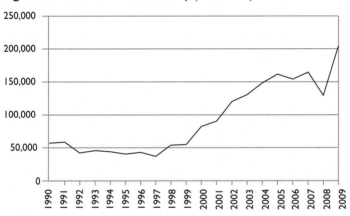

Source: Home Office British Citizenship Statistics UK 2009 (2010: Supplementary Table A)

Earned citizenship

Grants of British citizenship nevertheless rose to 165,000 in 2007 (see Figure 6.1), amongst the highest levels in Europe (Eurostat, 2009). Whether or not in response to that trend, the threshold was raised. Where citizenship had been seen as a means to promote integration, it must now be seen to be earned, with applicants demonstrating an economic and social contribution through volunteering and evidence of tax and law abidance. A new stage of 'probationary citizenship' (Borders, Citizenship and Immigration Act 2009) would, from 2011, lengthen the time taken to acquire full citizenship, during which time access to benefits and services would now be restricted (Home Office, 2008). This extended period would allow the individual 'to demonstrate their commitment to the UK and earn the privileges of citizenship' and in so doing improve public perception of the contributions migrants can make (UKBA, 2008: 21; 2009: Annex A). A 'good character' requirement for citizenship had already been tightened up in 2008, excluding those who have all but the most minor conviction for an offence that is not 'spent'. A more radical proposal to refuse or delay citizenship for those whose children committed criminal offences was dropped (Thorp and Garton Grimwood, 2009). Students, temporary workers and those on youth mobility schemes do not, as before, have access to citizenship status.

The reforms proved controversial in Parliament, in particular the extent to which details on implementation had been left to ministerial discretion, the additional complexity of the rules on access to benefits and the criminal justice connotations of the term 'probation' (Thorp and Garton Grimwood, 2009). Beyond Parliament, critics questioned the assumption that migrants should necessarily want to be British, the logic of establishing further obstacles to that status and the ever-present threat 'that one slip may take you off the ladder and out of the country' (Dummett, 2008). The inclusion of a particular form of social participation, 'active citizenship', raised concern that increasingly prescriptive integration requirements would deny opportunities to those who fail:

> The paradox of this strategy is that, in the name of integration, migrants are left either with an inferior legal status, or are simply excluded from the UK altogether. The focus of integration policy is no longer on the equalisation of opportunity, but rather on the discouragement and

penalization of migrants who do not possess certain attributes. (Ryan, 2008)

Labour intended, nevertheless, to go further, regulating access to probationary citizenship through a points system designed, in particular, to limit access for labour migrants, now deemed necessary 'to manage population growth'. External lobbying had contributed to that shift in emphasis:

> "The size of the population is now part of the discussion. Migration Watch has contributed to that thinking. They are very wised up with their statistics, a powerful lobby group and influential with the media and through them with the public. Ministers are aware of that."[6]

Labour migrants would be awarded points for such factors as earning potential and having worked in regions such as Scotland in need of further immigration, while points would be deducted for anti-social behaviour 'or in circumstances where an active disregard for UK values is demonstrated' (UKBA, 2009: Exec Summary, para 10). Those who did not secure sufficient points for probationary citizenship would have to leave the UK once their visa had expired. Formal consultation found limited enthusiasm for the proposals and questioned the potential fairness of the system, but public polling found greater support (UKBA, 2010a).

What had arguably begun as an attempt to celebrate acquisition of citizenship without accentuating the divide between citizens and non-citizens, had become an attempt to create an inclusive civic Britishness for those who earn that status at the expense of those who do not. The Coalition government will not pursue the 'complicated, bureaucratic and ineffective' earned citizenship policy but nevertheless believes it is 'too easy' to move from temporary residence to permanent settlement (UKBA, 2010b). No doubt further measures will follow. Rather than reinforce a divide between citizens, permanent residents and non-citizens, an inclusive sense of identity could alternatively be forged on the basis of shared experiences, common interests and equal participation, while addressing the underlying causes of insecurity for which migrants get the blame: 'Citizenship and a sense of belonging cannot be built on nationalism but must be based on some common form of social, economic and democratic equality' (Lawson, 2008: 10). Evidence from local campaigns in which British citizens are strongly supportive of migrants suggests that policy could be designed to build solidarity rather than to create further divides (Squire, 2009).

Civic participation

While the citizenship reforms were intended to encourage volunteering, there has been little attempt to bring migrants within successive governments' broader civic participation agendas.

A review of integration policies across Europe did rate the UK favourably in relation to political participation: allowing migrants to join political parties and form associations that can attract public funds and granting more generous rights to vote and stand for election than in many EU states. Only in its lack of any formal mechanisms for consulting migrants or their associations did it score 0% (Niessen et al, 2007: 185). The UK does indeed allow citizens of Commonwealth countries to vote in national and local elections and EU citizens in local and European elections. The former arose historically from the UK's relationship with its colonies, the latter a requirement of membership of the EU. Neither thus derives from an intention to foster integration but, in allowing participation in the democratic process, has contributed to that goal. Beyond elections, the failure of many UK institutions to engage effectively with migrant community organisations has been documented, although there are instances where they have succeeded in shifting policy agendas (Anderson, 2010; Phillimore and Goodson, 2010).

Integration policy: whose responsibility?

We saw in Chapter 1 that fragmentation of responsibility between tiers of government can inhibit coherent policymaking and implementation. In relation to integration, we see not only the consequences of fragmentation in Whitehall but lack of consensus on the respective roles of central and local government.

There has been a strong view, reflected by the Select Committee that reported on migration and cohesion in 2008, that integration is primarily a local responsibility. Many issues are indeed most effectively addressed at that level: the Select Committee arguing, for instance, that negative public attitudes are fuelled by local misunderstandings and that local government could help prevent myths arising through transparent decision-making in relation to social housing and resource allocation (CLG, 2008b; SC Communities and Local Government, 2008: 23). Local action, however, cannot address the role played by national media, nor the role of central government in setting the tone of national debates (Maclaren and Johnson, 2004; Greenslade, 2005; Spencer, 2006b: 28; see also Chapter 2). It is also, moreover, only central government that can set the legal framework for integration, including equality law and the restrictions on migrants' conditions of stay; that can ensure an adequate evidence base, and the coordination of private, public and civil society partners to mainstream integration objectives nationwide.

There is nevertheless a key role for local government. Across Western Europe, cities have often taken the lead in developing integration programmes, with differing levels of central guidance, requirements and resources. There is a series of networks in which local authorities share experiences, independent of dialogue at national or intergovernmental level, and a growing body of knowledge on policy drivers, levers and outcomes (CLIP, 2008; British Council, 2010; Cities of Migration, 2010; Eurocities, 2010). In the UK, government has not encouraged local authorities to develop integration strategies per se, nor considered whether national policy supports or hinders local authorities in that role. It has, moreover, failed to resource them adequately to manage the challenges for new migrants and settled residents: 'local communities have been abandoned to manage these challenges alone' (Robinson, 2010b: 17). While some authorities nevertheless have policies relating to refugees and ad hoc initiatives with a broader target group, the Mayor of London is unusual in having supported a cross-cutting integration strategy for migrants, building on an earlier strategy for refugees, *London Enriched* (MOL, 2009, 2010).

The government consulted in 2009 on the desirability of extending the role of local authorities and devolved administrations. UKBA had already instructed the 11 regional refugee partnerships that it funded to broaden their remit to other migrants but only to facilitate cooperation, with a budget to match: for the East Midlands, for instance, just £130,000 a year (Local Government East Midlands, 2009). The remit of those partnerships nevertheless had the potential to support the mainstreaming of integration objectives across the work of local agencies, to build an evidence base and spread good practice, if prioritised to do so (MOL, 2010). UKBA has used this structure to talk to local agencies; channels not available when A8 migration aroused their concern. The 2009 proposals suggested that local authorities could provide more advice and signposting to migrants (on a full cost recovery basis). Mentoring schemes and orientation days were among the limited options proposed. The latter could be on a compulsory basis, attract points towards probationary citizenship and provide information about services, volunteering and 'British values'. They would have the side benefit of providing local authorities with data about newcomers in their area (UKBA, 2009). Being a low-key exercise, the proposals attracted scant attention. Nor were they intended to lead to any shift in scale, either in the development of a national integration strategy or in a programme to deliver it (UKBA, 2010a). The severe budget cuts now facing local authorities threaten their capacity to retain even current levels of engagement, including the financial support on which many refugee and migrant community organisations depend.

Conclusion

The intense political debates on migration are fuelled by perceptions of migrants' impacts after arrival yet policy to foster economic, social and civic participation has been neglected and marginal to those debates. In the UK, there has been no strategy to foster the integration of migrants, only piecemeal interventions that lack the clarity of objectives and coherence in approach that such a strategy could provide. No department has been charged with providing leadership, neither the Home Office nor CLG having been given the mandate or resources to do so, leaving an extraordinary lack of coherence across Whitehall and between central and local government. The relationship between migrants and social policy agendas addressing exclusion, poverty or inequality, 'place shaping' or most recently 'the Big Society' has been left unexplored. Encouragement from the EU to develop a coherent approach has had little influence on developments in the UK.

Beyond a limited strategy for refugees, English language provision and an increasingly divisive 'earned citizenship' agenda, policy has focused on ethnic minorities, not on those who have recently arrived. Integration goals have not been embedded in mainstream agendas such as civic participation, so that key elements of an effective strategy are missing and mainstream provision can be out of tune with migrants' particular needs. Little attention has been paid to understanding the causes of public hostility or the means by which it could be addressed. Rather, there has been an assumption that concerns can be assuaged through the robust and repeated assertion that migration is now more tightly controlled, coupled with an assurance that migrants will only access services and resources to which their contribution makes them entitled. Evidence that the percentage of the public who deem immigration and race to be among the 'most important issues facing Britain today' rose in the 10 years after Labour came to power from 3% to 40% in June 2007 (MORI, 2009) suggests that approach has not been successful.

Confusion within government on the meaning of integration, from the Home Office's refugee definition emphasising economic and social participation to CLG's narrow focus on 'getting on' with other residents, has muddied the water, demonstrating that the way in which an issue is conceptualised in government can limit its capacity to act. The model developed in response to Commonwealth immigration has proved ill adapted to the diversity of modern migration and left a legacy of scepticism on the language of 'integration' that any new strategy would need to overcome.

Experience abroad and in the UK suggests that local authorities could be key players. Employers and civil society could also be mobilised to make a far greater contribution, not least in the context of the severe limits on public funds that will constrain any future intervention. Nevertheless, government cannot simply devolve responsibility to the local level. It needs to identify those barriers that can only be addressed at the national level, ensure that integration goals are built into mainstream programmes and, crucially, set the tone of public and media debates. The new duty on public bodies to promote equality and good community relations could be one lever to drive this agenda forward.

The lack of a strategic overview of integration processes and of an evidence base on the impact of existing interventions has enabled contradictory policies to emerge: contradictions that reflect competing pressures on government but whose impact could be mediated if acknowledged and addressed. Notable here are the conditions attached to immigration status, which for many new migrants limit participation; conditions that could be reviewed to assess whether, in the light of evidence on their impact, all of the restrictions are necessary and proportional.

An evidence-based review could lead to a holistic strategy across the labour market, social, cultural, political and identity domains in which integration processes take place; facilitating a level of participation by all migrants, not only those with the right to settle. Integration processes start on day one, not least through interaction with neighbours, employers and service providers and it is in the early months that challenges can be most evident.

There is a plethora of advice on what such a strategy might contain in relation to integration in the labour market (LDA, 2005; Rutter et al, 2008; Phillimore and Goodson, 2008a; OECD, 2009) and other domains (Grover, 2006; Spencer et al, 2007; CLIP, 2008; European Commission, 2010; Haque, 2010). The goal would be to identify and address barriers to participation in each sphere, for which responsibility would lie not only with government and public agencies but with a broad range of actors from employers and trades unions, voluntary and community-sector organisations, to neighbours and migrants' families and communities (Spencer, 2006b: 9). In that way, the focus of the strategy would not be top-down instruction from national government but the mobilisation of key partners at the national and local level to foster integration processes as a shared responsibility, to the mutual benefit of the economy and society as a whole. Within the 'Big Society' umbrella, an integration agenda could foster an inclusive civic identity based on shared experiences, rather than a divided society in which some are never allowed to feel that they have earned the right to belong.

Notes

[1] Interview with Home Office official, 6 August 2009.
[2] Interview with Home Office official, 6 August 2009.
[3] Interview with Home Office official, 6 August 2009.
[4] Interview with former CLG official, 18 August 2009.
[5] Interview with former CLG official, 18 August 2009.
[6] Interview with Home Office official, 6 August 2009.

References

ABNI (Advisory Board on Naturalisation and Integration) (2008) 'Final Report of the Advisory Board on Naturalisation and Integration November 2004–November 2008'. London: Home Office.

Ager, A. and Strang, A. (2004) *Indicators of Integration: Final Report*. Home Office Development and Practice Report. London: Home Office.

Alibhai Brown, Y. (2000) *After Multiculturalism*. London: Foreign Policy Centre.

Alibhai Brown, Y. (2006) 'This Country is Already Integrated, Ms Kelly, but in Ways Your Government Would Not Like', *The Independent*, 28 August.

Anderson, B. (2010) 'Mobilising Migrants, Making Citizens: Migrant Domestic Workers as Political Agents', *Journal of Ethnic and Racial Studies* 33(1): 60–74.

Audit Commission (2007) *Crossing Borders: Responding to the Local Challenges of Migrant Workers,* London: Audit Commission.

Bader, V. (2001) 'Institutions, Culture and Identity of Transnational Citizenship: How Much Integration and "Communal Spirit" Is Needed?', in C. Crouch, K. Eder and D. Tambini (eds) *Citizenship, Markets and the State*. Oxford: Oxford University Press, pp 197–212.

Banting, K. and Kymlicka, W. (2006) *Multiculturalism and the Welfare State: Recognition and Redistribution in Contemporary Democracies*. Oxford: OUP.

BIC (Business in the Community) (2008) *Voluntary Code of Practice on Employing Migrant Workers / Overseas Staff in Great Britain*. London: Business in the Community.

Blair, T. (2006) 'The Duty to Integrate: Shared British Values', Speech, 8 December, London, 10 Downing Street.

Bloch, A. (2002) *Refugees: Opportunities and Barriers in Employment and Training.* Research Report 179. London: Department for Work and Pensions.

Bloch, A. (2004) *Making it Work: Refugee Employment in the UK.* London: Institute for Public Policy Research.

British Council (2010) 'Open Cities'. Available at: http://opencities. britishcouncil.org/web/index.php?home_en (accessed 9 May 2010).

Brubaker, R. (2001) 'The Return of Assimilation? Changing Perspectives on Immigration and Its Sequels in France, Germany and the United States', *Journal of Ethnic and Racial Studies* 24(4): 531–48.

Cangiano, A. (2007) 'Employment Support Services and Migrant Integration in the UK Labour Market', HWWI Policy Paper 3–7, Hamburg Institute of International Economics.

Cantle, T. and Community Cohesion Review Team (2001) *Community Cohesion: A Report of the Independent Review Team*. London: Home Office.

Carrera, S. (2008) *Benchmarking Integration in the EU: Analyzing the Debate on Integration Indicators and Moving It Forward*. Brussels: Centre for European Policy Studies.

Carrera, S. and Wiesbrock, A. (2009) *Civic Integration of Third Country Nationals: Nationalism versus Europeanisation in the Common EU Immigration Policy*. Brussels: Centre for European Policy Studies.

Castles, S. (2001) *Assessment of Research Reports Carried Out Under the European Commission Targeted Socio-Economic Research (TSER) Programme*, Brussels: European Commission.

Castles, S., Korac, M., Vasta, E. and Vertovec, S. (2002) *Integration: Mapping the Field*. London: Home Office.

CEU (Council of the European Union) (2004) *Report of the Meeting of the European Council on 19 November 2004*. Brussels: Council of the European Union.

CIC (Commission on Integration and Cohesion) (2007a) 'Our Interim Statement', London: CIC.

CIC (2007b) *Our Shared Future*, London: CIC.

Cities of Migration (2010) 'About Cities of Migration'. Available at: http://citiesofmigration.ca/about/lang/en/

CLG (Department for Communities and Local Government) (2006) *Improving Opportunity, Strengthening Society: One Year on – A Progress Report on the Government's Strategy for Race Equality and Community Cohesion*. London: Department for Communities and Local Government.

CLG (2008a) 'The Government's Response to the Commission on Integration and Cohesion'. London: CLG.

CLG (2008b) *Managing the Impacts of Migration: A Cross-Government Approach*. London: CLG.

CLG (2008c) *Review of Migrant Integration Policy in the UK (Including a Feasibility Study of the Proposal for an Integration Agency)*. London: CLG.

CLIP (Cities for Local Integration Policy) (2008) *Equality and Diversity in Jobs and Services: City Policies for Migrants in Europe.* Dublin: European Foundation for the Improvement of Living and Working Conditions.

Collett, E. (2009) *Beyond Stockholm: Overcoming the Inconsistencies of Immigration Policy.* Brussels: European Policy Centre.

Commission on the Future of Multi-Ethnic Britain (2000) *The Future of Multi-Ethnic Britain.* London: The Runnymede Trust.

Dench, G., Gavron, K. and Young, M. (2006) *The New East End: Kinship, Race and Conflict.* London: Young Foundation.

DIUS (2009) *A New Approach to English for Speakers of Other Languages.* London: Department for Innovation, Universities and Skills.

Doormernik, J. (2003) 'Integration Policies towards Immigrants and their Descendants in the Netherlands', in F. Heckman and D. Schnapper (eds) *The Integration of Immigrants in European Societies: National Differences and Trends of Convergence.* Stuttgart: Lucius and Lucius, pp 165–83.

Dummett, A. (2008) 'Changes to Citizenship', *Journal of Immigration Asylum and Nationality Law* 22(3): 213–17.

Dummett, A. and Nicol, A. (1990) *Subjects, Citizens, Aliens and Others: Nationality and Immigration Law.* London: Weidenfeld and Nicolson.

Dustmann, C. and Fabbri, F. (2005) 'Immigrants in the British Labour Market', *Fiscal Studies* 26(4): 423–70.

Dustmann, C., Fabbri, F., Preston, I. and Wadsworth, J. (2003) *Labour Market Performance of Immigrants in the UK Labour Market*, online report, London: Home Office, 05/03.

DWP (Department for Work and Pensions) (2005) *Working to Rebuild Lives: A Refugee Employment Strategy.* London: DWP.

Entzinger, H. (2000) 'The Dynamics of Integration Policies; A Multidimensional Model', in R. Koopmans and P. Statham (eds) *Challenging Immigration and Ethnic Relations Politics: Comparative European Perspectives.* Oxford: Oxford University Press, pp 97–118.

Entzinger, H. and Biezeveld, R. (2003) *Benchmarking in Immigrant Integration*, Brussels: European Commission.

Eurocities (2010) 'Eurocities'. Available at: http://www.eurocities.eu/main.php (accessed 9 May 2010).

European Commission (2010) 'European Website on Integration'. Available at: http://ec.europa.eu/ewsi/ (accessed 9 May 2010).

Eurostat (2009) 'Acquisition of Citizenship in the European Union', *Eurostat Data in Focus* 44/2009, Brussels: European Commission.

Evans, G. (2006) 'Is Multiculturalism Eroding Support for Welfare Provision? The British Case', in K. Banton and W. Kymlicka (eds) *Multiculturalism and the Welfare State: Recognition and Redistribution in Contemporary Democracies.* Oxford: OUP.

Evans, O. and Murray, R. (2009) *The Gateway Protection Programme: An Evaluation*, Research Report 12, London: Home Office.

Favell, A. (2001a) 'Multi-Ethnic Britain: An Exception in Europe?' *Patterns of Prejudice* 35(1): 35–57.

Favell, A. (2001b) *Philosophies of Integration: Immigration and the Idea of Citizenship in France and Britain.* 2nd edition. Basingstoke: Palgrave.

Finney, N. and Simpson, L. (2009) *Sleepwalking to Segration? Challenging Myths about Race and Migration.* Bristol: The Policy Press.

Flint, J. and Robinson, D. (2008) *Community Cohesion in Crisis? New Dimensions of Diversity and Difference.* Bristol: The Policy Press.

Goodhart, D. (2004) 'Too Diverse?', *Prospect* 95, February.

Greenslade, R. (2005) 'Seeking Scapegoats: The Coverage of Asylum in the UK Press', Asylum and Migration Working Paper 5, London: Institute for Public Policy Research.

Grover, D. (2006) *More than a Language: NIACE Committee of Inquiry on English for Speakers of Other Languages. Final Report.* Leicester: National Institute of Adult and Continuing Education.

Haque, Z. (2010) *What Works for Integrating New Migrants: Lessons from International Best Practice.* London: Runnymede Trust.

Heckman, F. et al (2001) *Effectiveness of National Integration Strategies towards Second Generation Migrant Youth in a Comparative European Perspective (EFFNATIS).* Bamberg: European Forum for Migration Studies, University of Bamberg.

Heckman, F. et al (2006) 'Integration and Integration Policies: IMISCOE Network Feasibility Study'. Amsterdam: IMISCOE.

Home Office (1999) *Consultation Paper on the Integration of Recognised Refugees in the United Kingdom.* London: Home Office.

Home Office (2000) *Full and Equal Citizens: A Strategy for the Integration of Refugees into the United Kingdom*. London: Home Office.

Home Office (2001) *The Denham Report: Building Cohesive Communities*. London: Home Office.

Home Office (2002) *Secure Borders, Safe Haven: Integration with Diversity in Modern Britain*. Cm 5387. London: Home Office.

Home Office (2005) *Integration Matters: A National Strategy for Refugee Integration*. London: Home Office.

Home Office (Border and Immigration Agency) (2008) *The Path to Citizenship: Next Steps in Reforming the Immigration System*. London: Home Office.

Home Office (2010) *Control of Immigration Quarterly Statistical Summary United Kingdom July–September 2010*, London: Home Office.

IDEA (Improvement and Development Agency) (2010) 'Migration Programme: Sharing Good Practice'. Available at: http: //www. idea.gov.uk/idk/core/page.do?pageId=5961509 (accessed 17 March 2010).

Ireland, P. (2004) *Becoming Europe: Immigration, Integration and the Welfare State*. Pitsburgh: University of Pittsburgh Press.

Keith, M. (2008) 'Between Being and Becoming? Rights, Responsibilities and the Politics of Multiculture in the New East End', *Sociological Research Online* 13.

Kloosterman, R. and Rath, J. (eds) (2003) *Immigrant Entrepreneurs: Venturing Abroad in the Age of Globalization*. Oxford and New York: Berg.

Kofman, E. and Phizacklea, A. (2000) *Gender and International Migration in Europe*. London and New York: Taylor and Francis Ltd.

Kundani, A. (2007) *The End of Tolerance: Racism in 21st Century Britain*. London: Pluto Press.

Lawson, N. (2008) 'The Wrong Dilemma', in D. Flynn and Z. Williams (eds) *Towards a Progressive Immigration Policy*. London: Compass, Migrants Rights Network and Barrow Cadbury Trust, pp 9–11.

LDA (London Development Agency) (2005) *Local Integration of Immigrants into the Labour Market: UK Case Study – The Case of Refugees in London*. London: London Development Agency and OECD.

Life in the UK Advisory Group (2002) *The New and the Old: The Interim Report for Consultation of the 'Life in the United Kingdom' Advisory Group.* London: Home Office.

Life in the UK Advisory Group (2003) *The New and the Old: The Report of the Life in the United Kingdom Advisory Group.* London: Home Office.

Local Government East Midlands (2009) 'East Midlands Regional Strategic Migration Partnership Annual Report 2008–2009', Melton Mowbray.

Maclaren, L. and Johnson, M. (2004) 'Understanding the Rise of Anti-Immigrant Sentiment', in A. Park, J. Curtis, E. Clery and C. Bryson (eds) *British Social Attitudes: The 21st Report.* London: Sage.

Malik, K. (2005) 'Making a Difference: Culture, Race and Social Policy', *Patterns of Prejudice* 39(4): 361–78.

Markova, E. and Black, R. (2007) *New Eastern European Immigrants and Social Cohesion.* York: Joseph Rowntree Foundation.

McCarvill, P. (2011) *Who's Still Missing: Refugees, Migrants and the Equality Agenda.* London: Equality and Diversity Forum.

MOL (Mayor of London) (2009) *London Enriched: The Mayor's Refugee Integration Strategy.* London: Mayor of London.

MOL (2010) 'London Strategic Migration Partnership Terms of Reference'. Available at: http://legacy.london.gov.uk/mayor/migration/lsmp/terms-ref.jsp

MORI (2009) 'Trends since 1997: The Most Important Issues Facing Britain Today'. Available at: http://www.ipsos-mori.com/researchpublications/researcharchive/poll.aspx?oItemId=56&view=wide (accessed 4 January 2010).

NEP (National Equality Panel) (2010) *An Anatomy of Economic Inequality in the United Kingdom: Report of the National Equality Panel.* Case Report 60. London: National Equality Panel.

NIACE (National Institute of Adult and Continuing Education) (2008) 'Response to the DIUS Consultation "ESOL and Community Cohesion"'. Leicester: NIACE.

Niessen, J. (2001) *Diversity and Cohesion: New Challenges for the Integration of Immigrants and Minorities.* Strasbourg: Council of Europe.

Niessen, J., Huddleston, T. and Citron, L. (2007) *Migrant Integration Policy Index*. Brussels: British Council and Migration Policy Group.

Niessen, J., Kate, M.-A. and Huddleston, T. (2009) *Developing and Using European Integration Indicators: Background Paper for Swedish Presidency Conference Integration of New Arrivals: Incentives and Work in Focus*, Malmo, 14–16 December. Brussels: Migration Policy Group.

OECD (Organisation for Economic Cooperation and Development) (2009) *The Labour Market Integration of Immigrants and their Children: Key Findings from OECD Country Reviews. High-Level Policy Forum on Migration*. Paris: OECD.

ONS (Office for National Statistics) (2010) 'Statistical Bulletin: Labour Market, April 2010', London: Office for National Statistics.

Penninx, R. and Martiniello, M. (2004) 'Integration Processes and Policies: State of the Art and Lessons', in R. Penninx, K. Kraal, M. Martiniello and S. Vertovec (eds) *Citizenship in European Cities: Immigrants, Local Politics and Integration Policies*. Aldershot: Ashgate.

Phillimore, J. and Goodson, L. (2008a) *New Migrants in the UK: Education, Training and Employment*. Stoke on Trent: Trentham Books.

Phillimore, J. and Goodson, L. (2008b) 'Making a Place in the Global City: The Relevance of Indicators of Integration', *Journal of Refugee Studies* 21(3): 305–25.

Phillimore, J. and Goodson, L. (2010) 'Failing to Adapt: Institutional Barriers to RCO's Engagement in Transformation of Social Welfare', *Journal of Social Policy and Society* 9(2): 1–12.

Phillips, T. (2005) *After 7/7: Sleepwalking to Segregation*. London: Commission for Racial Equality.

Refugee Council (2009) 'Policy Statement on Moving on Together: Government's Recommitment to Supporting Refugees', London: Refugee Council.

Robinson, D. (2010a) 'New Immigrants and Migrants in Social Housing in Britain: Discursive Themes and Lived Realities', *Policy and Politics* 38(1): 57–77.

Robinson, D. (2010b) 'Migration in the UK: Moving Beyond Numbers', *People, Place and Policy Online* 4(1): 14–18.

Robinson, D. and Reeve, K. (2006) *Neighbourhood Experiences of New Immigration*. York: Joseph Rowntree Foundation.

Rose, E. et al (1969) *Colour and Citizenship: A Report on British Race Relations*. London: Oxford University Press.

Rutter, J., Cooley, L., Jones, N. and Pillaj, R. (2008) *Moving up Together: Promoting Equality and Integration among the UK's Diverse Communities*. London: Institute for Public Policy Research.

Ryan, B. (2008) 'Integration Requirements: A New Model in Migration Law', *Journal of Immigration, Asylum and Nationality Law* 22(4): 303–16.

SC Communities and Local Government (Select Committee on Communities and Local Government) (2008) *Community Cohesion and Migration*. Tenth Report Session 2007–08. London: House of Commons.

Spencer, S. (2006a) 'Refugees and Other New Migrants: A Review of the Evidence on Successful Approaches to Integration'. Oxford: COMPAS.

Spencer, S. (2006b) 'The Challenge of Integration in Europe', in D. Papademetriou (ed) *Europe and its Immigrants in the 21st Century*. Washington: Migration Policy Institute and Luso-American Foundation.

Spencer, S. (2007) 'Immigration', in A. Seldon (ed) *Blair's Britain 1997–2007*. Cambridge: Cambridge University Press.

Spencer, S. and Cooper, B. (2006) *Social Integration of Migrants in Europe: A Review of the European Literature*, Oxford: COMPAS.

Spencer, S. and Di Mattia, A. (2004) *Introductory Programmes and Initiatives for New Migrants*, paper for Ministerial Conference on Integration, Groningen, November 2004.

Spencer, S. and Pobjoy, J. (2011) *Immigration Status and the Allocation of Rights: Exploring the Rationale*. COMPAS Working Paper. Oxford: COMPAS.

Spencer, S. and Rudiger, A. (2003) 'Social Integration of Immigrants and Ethnic Minorities, Policies to Combat Discrimination', Paper presented to the conference 'The Economic and Social Aspects of Migration' organised by the European Commission and OECD, Brussels, 21–22 January, OECD/European Commission.

Spencer, S., Ruhs, M., Anderson, B. and Rogaly, B. (2007) *Migrants' Lives beyond the Workplace*, York: Joseph Rowntree Foundation.

Squire, V. (2009) *Mobile Solidarities: The City of Sanctuary Movement and the Strangers into Citizens Campaign*. Milton Keynes: Open University.

Thorp, A. and Garton Grimwood, G. (2009) 'Borders, Citizenship and Immigration Bill [HL]', Research Paper 09, London: House of Commons Library.

UKBA (United Kingdom Border Agency) (2008) 'Multi-Annual Programme for the European Fund for the Integration of Third-Country Nationals for the Period 2007–2013 as part of the General Programme "Solidarity and Management of Migration Flows"', as revised 4 November 2008. London: Home Office.

UKBA (2009) *Earning the Right to Stay – a New Points Test for Citizenship*. London: Home Office.

UKBA (2010a) *Earning the Right to Stay, a New Points Test for Citizenship: Analysis of Consultation Responses*. London: Home Office.

UKBA (2010b) 'Government Announcement on Settlement Reforms', Press notice, 5 November, London: Home Office.

Vermeulen, F. and Penninx, R. (2000) *Immigrant Integration: The Dutch Case*. Amsterdam: Spinhuis.

Vertovec, S. (2007) 'Super-Diversity and its Implications', *Journal of Ethnic and Racial Studies* 30(6): 1024–54.

Vertovec, S. and Wessendorf, S. (eds) (2010) *The Multiculturalism Backlash: European Discourses, Policies and Practices*. London and New York: Routledge.

Waters, M. and Jimenez, T. (2005) 'Assessing Immigrant Assimilation: New Empirical and Theoretical Challenges', *Annual Review of Sociology* 31: 105–25.

WMSMP (West Midlands Strategic Migration Partnership) (2009) 'A Regional Strategy for the Social Inclusion of Refugees and Asylum Seekers in the West Midlands 2006–2009: Review Report 2009', West Midlands Strategic Migration Partnership.

Zetter, R., Griffiths, D., Sigona, N. and Hauser, M. (2002) 'A Survey of Policy and Practice Related to Refugee Integration in the EU'. Oxford: Oxford Brookes University.

7

Conclusion

In the course of this book I have looked at the context in which migration and integration policies are developed; at policies towards those seeking asylum, migrant workers, international students, family members and irregular migrants before turning to migrants' economic, social and civic participation. In this chapter I draw out the common themes that have emerged, look at what we have learnt about policymaking on migration, address some overarching debates and conclude with an alternative way forward.

We saw in Chapter 1 that the UK is far from alone in experiencing migration on a significant scale; the outcome of global, economic, social and political forces which will ensure that, at differing levels and in evolving forms, migration will be a permanent part of our future. Recognising that structural context does not mean that governments are powerless to intervene but is to understand that managing migration necessitates addressing underlying causes, at home and abroad, and devising policy tools that reflect the complexity of the processes at play. Despite decades of experience, however, successive governments have reacted to migration with ad hoc initiatives; presenting no vision of what they want to achieve or coherent strategy to deliver it. In this chapter I suggest how that could change.

There are influential voices who argue that the overriding priority for government should be to limit entry and settlement severely in order to curb population growth. Tighter controls are needed, it is suggested, to reduce pressure on housing and public services, protect jobs for existing residents, strengthen cohesion and avoid support growing for far-right parties. Regardless of the weight that government gives to the case for further limits on migration, however, there are competing priorities to which it has to give credence. There are also significant constraints on its capacity to determine who comes to the

UK, and who stays. Any analysis of the efficacy of migration policy must take account of the ways in which it can unravel, at national or local level, when it moves on from policymakers to the operational phase.

Competing priorities and constraints

We saw that the first constraint is that the very nature of migration means UK policy cannot be devised in isolation from that of other states, or from the UK's broader international interests. Relationships with Commonwealth countries had to be taken into account in the early decades after the Second World War; their influence subsequently giving way to that of our European neighbours on whose cooperation the UK relies to strengthen the EU's external borders, prevent 'asylum shopping' (as it is perceived) and facilitate removals. Nevertheless, the optional 'opt-out' from EU provisions has allowed the UK to pick and choose those policies deemed in the national interest (albeit at some political cost), so that UK policy developments have often proceeded in parallel to those at EU level rather than dictated by them.

With EU membership, however, comes non-negotiable free movement of EU citizens to work in Britain. In 2004, the UK could have chosen to take advantage of transitional arrangements to limit the entry of the 'A8' nationals of the enlarged EU for seven years. The decision not to do so brought economic benefits but subsequently a high political cost, not mitigated by the quid pro quo that UK citizens could then study or take up employment in 24 other member states. Free movement for EU citizens means that restrictions to limit the numbers who enter can generally only apply to those coming from beyond the EU (or indeed EEA) borders. Yet it is the highly skilled workers and international students among them from whom many of the benefits to the UK economy derive.

Bilateral relationships can equally be crucial, as in securing the cooperation of France to close the Sangatte refugee camp in Calais (in a way that met the UK's immediate need to curtail entry, not the needs of the refugees concerned). But international relations work through reciprocity: the Coalition government finding in 2010, for example, that the price for India's cooperation on favourable terms of investment was to be given a say in how its citizens would be treated by the cap on non-EEA migrant workers. Reciprocity in broader international agreements can equally be a constraint; business benefiting from the UK's participation in the General Agreement on Trade in Services (GATS), for instance, but that in turn imposes limits on the extent to which intra-company transfers of staff can be curtailed by the cap (see Chapter 3). The absence of a UN framework for the broader governance of migration has led to a proliferation of mechanisms for dialogue and collaboration, demonstrating that migration cannot be addressed effectively on a unilateral basis (see Chapter 1).

Human rights obligations

Governments are further constrained by obligations under international human rights treaties and by the ethics that underlie their existence: public acceptance in a liberal democracy that people should be able to choose their life partners and children allowed to live with their parents, for instance, imposing some constraint on government's freedom to curtail family migration beyond any impact of human rights law. There are instances where government has felt it necessary to address the conflict between immigration controls and those principles: Labour honoring its 1997 manifesto commitment to remove the 'primary purpose' rule, for instance, taking action to curb the excessive delays faced by families waiting in the Indian subcontinent and removing the bar on entry for same-sex partners. At other times thinly disguised attempts have been made to bypass such ethical considerations, leading to scepticism that steps taken to protect individuals (such as those to prevent forced marriages) are in fact designed to limit the number of people allowed to enter (see Chapter 4).

The UN Convention on Refugees is one significant constraint on policy options on asylum. There has remained a commitment in principle to its core requirement that all who ask for sanctuary should have their case considered and not be returned to a country where they could face persecution. When the number of applicants rose significantly in the 1990s, however, the then Conservative administration began to erect barriers to entry, remove safeguards in the determination process and use exclusion from welfare provision as a means of immigration control, a process taken to extraordinary lengths by the Labour government over the next decade.

The Human Rights Act 1998 enabled individuals more readily to challenge immigration rules breaching the European Convention on Human Rights and, to ministers' regret, their decisions have repeatedly been subject to court challenge under this and other statutes. Some significant changes in policy and practice have had to be made as a result, not least to provide a level of support to refused asylum seekers and to refrain from removals to countries where the individual could face torture (see Chapter 2). Such reforms have not changed the direction of policy but have relieved some of its harshest effects on people's lives.

The considerable strengthening of discrimination law has created the potential, if not yet the reality, that migrants will derive benefit from that protection. Yet the statutory discrimination against new arrivals, in the patchwork of restrictions attached to conditions of entry that limit access to work, services, benefits and the democratic system, militates against equality of opportunity and thus economic, social and civic integration.

Legacy of the past

We saw, furthermore, that new governments do not start with a clean slate and their scope for action is limited, to a degree, by the legacy they inherit. Historic patterns of immigration have created networks of co-nationals, family and friends that influence the paths of future migrants; and policy frameworks are already in place, bringing with them the constraining paradigm in which they were conceived.

A new government, moreover, inherits a system for administering and enforcing immigration controls that is more or less fit for purpose. Labour's inheritance in 1997 included rising numbers of asylum seekers, a backlog of 50,000 applications and a system of administration severely ill equipped for policymaking or the operation of immigration control. Its legislative hyperactivity then exacerbated the problems staff faced, with no less than seven major pieces of legislation on immigration, asylum and citizenship in the decade 1999–2009. More fundamentally, it inherited a way of thinking about migration as a problem not an opportunity, which in part it overcame; and a way of thinking about integration, which it did not.

Economy rules

Most significantly, as the Coalition government is finding to its cost, government cannot shut the door to migration because of the economic price that the country would pay. Even the British National Party agrees that the UK should remain open to 'genuine' international students and to labour migrants if there is 'a need to rebuild British industry or when there is a genuine shortage of skills' (BNP, 2010: 19).

In its shift to 'managed migration', Labour departed from the ad hoc expansion of work permits that the Conservative administration had overseen in the 1990s, to an overt strategy of making the UK competitive in the global market for talent, intent on maximising the economic gains and expansion of public services that the mobility of the highly skilled could bring. Recruitment from developing countries raised concerns about the impact of that 'brain drain', leading to a modest shift in NHS recruitment practice. Yet few questioned the benefits to Britain when the NHS plan, launched in 2000, heralded an increase of 9,500 doctors and 20,000 nurses that could only be delivered by staff from abroad; or disagreed when business, in a period of economic growth, demanded red tape be scrapped to enable them to hire the IT specialists and engineers they needed and to bring in their own staff from abroad (see Chapter 3).

Nor did the Opposition challenge the wisdom of Blair's campaign, launched in 1999 and reinforced in 2006, to secure 25% of the English-speaking student market. International students make a substantial economic contribution, expand the range of courses available to UK students and bring cultural benefits to education that are more difficult to quantify. Students from EU countries, through reciprocal arrangements, pay the same fees as UK students; hence those most lucrative as a source of income are those from beyond the EU's borders – the very people whom a tight limit on numbers would need to control (see Chapter 3).

Economic growth brought demand for high-skilled workers for the knowledge economy but also an expansion in low-wage jobs. In opening up entry channels for low-skilled workers and later for A8 'migrants' from an enlarged EU, Labour recognised that the absence of legal channels in face of strong demand for labour in sectors like construction, agriculture and hospitality could only fuel demand for irregular workers. The consistently high employment rate of A8 workers demonstrates that the jobs were indeed there to be had.

In its openness to the economic benefits of migration, Labour transformed the parameters of policy and debate, its success in marking Britain as a country open to overseas talent confirmed by the insistence of the Coalition's first Home Secretary, Theresa May, that the government would ensure the country continued to attract the 'brightest and the best'. Nevertheless, as we emerge from recession, there is less consensus now on the overall benefits of labour migration and greater awareness that the benefits to employers do not necessarily equate to benefits for all.

Managing demand

'Demand' for migrant workers can reflect a shortage of people in the resident workforce with suitable skills but also the pay and conditions employers are willing to provide. Upskilling at the high end of the labour market has, to an extent, been a priority: expansion of training places for doctors and nurses did substantially address the NHS's heavy reliance on overseas health professionals. No such intent, however, has been evident in reducing the need for migrants in occupations such as social care, where in London more than 60% of care workers are foreign-born. In sectors facing public expenditure constraints, cutting off the supply of migrant workers will thus not necessarily lead to an increase in suitable domestic supply. Improvements in pay and conditions, training, and support in making the transition from benefits to work are key elements of that equation.

Where employers and agencies are determined to exploit irregular migrants, paying below the going rate, tackling the incentives for migrants to overstay and work without permission (and for traffickers to profit) means closing down the spaces where this can happen. The Gangmasters Licensing Authority and enforcement of the minimum wage play a key role but are inadequate in their reach to prevent vulnerable workers from exploitation (whether migrants or not), and hence the ongoing demand for their labour. Protecting the rights of migrant workers alongside those of other staff is essential to prevent their employment undercutting the rate for the job. It is also in the interests of employers who do not want to face unfair competition from those willing to break the rules.

The solutions to the level of demand for skilled and low-skilled migrant labour thus lie in education, skills and employment policy more than in migration policy. Hi-tech border controls to keep unauthorised workers out are no substitute for tackling the incentive for them to be there. The Points-Based System provides a mechanism to match supply to demand but the core issue is managing demand (see Chapter 3).

There are thus, as in other areas of migration policy, competing priorities and interests at stake. Government must consider the pros and cons of importing skilled migrants to address gaps in the labour market for which there may be alternative solutions; and assess the value of tackling demand for irregular migrants by enforcing employment standards, against labour market flexibility in a deregulatory climate. It must consider, with developing countries, the risk of denuding those countries of skilled staff, against the value of migrants' remittances to their economies and of migrants' skills and ideas if they return: development goals need not be antithetical to a labour migration policy but do need to be reflected within its objectives.

We saw that those whose primary concern is to limit population growth now focus not solely on the numbers who enter but on those allowed to settle, arguing that Britain could continue to benefit from skilled workers from abroad as long as there are tight restrictions on who is allowed to stay. Yet here again there is a downside to consider: the most sought-after workers might be expected to choose a country that allows them to put down roots (why disrupt your career and family with a further move?). Those who know they will have to leave may moreover be less motivated to make a full social and civic contribution while in the UK; while for employers, temporary staff entail the cost and disruption of replacement when they leave.

Limits of border controls

Governments also face limits on what can be achieved by border controls and not only because of the pull factor of labour market demand. More than a hundred million people arrive at the UK's borders each year, of whom the majority are British and European citizens enjoying freedom to travel for work, leisure or family reasons, but who nevertheless need to pass through passport control. More than 12 million are people subject to immigration controls, many of them contributing to the £16 billion the tourism industry earns from international visitors each year, helping to sustain Britain's fifth largest industry, which is forecast to support nearly three million jobs by 2020 (see Chapter 5). We saw that each minute of delay in passing through immigration control has an economic cost. Government cannot afford to threaten that income: plans to curb the time limit for tourist visas from six to three months in 2008 were reportedly dropped on those grounds. Managing the entry and exit of that volume of people does not permit 100% surveillance because of the time and level of intrusion; border control is thus, of necessity, a risk management exercise. No government is likely to want to go so far as one columnist has suggested and say that it is powerless in the face of porous borders (Toynbee, 2010). Nor would that be true. Yet a reality check suggests that government should not over-promise what cannot be delivered.

This is not to say that more could not be done to manage borders effectively. The E-borders information system should by 2014 provide information on whether each migrant has left the UK by their appointed date. Significant resources would, however, then be required to track down and remove those who have not and a cost borne if the individual was by then fulfilling an essential role. Migration Watch suggests that a far greater number of prospective students should be interviewed before receiving a visa in order to improve detection of those who are not genuine in their intent to study (Migration Watch, 2010). This could be done but government has to balance the potential advantage of so doing against the staff costs, delays and deterrence effects that this would entail in an increasingly competitive market for international students.

We saw in relation to asylum that it is difficult to assess how effective policy has been overall in curtailing numbers because there are so many variables at play, not least the cessation of conflicts that were the immediate cause of flight and the time-lag in the effects of new measures. Extension of visa requirements and carrier sanctions has undoubtedly prevented an unknown number of would-be asylum seekers from reaching the UK. Whether that counts as success depends on whether one considers the impact on the individuals among them who were in need of protection and who thereby failed to receive it.

Ethics and efficacy of internal controls

Finally, governments are constrained by the ethics and efficacy of internal controls intended to ensure that people observe their conditions of stay and leave when their visa has expired. We saw in Chapter 5 that the vast majority of irregular migrants (estimated at 618,000 in 2007) arrived legally but overstayed; and that there is a further number who are 'semi-compliant': irregular because they are working or accessing services to which they are not entitled. The law defines all of these as criminal offences for which the individuals are subject to removal, making no distinction between those who arrived in the back of a lorry and those who are simply working longer hours per week than permitted – an inflexible legal framework in need of reform. Removals are also costly and beset with difficulties, hence the numbers removed scarcely touch the numbers who remain, whose removal would in itself be highly disruptive and controversial. Public support for curbing migration does not, moreover, preclude fervent resistance to the removal of families settled within a local community.

When the Coalition government dropped plans to introduce identity cards for British citizens it retained them for foreign nationals. This leaves open the continuing expectation on local service providers that they will police entry to services, informing the immigration authorities if they suspect irregular migration status. That approach has met with some resistance from service providers, not least health professionals who do not consider this to be their role; and it carries social as well as individual costs, including to public health if individuals cannot access essential services. An information 'firewall' barring transfer of information relating to key services does and could further protect access regardless of immigration status where it is deemed that social policy objectives or human rights protection need to be accorded greater priority than immigration control.

Policy trade-offs to meet competing objectives

The government's freedom of manoeuvre in devising migration policy is thus circumscribed by competing pressures and constraints. Governments can shift priorities and occasionally the paradigm, as Labour did in opening up Britain to 'the brightest and the best', but refining entry channels and border controls does not address the structural factors that drive migration; and each shift in priorities can carry a cost, whether or not explicit in the policy debate.

The decision to impose a cap on migration from outside the EEA has brought into the open some core tensions, notably between the immediate economic benefits of overseas labour and students and the long-term goals of reducing the dependency on migrant labour and curbing population growth. A less explicit trade-off is the exclusion of most new migrants from 'recourse to public funds', with a prior requirement to demonstrate that such support will not be needed if entry is allowed. That exclusion from services and welfare benefits protects the public purse from those who have not contributed to it and is intended to reassure the taxpayers who have. The downside is that excluding newcomers from that safety net lays them open to exploitation at work and to violence within the home (by limiting their freedom to walk away), while exclusion from free health care may also have public health implications. Underlying this particular debate lie differing views on the basis of entitlement, most evident in relation to a tightly rationed resource, social housing: whether access should be on the basis of need (where those of newcomers could trump those of longer-term residents) or on the basis of residence, belonging and previous contribution to the public purse (or, at its most extreme, ethnicity, the BNP asserting in this context 'the importance of the prior status of the indigenous people'; BNP, 2010: 21). The question is whether, in a society that will continue to have a diverse section of the community who do not hold UK nationality or permanent residence, exclusion from the safety net of the welfare state is a means to secure their acceptance or more likely to perpetuate economic inequality and social divides.

Lack of a governance structure to match the task

Trade-offs, winners and losers are the stuff of politics but migration policy has lacked a governance structure that has the competing interests facing each other around the table, to make those choices, and the costs attached, transparent.

Transferring responsibility for labour migration across to the Home Office in 2001 made it possible, in theory, to develop a holistic migration policy – linking labour migration, family, asylum and integration for the first time. The downside is its isolation in the Home Office from departments that could tackle the causes of demand for migrant labour, and continuing separation from departments responsible for international development, justice, education and health, for instance, which urgently need to be given a say. Officials communicate where their agendas meet but there is no mechanism to recognise and reconcile competing national policy objectives, to engage the devolved administrations and local government whose interests can diverge from those of central government, or to ensure that broader local impacts are consistently taken into account – hence the kickback when the number of A8 migrants brought unanticipated consequences for local services.

The weakness in governance arrangements has often allowed the imperatives of migration control, felt keenly in the Home Office, to override other considerations, and to conflict with mainstream policy objectives. Where departments have held the Home Office back, as in the influence the Department for Business, Innovation and Skills exerted to rein in steps to curb student numbers in 2009, it has tended to happen behind the scenes with little public debate on the pros and cons, winners and losers, of that decision. One counter-factor has been the space provided by the Migration Advisory Committee (MAC). Taking evidence and applying rigour to its analysis of the need for and implications of labour migration, the MAC has since 2007 brought greater transparency and reasoned debate to this one aspect of migration policy, the value of which was recognised in the Coalition government's decision to retain access to its advice. When the MAC asked, in the context of its consultation on the cap, *how* it should balance conflicting economic and social impacts, it began to open up that debate (see Chapter 3). Yet it is also necessary to consider broader impacts, on international relations or development, for instance; and what impacts there *could* be if there was an effective integration strategy for new migrants, reducing the social and economic costs of adjustment in the early months after arrival.

The quid pro quo of the lack of joined-up policymaking has been the near exclusion of migrants (and migrant voices) from consideration in mainstream policies. Where it is now expected that policymakers will consider the potential implications of policy on women, ethnic minorities or disabled people (and that their voices will be heard in the policymaking process), there has been no such expectation in relation to migrants: hence policies that could help to foster integration processes, like initiatives on civic participation or employment services, have largely not been expected to take that role on board.

The Home Office has been given huge discretion to change the Immigration Rules with scant parliamentary scrutiny. The scope of that freedom, however, differs across the system, the expansion of labour migration largely delivered by changing the rules but asylum reform requiring primary legislation, bringing media attention as well as parliamentary debate. Parliamentary Select Committees have played a key role, focusing a spotlight on the operation of the system and its impact on individuals and human rights norms that would not otherwise have occurred. NGO voices have consistently identified the impact of immigration controls on migrants' lives and, with ethnic minority communities, have secured some changes to policy and practice where the evidence left government little option but to respond.

Weak evidence base

The trade-offs implicit in migration policies are rarely explicit in policy debates. Nor is the evidence base on which to make reasoned choices available in many instances because of a lack of data or research addressing the questions to which policymakers need answers. In recent years the evidence gap has begun to be addressed in relation to labour migration and asylum but it is still severely limited in relation to family migration, irregular migration, students and integration. Hence we know surprisingly little, for instance, about the impact of 'no recourse to public funds' on those subject to that constraint in their early years (is it a proportional response to the need to protect public funds or a counterproductive barrier to integration?); or about the ways in which, and reasons why, those who come legally to the UK subsequently acquire irregular status. A stronger evidence base is needed to underpin a more effective policymaking process – and a more informed public debate.

Polarised public debate

The constraints that government faces in managing migration have largely not been shared with the public. Where the door remains open, the rationale has not been explained. Governments have not chosen or felt able to share with the public the opportunities and constraints, the conflicting objectives, winners and losers, and tough choices to be made. They have not given the public the information that explains the apparently inexplicable, why government cannot simply shut the door.

Instead, successive governments have sought to reassure the public that migration is under control when rising numbers suggested it was not. Tabloid media pressure is at times intense, ready to exploit any instance of abuse (and sometimes to invent it; see Chapter 2), creating a climate in which it is difficult for government or external voices to foster an evidence-based examination of the options. In face of that challenge, the response – in promising ever-tougher measures to address abuse – has arguably served to reinforce concerns among a public sceptical that the next measure will be any more effective than the last. In reinforcing the anxiety they sought to assuage, ministers have exacerbated their own predicament.

Ministers have thought it possible, moreover, to send a mixed message: that some migrants are good for Britain while others are unwelcome. At the very time that government was reinforcing negative perceptions of asylum seekers in 2000–05, it was campaigning to attract more international students and skilled workers, in some cases from the same source countries. There was no recognition that the public might need some explanation. The economic contribution of workers and students at a national level might be very different from that of asylum seekers (who are, after all, not allowed to work); but the perception of these newcomers at the local level may not mirror that distinction.

Highly problematic for government is that the heat of the 'debate' encourages those who benefit from migration policy to keep their head below the radar, employers' representatives rarely speaking up publicly in favour of relaxing controls, choosing to lobby in private rather than attract unwelcome publicity for an unpopular sentiment. NGOs, meanwhile, find significantly more to criticise in government decisions than to praise. Hence government regularly finds itself isolated in this policy field, on the defensive, apparently unable to please regardless of ever-greater levels of legislative reform and resources deployed in its attempt so to do.

Lack of a strategy to promote 'integration'

Public concern about migration numbers reflects perceptions about their impact after arrival. Yet an extraordinary policy omission has been the lack of any strategy to foster the economic, social and civic participation of new migrants – the 1,500 people who, on average, have arrived each day to stay for more than a year. Fostering participation requires engagement from the institutions and people in mainstream society as well as migrants, and policy intervention can facilitate – or hinder – that process (see Chapter 6).

With the exception of refugees, there has been a policy vacuum on this agenda: no department charged with leadership, no clarity of objectives and no framework in which to mobilise employers and civil society partners or support local authority initiatives. In Chapter 6 we saw how early measures relating to Commonwealth immigrants remained focused on those communities as minority ethnic groups, no longer addressing issues related to newcomers; and how latterly 'integration' was subsumed within the narrower cohesion agenda. For long-term residents, encouragement to learn English and knowledge of 'life in the UK' gave way to 'earned citizenship' provisions likely to further marginalise migrants from the mainstream. The relationship between migrants and broader social policy agendas addressing exclusion, poverty, inequality, place-shaping and most recently the 'Big Society' is as yet unexplored. Those concerned that migration may undermine cohesion have been more likely to argue for less migration than to consider the policy levers that can ensure communities are strengthened by the cultural diversity migration brings.

Moving forward

What does this suggest could be done to detoxify migration as a divisive issue and design policies that find a better balance in meeting conflicting policy objectives?

First, there is no alternative to engaging the public in a debate that is honest about the options and what can and cannot be delivered: the trade-offs and constraints that explain why bringing migration down to zero is not an option – the costs to the tourist industry; to small businesses, universities and prospective UK students; to families divided from loved ones; to refugees denied sanctuary; to families unable to find a carer for an elderly relative; and to Britain's international reputation. The public has been given no explanation, no rationale. They have not been consulted on the choices to be made. Knowing the reasons may not change minds but it could form the basis of a more reasoned, inclusive, debate.

This will not be easy. There are genuine conflicts of interest for some sections of the public that cannot be ignored. There is also a lack of information, some misinformation and epistemic uncertainty, as well as unhelpful divisive rhetoric. That could be redressed in a communication strategy designed to ensure that the public has the facts, without caveat and without exaggeration. The communication, however, needs to be two-way. Regular consultation, in fora that enable differing viewpoints to be heard on the basis of evidence on the choices at stake, should inform future policy reform.

Second, a step that lies entirely within government control: a governance system that ensures across central, devolved and local government that the implications of migration and conflicting policy choices can be aired and resolved, and barriers to implementation identified and addressed. Migrants, and those who engage with them as employers and union representatives, service providers and community groups, also need to be heard. No longer should it then be possible to plan an expansion of migration without considering the implications for housing or education provision; a curtailment of numbers without considering the costs to those sectors of the economy, devolved nations or families affected; or to devise procedures relating to vulnerable migrants divorced from the standards of care considered acceptable for other members of the public. Migration cannot be managed effectively or humanely without the cooperation of EU neighbours, and the UK also needs to consider whether its repeated opt-out of agreements (which would often in practice only require modest changes in policy) is the best way to secure it.

Third, on the basis of those deliberations and public consultation, government should identify and make explicit the positive objectives that its migration and integration policy is intended to achieve. If limiting the growth of the population is an objective it should be explicit here, alongside the commitment to uphold the UK's obligations under international law and, one might hope, to ensure that families are not divided; while creating conditions conducive to the economic, social and civic participation of migrants and an inclusive sense of belonging for all residents at the national and local level.

Having identified its objectives and sought a stronger evidence base, government could develop a comprehensive migration policy. The chapters of this book have been replete with suggestions on what it could entail, both within the migration system itself and, in relation to labour migration, in addressing the underlying conditions that create demand for legal and irregular migrant labour.

On labour migration, the optimal first step is to secure investment in skills training and improvements in pay and conditions in low-wage occupations, and more effective supervision of employment standards, to reduce demand for migrant workers. If, as seems likely in a time of severe public expenditure constraints, that is not going to happen, then we need honesty that there will be a continued reliance on migrants and make provision accordingly, not least to ensure access where needed to English language tuition. There is infinite scope for nuancing the criteria for access to labour market entry channels to raise the threshold for entry, but the absence of mechanisms to match demand from among local workers can only incentivise employers and migrants to break the rules. On students, the alternative to lucrative international fee-payers is less clear. Universities and colleges rely on that income to keep courses open for UK students and there are broader, less quantifiable benefits to international relations and trade. Further steps could be taken in issuing visas to ensure a genuine intention to study; and further measures taken within the UK to foster a positive experience in education and employment to support their studies, enabling the UK to continue to attract students in an increasingly competitive international market.

On asylum, there has been no shortage of suggestions for restoring safeguards in the refugee determination system; for raising levels of welfare support to end destitution; and for alternatives to detention and forced returns (where incentives for voluntary return have been shown to be both more cost-effective and humane). For those who are vulnerable, not least children and women in need of maternity care, the government should ensure that standards of care are no less than considered acceptable for other people in the UK (see Chapter 2).

On family migration, we saw the strongest need for an evidence base to inform future policy: on the implications of dividing or uniting families, age restrictions on marriage, lack of recourse to public funds and English language requirements before entry and settlement. We need to know what impact family migrants have on the labour market, what facilitates participation at a level commensurate with education and skills and what the most effective means might be to facilitate their full social and civic participation. Armed with that evidence, family migration – including dependants of labour migrants and students – could be fully integrated into a holistic migration policy (see Chapter 4). A major concern in the current strategy to cut net migration is that the axe will fall on family migrants for whom, unlike labour and student migration, there is no powerful interest group to fight back. Yet it is cuts in this entry channel that would have the most direct impact on people's lives in the UK.

On irregular migration, I argued that the 1971 legal framework, which criminalises minor breaches of conditions of stay alongside evasion of immigration control, contributes to a focus on enforcement at the expense of prevention and militates against a proportionate and hence effective response. Recategorising minor breaches so that they attract civil penalties, with a view to ensuring future compliance, would enable criminal enforcement activity to focus where it is most needed. The core strategy, nevertheless, should focus on prevention, reducing demand for irregular migrant workers and identifying ways in which the design and operation of entry controls and conditions of stay foster the propensity to irregular status. The government should ensure that those whose status is irregular can get access to basic services (essential on social as well as human rights grounds), and identify pathways for some of the estimated 618,000 irregular migrants, just 1% of the population, to return to legal status (see Chapter 5).

On integration, I argued that the capacity to facilitate economic, social and civic participation and a mutual sense of belonging is primarily that of organisations and individuals at the local level, from employers and unions through to community groups, neighbours and migrants' own families. Nevertheless, government needs to provide a conducive legal and policy framework, clarity on objectives and an inclusive rhetoric to facilitate that process (see Chapter 6). The government's rationale for the drive to create a 'Big Society' is that 'we need to draw on the skills and expertise of people across the country as we respond to the social, political and economic challenges Britain faces' (Cabinet Office, 2010). Integration is one of those challenges and could be at the heart of that agenda.

I noted in Chapter 1 that policymaking is not a linear or necessarily rational process, hence I am not imagining that the path to reform could progress in the logical way that I have suggested. Nevertheless, if the government is to break the pattern of reactive reforms in which its room for manoeuvre is severely constrained by a poorly evidenced, polarised debate, then it could do worse than to start by sharing with the public the opportunities and constraints that it faces; by establishing a governance system that enables the full range of competing issues to be considered and resolved; and by setting clear public objectives for migration policy on which it could attempt to build the consensus that has been, and remains, so evidently lacking in this policy field.

References

BNP (British National Party) (2010) *Democracy, Freedom, Culture and Identity: British National Party General Election Manifesto 2010.* Welshpool: British National Party.

Cabinet Office (2010) 'Building the Big Society'. Available at: http://www.cabinetoffice.gov.uk/media/407789/building-big-society.pdf (accessed 9 September 2010).

Migration Watch UK (2010) 'What Can Be Done?'. Available at: www.migrationwatchuk.org/whatcanbedone.

Toynbee, P. (2010) 'Our Borders Are Porous. Why Can't Our Politicians Admit It?', *The Guardian*, 27 February.

Index

The letter f following a page number indicates a figure

N